D1519757

Economics as Discourse

Recent Economic Thought Series

Editor: Warren J. Samuels
Michigan State University
East Lansing, Michigan, U.S.A.

Economics As Discourse

An Analysis of the Language of Economists

Edited by
Warren J. Samuels

Kluwer Academic Publishers
Boston/Dordrecht/London

Distributors for North America:
Kluwer Academic Publishers
101 Philip Drive
Assinippi Park
Norwell, Massachusetts 02061 USA

Distributors for all other countries:
Kluwer Academic Publishers Group
Distribution Centre
Post Office Box 332
3300 AH Dordrecht. THE NETHERLANDS

Library of Congress Cataloging-in-Publication Data

Economics as discourse: an analysis of the language of economists/
    edited by Warren J. Samuels.
        p.   cm. — (Recent economic thought series)
    Includes bibliographical references.
    ISBN 0-7923-9046-6
    1. Economics—Language.   2. Discourse analysis.   I. Samuels,
Warren J., 1933–   .   II. Series.
HB71.E268   1989
330'.014—dc20   89–20008
                                                            CIP

Printed in the United States of America.

In memory of Thorstein Veblen,

whose essays on the place of science in
modern civilization, the prospect of economics
as an evolutionary science, and the
preconceptions of economic science, among
others, represent early and major efforts in
understanding economics as a system of
discourse and the consequences of economics
serving the functions of knowledge, social
control, and psychic balm.

Contents

Contributing Authors

Jack Amariglio
Department of Marketing
Merrimack College
North Andover, MA

C. Edward Arrington
Department of Accounting
University of Iowa
Iowa City, IA

Raymond Benton, Jr.
Department of Marketing
Loyola University
Chicago, IL

Pamela Cook
Department of French Literature
Yale University
New Haven, CT

John B. Davis
Department of Economics
Marquette University
Milwaukee, WI

Sheila C. Dow
Department of Economics
University of Stirling
Stirling, Scotland

Robert L. Heilbroner
Department of Economics
New School for Social Research
New York, NY

Arjo Klamer
Department of Economics
George Washington University
Washington, DC

Don Lavoie
Department of Economics
George Mason University
Fairfax, VA

Philip Mirowski
Department of Economics
Tufts University
Medford, MA

Edward Puro
Department of Economics
Michigan State University
East Lansing, MI

Jane Rossetti
Department of Economics
Williams College
Williamstown, MA

Janet A. Seiz
Department of Economics
Grinnell College
Grinnell, IA

E. Roy Weintraub
Department of Economics
Duke University
Durham, NC

Paul Wendt
Department of Economics
Clark University
Worcester, MA 01610

Nancy Wulwick
Levy Economics Institute
Bard College
Annandale, NY

Economics as Discourse

1 INTRODUCTION

Warren J. Samuels

The study of economics as discourse requires a perspective that focuses on the relationships among knowledge (or truth), discourse (or language), and meaning. Central to this task is the recognition that the conduct of economic analysis uses words and that words embody meanings that are applied to the object of study, but do not necessarily derive from that object although they define that object for us.

Knowledge

Economists are engaged in efforts to understand and explain the economy. In the pursuit of this knowledge they have attempted to make coherent the respect(s) in which belief is to be accepted as knowledge, or the sense(s) in which this knowledge has the quality of "truth." The field of methodology in economics parallels the fields of epistemology and philosophy of science in the attempt to make sense of and to prescribe the terms on which efforts at knowledge may be accepted as "true," or the terms on which statements can be accepted as "knowledge." The conduct of such methodological inquiry typically treats economics as a science

1

engaged in the pursuit of truth as an epistemological category — though there have almost always been economists who were skeptical of the status of economics as a science, and the pursuit of knowledge is only one of three putative function of economics, the other two being psychic balm and social control.

The end result of such methodological inquiry, however, depends upon one's perspective and can be understood in two different ways–prescriptivism and credentialism. Prescriptivism involves the identification and clarification of presumably increasingly demanding and presumably increasingly rigorous and reliable epistemological criteria thence to be *prescriptively* established as *the* specific canons of practice (for example, science versus idealist intuition, induction versus apriorist deduction, falsification versus verification, and so on). Credentialism involves the establishment, more permissively or more pluralistically, of varying alternative technical epistemological credentials by which statements can be accredited as having differing claims to the status of "knowledge" without identifying either a conclusive hierarchy thereof or the singular preferred and honorific credentials. In the former case, only one definition of scientific truth or knowledge is accepted; in the latter, different sets of credentials can be established and assigned, with the question of the putative relative status of each left open.

Epistemological controversy in all fields of scientific inquiry has included conflicts over the relative importance of deduction and induction (rationalism and empiricism) and the relation of each to the other; the status of logical positivism and/or logical empiricism; the possibility of conclusively verifying or refuting an hypothesis or theory; the nature of explanation and the relation of explanation to predictive capacity; and so on. In the process, among other things, the notions of validity, truth, desirability and workability have generally been distinguished from each other, although in varying ways. Also distinguishable are knowledge for its own sake (as explanation), for prediction, and for control.

Prescriptivist epistemology has been challenged as inconclusive, for example, resting ironically on subjective meta-epistemological foundations. In recent decades, prescriptivist epistemology has been challenged as misrepresenting the actual practice of science, however it claims science should be practiced. These challenges have taken many forms, including the claims that scientists have not practiced and/or could not practice the logical empiricism that they have preached; that conventionalism has been more important than epistemological objectivity and rigor; that scientists practice normal science, thereby giving effect to and reinforcing the dominant paradigm; and, *inter alia*, that science is in

practice essentially a sociological rather than epistemological phenomenon, not unlike everything else human.

For both technical epistemological and practical sociological reasons
but contrary to some of the claims of prescriptivist epistemology contingency and problematicity have become widely accepted as the inexorable characteristics of scientific knowledge. Scientific truth is always
partial, probabilistic, and provisional, not necessarily, if ever, a complete,
exhaustive, and definitive explanation or description of reality. In economics and other disciplines, principles or laws are understood to be
constrained statements of tendency.

Further controversy exists as to whether economists are engaged in the
pursuit of truth, the establishment of belief, or the instrumentalist utilization of tools. In all these and other respects, there is an ubiquitous x:X
problem: If X is reality, or the object of study, and if x is our knowledge
of X, the key questions are, first, is there really (and if so, in what sense)
an X independent of our perception and contemplation; second, is such
a reality knowable; and third, inasmuch as our only knowledge of X is x,
how do we know that x is representative of X? The attempt to identify
and perhaps to prescribe epistemological credentials is an effort to come
to grips with these and other fundamental questions and is an important,
indeed essential, human activity.

Discourse

Contrary to our conventional understanding, perhaps knowledge or truth
is not what is actually going on in the conduct of scientific inquiry and the
pursuit of epistemological credentials. It is possible to consider epistemological considerations as part of a larger human effort, namely, the theory
and practice of discourse, or "rhetoric," in which attention is directed
to the art of persuasion — persuasion of oneself and of others. In this
regard, the effort to identify, and certainly also to prescribe epistemological credentials is ipso facto also, and perhaps preeminently, an effort
to use those credentials to persuade, to lend credence to whatever statements, models, theories, analytical techniques, and so on are taken to
conform to the one or another or the established and prescribed credentials. Epistemological theory and conventional practice determine what
explanation is plausible and therefore functions to persuade. Doing epistemology is thus no different than doing rhetoric: one is either studying
persuasion or practicing it.

In the light of these considerations, it is possible and arguably even

necessary if not also desirable to contemplate economics (and other
disciplines) as comprising modes of discourse embracing and giving effect
to a system(s) of belief, to a particular paradigm(s) with its distinctive
set(s) of preconceptions. The distinctive feature of the mode of discourse
is language. Economists use language, that of ordinary speech, technical
jargon, or mathematics. As a mode of discourse, economics, the stories
that economists tell, and/or the knowledge that economists purport to
affirm are all affected by the structure and content of the words that they
use — by their language.

In recent years economists such as Todd Lowry and Keith Tribe, for
example, have attempted to identify and explore the different deep structures of economic thought, embodied noncognitively in the language of
economists, that have characterized premodern and modern economics,
often combined in one way or another. These developments comport with
and indeed have been influenced by the work of writers in philosophy,
literary criticism, hermeneutics, philosophy of language, deconstruction,
sociolinguistics, semiotics, and the psychology of perception. The most
important figures outside economics have been Louis Althusser, Gaston
Bachelard, Roland Barthes, Peter L. Berger, Richard J. Bernstein,
Jacques Derrida, Mary Douglas, Umberto Eco, Michel Foucault, Hans-
Georg Gadamer, Jurgen Habermas, Jacques Lacan, Claude Levi-Strauss,
Christopher Norris, Paul Ricoeur, Richard Rorty, Ferdinand de Saussure, James Boyd White, and others. The other principal economists
engaged in such activities, although not all in the same way, have been
Jack Amariglio, Arjo Klamer, Don Lavoie, Donald McCloskey and Roy
Weintraub, among others. It has been McCloskey who has led the way,
with the others, especially Klamer, close behind. But even these writers
were preceded by Thorstein Veblen, Vilfredo Pareto, Kenneth Boulding
(most notably in *The Image*), and Ben Ward, as well as John Kenneth
Galbraith and Fritz Machlup, among others.

Not surprisingly, there has been an uneasy tension in economics and
in other disciplines between the advocates and practitioners of the traditional study of methodology and those who advocate the study of economics as the practice of discourse or rhetoric. This has especially been the
case because McCloskey has presented rhetoric as a powerful successor
to what he considers to be failed modernist methodology, but the conflict
would have emerged in any case, involving what Joseph Schumpeter
called a contest for social space. Interestingly, during the past decade,
studies by economists of both methodology and rhetoric-discourse have
flowered. It is not certain whether the analysis of rhetoric-discourse is
part of traditional epistemology or whether (as suggested above) epistem-

ology is part of rhetoric-discourse — which itself has a long and honorable history stemming back to the great thinkers of ancient Greece.
Economics imposes and economists work with a discursive order, an
order that may or may not bear any connection with the actual economy.
Indeed, rival modes of economic discourse, rival stories or discursive
orders, may all relate to the actual economy. In any case, the relation
ship between discourse and truth is presently, and perhaps will be peren-
nially, an open and contested one. When is a metaphor a metaphor and
for what, and when is it a statement of reality itself?

Meaning

It is perhaps not too much to say that the aggregate of all such work
(epistemology and rhetoric understood as the analysis of discourse) has
resulted in the identification of the quest for *meaning* as the fundamental human activity. Truth itself becomes a subcategory of meaning. The
paramount status of meaning is the case whether economic reality is given
in the senses that the philosophical realist and idealist affirm or is a
matter of social, human construction; or whether one follows the road of
epistemology or rhetoric-discourse.

Aspects of Economics as Discourse

The principal directions that the development of the analysis of discourse
has taken include: economics as a system of rhetoric, including metaphor;
economics as a system of discourse per se; economics as a paradigm or
world view or ideology; economics as a facet of intellectual history (history of ideas); and economics as a system of belief or interpretation.
Earlier work on ideology in economics and the sociology of knowledge
and contemporary work on the sociology of intellectual disciplines have
contributed to or reinforced these developments. But the developments
of principal interest here are often quite differently directed and formulated, dealing principally with the analysis of the use of technical and
other terminology, or language in general. One dimension of this work
has been to identify the preconceptions, implicit premises, and/or fundamental ambiguities resident in even the most supposedly rigorous technical analysis. Another has been to demonstrate the deep structural
configurations and understandings underlying conventional usage in economics. Still another has been to identify how discursive or rhetorical

practices are used, consciously or unconsciously, both to establish privileged positions for certain theories, paradigms, models, or lines of reasoning and to rule certain questions, theories, etc. out of disciplinary bounds.

The purpose of this book, as with all volumes in the Recent Economic Thought Series, is to help identify, make sense of, and assess the present status of these developments as a whole in terms of its substance, strengths and weaknesses, as well as to provide some indication of where future work might lead.

The program, or project, of the study of economics as discourse is, simply put, to determine what we are doing when we do economics, as we must, using language. Such a task, however further specified, is inevitably closely related to the question of the meaningfullness and coherence of what we know when we produce, through the use of language, economic knowledge. The question, it must be understood, applies to *all* schools of economic thought. The question also applies to the analysis of discourse itself — it is self-referential.

Several considerations inexorably enter the study of economics as discourse that are of fundamental philosophical, ontological, and, yes, practical significance. The effective positions on these considerations held by economists constitute the operative preconceptions channelling the formation, development, and use of economic knowledge. Positions on these considerations may be held deliberately or noncognitively. These considerations include the following, which necessarily overlap and are discussed in no particular order:

1.   Data as interpretive construction

To describe, to use words to describe, is to theorize and to do so within some particular paradigm. Knowledge is largely paradigm-specific. Facts are discourse specific: facts are paradigm- and theory-specific. Theories have paradigm-specific meaning. There is an interdependence between theory and fact, mediated by culture, paradigm, and experience, that govern perception and that are themselves products, not independently given. Facts do not speak for themselves. (Statistics, for example, appear as hard numbers but are artifacts contingent upon theory, concept formation, collection technique, and statistical processing techniques. Mathematics is a language that can impose its own limits and structuring on our perception of reality.) This is not to say that certain aspects of natural reality (whatever that term may mean) do not impose themselves upon us, at least in some sense, but it does signify that their imposition be understood, or at least used, by us as a matter of interpretive construction.

2. Economics as language

To write about the economy is to use language to describe, interpret, and explain the economy, that is, to use one artifact to write about another artifact. Language is an artifact, not necessarily if ever a "natural" expression of reality or anything else. It is a means of communication without any necessary presumption or pretense with regard to the status of what is communicated. Economics, as McCloskey has urged, is very much a system of metaphors. The choice between schools of thought is thus between their respective modes of discourse, their respective system of metaphors.

Economics as language is part of the total communication system of society, part, therefore, of the total symbolic, myth, and code system of society that governs meaning and signification. Science is a linguistic community, using language as a bond as well as a means of communication and using paradigm-consonance expressed in terms of language as a test of what is acceptable (Thomas Kuhn's "normal science").

As a language, economics is laden with preconceptions and presuppositions of both a substantive and structural variety. These include such juxtapositions as teleology versus matter-of-fact; oeconomics versus economics; economy versus polity; private versus public; and the rival distributional paradigms: productivity, exploitation, and appropriation. Coupled with the overall structuring produced by these preconceptions is the practice of selective perception and attribution. The result is the maintenance of deep conceptual structural elements and the changing substantive content of fundamental concepts, such as capital, market, invisible hand, freedom, unemployment, government, and so on.

3. The meaning of "economic reality"

There are several fundamentally important questions here: What is "economic reality" and in what sense is it "real"? What is the significance of the putative fact that the economy is an artifact, unlike the solar system that is given to man? Is the economy self-subsistent, and if so in what sense? Is there an "economy" that somehow transcends specific forms in which particular economic systems exist, for example, mercantilism, fascism, socialism, and capitalism? Is the economy something other, perhaps more concrete, than a process in which questions such as resource allocation get worked out? What is the relationship of economic reality to various modes of economic discourse, or to economic discourse per se?

Epistemologists and rhetoricians have cautioned against equating the assumption that there is something independent of and transcendental to man and to human discretion with either the less demanding assumption that there is something to study or the more demanding assumption of a particular paradigmatic or other formulation of that independent reality. Even if all analysts and scientists were philosophical realists, believing that the real exists independent of our idea of it, there is still an inexorable necessity of having to choose between alternative specifications of the real. And our choices are profoundly influenced by linguistic formations, as well as by ideological predispositions.

In addition to the fundamental question, whether humankind can have any direct knowledge of economic reality unmediated by the human mind, there is the less portentous but still important question of selective perception of social, if not also physical, reality. For example, (1) the desk is hard to our touch, but it is also comprised of atoms with subatomic particles in motion, which connotes the very different notion of softness and (2) the brain can be explained in chemical, physical, biological, and electronic terms, each with different nuances and connotations. Apropos the effort to transcend whatever meaning is found in phenomenal realism, the question arises, how do we know when theories are related to phenomena that actually exist, and in what sense? Apropos of social reality, what of the social and cultural bases of the perceptions of that reality? Language, paradigm, and culture mediate the x:X problem in practice.

4.   The relation of language to economic reality

Language is an artifact and not given by physical reality. Language is both cause and consequence of culture and perception. What is the relation of language to reality, including the very definitions as well as the nuances of the words we use? One of the most fundamental questions posed by the attention to science as discourse is this: In our work as economic scientists, how do we know when we are dealing with language solely or primarily as a linguistic construction and when as something to do with economic reality independent of language?

5. Multiple interpretations

We confront the fact that not only among philosophical realists does there exist a variety of specifications of reality between which we somehow must choose, but in every respect scientific work involves creation and selection among multiple interpretations. This is true of the economy per se and, indeed, of economic texts. It seems that the economy is characterized by enormous complexity, heterogeneity and kaleidoscopy of subject-matter. These aspects of diversity permit, perhaps indeed require, plural or multiple interpretations and analysis. In any event, students of the economy approach its subject-matter from a multiplicity of interpretive standpoints or perspectives. The result is multiple interpretations or specifications of economic reality, in whatever sense "real" is taken.

And these differences matter. Consider the very different perceptions of economic reality advanced by Thorstein Veblen, John Maynard Keynes, Friedrich Hayek, John Kenneth Galbraith, James Buchanan, Amartya Sen, Karl Brunner, Paul Samuelson, Paul Davidson, and Lester Thurow, among others. Pursuit of one or another of these different definitions of economic reality as the basis of policy will have profound consequences for what is called below the social (re)construction of reality.

What is true of the study of the economy is also true of the study of economic texts. The principal works of Adam Smith, David Ricardo, Karl Marx, and John Maynard Keynes, to name only the four most important cases, have been given radically different, indeed mutually exclusive, interpretations. What a writer "really meant" seems less significant, and less capable of reasonable solution than the fact that the meaning of a text is a joint product of the author and the reader. What a text is taken to mean is a function of both the text itself and what a reader gets out of it, and the latter is in part a function of what the reader brings to the reading of the text.

6. The social construction of reality

The problem of the social construction of economic reality arises in two quite different senses: first, the social perception of an economic reality itself presumably essentially independent of man, in which man imagines and makes images of economic reality on the basis of individual perception and social enculturation; and second, the actual (re)construction by man (re)creating what is essentially an artifact, not something given to man. The former understands social construction as limited to human perception and its vagaries; the latter, as involving human creative effort, whether deliberative or nondeliberative, whether individual or collective, or in whatever combinations thereof, but always emphasizing the role of human perception and its vagaries.

Another fundamental consideration posed by the attention to science as discourse is the subjective and normative nature of the economy in which the economy is indeed an artifact, a product of human action. In this regard, theories less explain and more define and thereby help generate economic reality, such that the putative objects of study are themselves at least partly constituted by human belief.

One implication of these insights is the possibility, if not the "reality," of comprehending both theory and government (as a chief mode of translating theory into reality) as objects of capture and use. Policy, ultimately understood in terms of the (re)creation of the economy, is a function of the operative definition of reality; and theory — economic knowledge — is a basis of the definition of reality and thus a suitable if not legitimate object of control in order to influence the (re)creation of the economy. There is a tautological relationship between the preconceptions and assumptions of a theory or paradigm and the policy implications that are drawn from it. These considerations are made infinitely complicated, in part by the operation of selective perception of the status quo — for example, with regard to rights, freedom, governance, sacrifice, coercion, and so on — and in part by the joint operation of the forces of socialization and individuation, focusing especially on whatever opportunity for individuation exists within the parameters permitted by culture, social control, and practice.

The key relevant social process is the relation of knowledge to social policy, especially the bringing to bear of what is putatively taken as knowledge to the question of the continuity versus change of the status quo. Insofar as the status quo is an artifact, it is a function of deliberative and nondeliberative choice, itself a function of the definition of reality, giving effect to judgments and conceptions of reality. Definitions of what *is*, however subjective and normative, function as the basis of what *ought to be* and thus channel what *becomes*.

Part of the social process of the relation of knowledge to social policy is the social function of obfuscating the fact of the artifactual, policy, and problematic nature of the status quo and its being subject, therefore, to the ongoing problem of having to reconcile continuity and change. This is sometimes referred to as the high priest function.

Another part of this process is the practice of deterministic science, which selectively accepts and reinforces the status quo, in part through assuming either the dominant or some other ideology (myth and symbol system) and in part through the selective perception and application thereof.

7. Language, cognitive process, and selective perception

Knowledge, or belief, is a function of a perceptual process, which is itself a function of power, culture, preconception, and ideology and is itself subject to manipulation. Selective perception is a key facet of the process of cognition and is channelled by interest, social location, ideology, belief system, and language. The key process, of which selective perception is a part, is cognition, and cognition is heavily channelled by language, including the myth and symbol system of society. There is fundamental interdependence between experience and perception. This interdependence is mediated by culture, institutions, and language; and culture, institutions, and language are themselves the product of experience and perception — a process of cumulative causation and infinite regress, with respect to which considerations of a given economic reality are highly problematic. Perception is not independent of language and of what structures language and vice versa.

8. The hermeneutic circle

Consider the proposition that interpretation is interpretative-system specific. Are we prepared to assume that this is the case, or do we prefer the presumption that one interpretation is the truth and is on that account to be given privileged status? It seems that there are no meta-criteria on which to choose between alternative theories, etc., with any serious degree of conclusivity, except by selecting the premise on which rests the theory thereby chosen. There is no independent interpretive, or evaluative standpoint. Critique is always a matter of infinite regress with regard to the basis of critique. Notice also that these arguments are self-referential: there is no independent interpretive base on which to conclusively affirm that interpretation is interpretative-system specific.

One function of ideology and the myth and symbol system of society is to obfuscate the fact of the arbitrary selection of interpretive base. The fundamental significance of both the selection and the obfuscation

involves positions with regard to the selective continuity versus change of
the status quo.

9.   *Attitudes toward ambiguity and contingency*

Attitudes toward both prescriptive epistemology and the study of science
as rhetoric or discourse to no small degree depend on individual ability
and willingness to forego absolute answers and accept contingency and
ambiguity. Closely related is the role of economics as psychic balm — to
set minds at rest (as George Shackle expresses it). Many people, including economic scientists, are antagonistic to analyses that are inconclusive
and demand some form of closure, however premature or presumptuous
that may be.

10.   *The problem of nihilism and relativism*

One objection to the analysis of economics as discourse (which interestingly can be applied to epistemology as well) is that such analysis leads to
nihilism and relativism. In response, consider the following: (1) Reality
may in fact be relativist. (2) As Frank Knight argued, most if not all
absolutes are only relatively absolute absolutes, and argument then must
ensue as to the respects in which they are only relatively absolute. (3) The
alternative to potentially nihilist and relativist analysis of discourse is to
attribute privileged status to the status quo, selectively perceived. Whereas, as a matter of putative fact, the status quo, however perceived, is
changing — a consideration that applies to language and to all other
institutions, prescriptivism being always in tension with practice. (4) Conducting the analysis of discourse in scholarly study is not tantamount to
advocating wholesale destruction of existing institutions. And who among
us is not in favor or of the destruction or fundamental reformation of
certain institutions, whether it be the corporation, the Federal Reserve
System, or the Soviet system? (5) Such opposition to the study of discourse is generally, but perhaps not always, high priestly advocacy or
pretense. It is, I submit, always functional with regard to the problem of
continuity versus change, the very problem that it would deny insofar as it
gives a privileged position to the status quo, selectively perceived (which
is of course the rub). (6) The value judgment is made that reality should
be faced rather than hidden from or obfuscated. Human arrangements
are in fact a matter of choice and design, and the deepest processes of
social choice involve the making and remaking of arrangements (institu-

tions), including language, notwithstanding selective pretensions of determinacy. (If human arrangements are not a matter of choice and design, then why the fuss over economic and social policy?)

This involves calling a spade a spade and letting it go at that: the psychic-balm and social-control, including status-quo legitimation, functions of economics can be and ought to be identified and analyzed wherever they arise, if economics is to merit the status of a self-reflective discipline. That this involves recognition of the inexorably political nature of economics is something that simply has to be faced. Even if one believes in absolutism (as opposed to relativism) and/or in the status quo (as opposed to nihilism), one still has to choose between alternative formulations of what is absolute and of the status quo. There is no escape from the necessity to choose in defining and in (re)making the status quo. This means, of course, that the analysis of economics as discourse need not, and perhaps should not, have a hidden political agenda — though if analysts of discourse did not have an eye to consequences they would be very different from all other types of analysts!

Emphasis on inconclusivity and on relativism and nihilism does not mean that economists (and all other people) cannot choose. It may be that not all economists need to have final answers to or positions on all questions. But economists can and indeed often must and do choose. What is often involved, given the foregoing analysis of economics as discourse, is choice that does not possess conclusivity. The idea of the hermeneutic circle reinforces the Duhem-Quine thesis in epistemology. One does not need absolute bases on which to severely discount or reject astrology or a particular economic theory or line of reasoning or to condemn the holocaust, the gulag, or apartheid; one makes, as one must, substantive and moral judgments. Individuals can live with both the belief that their analyses are substantively meaningful and the understanding that these analyses are characterized by the limits established by both epistemology and the analysis of discourse.

These are some of the major considerations raised by the contemplation of economics as discourse. The reader of the chapters that follow will do well to recall that when economists do economics they use either the words of ordinary language, the terminology of technical jargon, or the symbols of mathematics. The definition of reality is formulated and expressed through those words and symbols. The questions are, what are we to make of those words and symbols? What implicit theorizing, what preconceptions, what normative assumptions are deliberately or inadvertently entered into analysis by use of certain words? This book attempts to make sense of the present status of such inquiry into the nature and limits of economics as discourse. The considerations raised above are controversial and can be approached from a number of different points of view. The analysis of economics as discourse, moreover, can be undertaken in different ways. Such matters are clearly evident in the chapters and comments. The facts of these controversies and of these different perspectives, and the bases on which these "facts" are accepted as facts as well as the meaning adduced to them (the self-referentiability consideration stressed above), are what the study of economics as discourse is substantially all about.

2 Economics as a Postmodern Discourse

Jack Amariglio

Postmodern science — by concerning itself with such things as undecidables, the limits of precise control, conflicts characterized by incomplete information, "fracta," catastrophes, and pragmatic paradoxes — is theorizing its own evolution as discontinuous, catastrophic, nonrectifiable, and paradoxical. It is changing the meaning of the word knowledge, *while expressing how such a change can take place. It is producing not the known, but the unknown.*

— Jean-François Lyotard (1984, p. 60)

Mainstream economic discourse today is "modern"; it is also becoming, in fits and starts, "postmodern."[1] While economic discourse is characterized by a self-consciousness of modernism, within this modernism we can discern various postmodern "moments." The postmodern moments of mainstream economics consist of the more "nihilistic," paradoxical, and parodic[2] connotations of the concepts of uncertainty and expectations, bounded rationality, disequilibrium, game theory,

15

chaos, and catastrophe theory, as well as of post-analytic approaches to epistemology and methodology.

This chapter's mode of analysis is, itself, inscribed within the tensions and contradictions between modernism and its postmodern moments. This chapter is intended as a case in point to establish the necessity to move economics away from modernism's fetishism with "science" and "truth" and toward postmodernism's concern for "discourse analysis." Postmodernism brings to light the discursive nature of all knowledge (including economic theory), and it refuses to see the division between knowledge and other discursive forms as one between the operation of science and reason and that of emotion, sensuality, and so on. Discourse analysis of economic theory, at least in postmodern thought, is not a question of ascertaining the scientific core of concepts and methods; rather it is a question of seeing how language and other discursive forms can produce the meanings that determine partly our cognitive experiences of economic reality.

The chapter discusses how the introduction and elaboration of certain concepts such as uncertainty into economic analysis have increasingly made visible (to some) the discursive nature of economic "science." This is so because many of these concepts are themselves about cognitive experience, its formation, and its limits. The debates that have emerged over these concepts have produced, in some important cases, challenges to the dominant modernist biases of current economic discourse, and they have called attention to the ways in which meaning, knowledge, and cognition are formed within and by economic thought. As as example, the "nihilistic" connotations of uncertainty in neoclassical and Keynesian economic theory are discussed below. Where modernism chooses to side-step challenges such as the nihilistic interpretations of uncertainty pose, postmodernism, with its emphasis on discourse and its formation, suggests alternative foundations for economic theory that can embrace rather than repel the nihilism of uncertainty. If concepts such as uncertainty, chaos, and the like are to flourish within economic thought, a new (postmodern) approach to economic analysis will be required, one that recognizes the discursivity rather than the supposed scientific veracity of all we know.

If this chapter comprises an argument for discourse analysis, it does so in a manner unlike that of Donald McCloskey's work (1985) on the "rhetoric of economics." Where McCloskey takes on modernism in economics by calling attention to the rhetorical and metaphorical elements of its construction, here the concern is to trace the way certain concepts within modernist economic discourse "deconstruct" the very modernism they are thought to reflect — to show how the concept of uncertainty unfolded in neoclassical and Keynesian thought in such a way as to bring into radical doubt the modernistic premises from which it sprung. The deconstruction of modernism by uncertainty and by other postmodern moments shows how scientific economic discourse can "undo itself" in its own elaboration: a point made most clearly by postmodernist discourse analysis. In order to explicate how this deconstruction occurs as the result of the logical elaboration of modernist economic discourse, a brief descriptive and historical account of modernism and postmodernism as cultural and theoretical movements is necessary.

The Cultural Legacy of Modernist Discourse

Modernism in the arts, literature, and architecture refers to the appearance of similar discursive elements from the late nineteenth century to the present[3]. The onset of modern art or modern music or modern architecture differed in historical time from one sphere of discursive practice to another. However, the onset of modernist movements in all spheres was related to a transformation in the "lived experience" and the discursive construction of time and space.

As Stephen Kern (1983) shows, during the period 1880–1918 the inventions of the automobile, electrical energy, the x-ray, and so on, were contemporaneous and interrelated with the dawning of impressionist and cubist art forms, atonality in music, the "stream of consciousness" novel, psychoanalysis, and other cultural innovations. Slightly later, in the 1920s and 1930s, modernism emerged in architecture with the "international style" and Bauhaus-led residential and industrial design. What these innovations represented, whether in building construction, the visual arts, transportation systems, or interpersonal relations, was an assault on former limits to the now transcendable dimensions of time and space. The boundaries of time and space were not simply reconceived; they were exploded and recomposed according to the new, "modern" discourses and practices.

The modernist experience, where "all that is solid melts into air," was discursively understood to express Man's[4] immanent power to transcend previous barriers in the conquering of time and space. Crucial to modernist movements were the metaphor of the machine as transcendent technology (as in futurism) and the vanguardism of the avant-garde — groups of diverse practitioners whose common goal was to leave behind the old in favor of the new and the previously unthought.[5] In modernist discourse, close attention was paid to form and most especially to those forms thought to express the essence of all things. Geometric form and spareness of expression constituted a "modernist aesthetic," as the belief spread that the traditional referents of art, music, and so forth were less universal and transhistorical than the formal dimensions of time and space. The formal dimensions of time and space permitted the representation of *all* referents, regardless of their spatial or historical "origin."

In its supposed transcendence of time and space — the making of an entire culture obsessed with this goal — modernism was not so much a rejection of traditional representation as it was a wholesale embrace of the formal strategies through which representation was actualized. Modern artists and architects, for example, sought to find the precise geometry and engineering principles that made art and architecture possible. In literary criticism, the "new criticism" of the 1930s and 1940s was an analogous modernist movement. The point of the "new criticism" was to locate in a text the internal, formal conditions that made a poem or novel possible. New critics were vehemently opposed to prior literary strategies that located the meaning of texts in the "external" conditions of their historical production, in the political and cultural artifacts to which the "story" referred, or in the biography of the author. In fact, new critics were less concerned with explaining the "meaning" of texts than in laying bare the formal structures that made meaning possible in the first place.

The various cultural formalisms imitated what was thought to be the structure of the mathematical and scientific discourses, such as subatomic physics.[6] Like science, the goal of art, architecture, etc., was to move from the merely transient (hence, the abandoning of the historically determinate "referent") to the universal and transhistorical. Modernism held out the promise that the unknown could be made known: time and space truly could be brought under human control through Reason.

Modernist discourse, then, combined at least five attributes.[7] First, it presented the view that time and space are existential dimensions that can be "controlled" through a discovery of their essential principles. Second, the theoretical and empirical "discovery" of these principles — the bracketing of time and space in discourse — displayed the power of human knowledge, especially science, to transcend history by capturing what is universally and eternally true. Third, modernist discourse asserted that the basic principles of time and space are formal in nature and can be expressed theoretically, solely by a discourse that emphasizes form (the abstract, the universal, the eternal) over content (the concrete, the transient, the historically contingent). The only content worthy of scientific exploration is form itself. Fourth, modernist discourse attempted to structure itself according to the same formal principles it had discovered. One of the characteristic features of modernism is the self-conscious structuring of its written and spoken mode of presentation as a reflection or demonstration of the formal principles it seeks to portray. Thus, in neoclassical economics, for example, modernism has meant mathematical and axiomatic forms of discursive presentation in order to represent adequately — like a mirror — the logical behavior it claims to have discovered.

Fifth, the point of modernist discourse and culture (including the sciences) was to remake the world according to the newly discovered universal and abstract principles. These abstract principles, if understood correctly, would provide any "concrete" society blueprints for beneficial change at any moment of their particular history. So, for example, the "international style" in architecture promised to transcend geological obstacles, spacial and political boundaries, and the historical time of specific social formations. It would do so by adopting a universal formal style, epitomized in the glass-paned skyscraper, capable of turning any landscape into a metropole and representing the happy combination of formal elegance, sleekness, efficiency, simplicity, and strength (Jencks, 1984; Hutcheon, 1986–87).

The desire to remake the world according to universal formal principles and corresponding aesthetic values gave modernist movements their pervasive utopianism. By demonstrating Man's ability to discover and use efficaciously the essential principles of time and space, modernism promised to revolutionize life while upholding the universality and eternality of Reason and Truth. Some avant-gardists warned of the tyranny of reason and delighted in revealing the irrational aspects in attempts to employ consistently the principles of formal composition, but others became the harbingers of a new age.

At the very heart of modernist culture and discourse, however, was the radical doubt that would erupt in the art, music, and architecture of the 1950s and 1960s as postmodernism. This doubt followed in the wake of modernism's endeavors to discover the unknowable itself. In the sciences, the "observations" and concepts of relativity, disequilibrium, and uncertainty pointed to the difficulty of constructing a stable discourse around a time/space axis. The scientific concepts of relativity, uncertainty, etc., suggested that time and space were unstable and, in some cases, internally contradictory and unmeasurable. Indeed, as they were incorporated into modernist discourses, these very notions of arbitrary change, contradiction, uncertainty, etc., represented the transcendable limits of knowledge (and, thus, new "frontiers" to be conquered) or the simply unknowable (thus contributing to a resurrection of metaphysics and religion, which had always asserted the essential "mystery" of the world).

The utopian optimism of modernist discourse was shaken by the extension of modernism to the unknowable, i.e., by the undertakings to discover the formal, abstract principles of an uncertain, everchanging, unmeasurable, and seemingly random world. In economic discourse, the typical modernist response to these undertakings has been to rescue modernism by "recuperating" or "domesticating" the notions of uncertainty, disequilibrium, paradox, and the like. However, in economics, as in art, architecture, etc., the recognition of the aporia at the core of modernist discourse — its inability to think the unknowable — has engendered doubts and criticisms of modernism.

Postmodern Discourse: Theory in a Fragmented Age

Although postmodernism was first applied to a new sensibility and practice in the arts and architecture, the concept of postmodernism has been extended to so many diverse activities and fields that it now designates a general discursive formation. The wide use of the concept of the postmodern, as with modernism, has given rise to a "theory of the postmodern." Often, this theory involves the claim that modernism and postmodernism represent cultural historical "ages." Postmodernity supposedly represents a break with the industrial capitalist past; it marks a break with "productivist" ideology (which emphasizes work and production to the exclusion of consumption and leisure); it marks a break with the modernist belief in efficacy of rationality and truth; and so forth.

Rather than delineating the precise epochal boundaries of modernity and postmodernity, Jean-François Lyotard (1984) explicates the "postmodern condition." For Lyotard, the "postmodern age" is more a conjunctural moment summing up the contemporary sensibility of "incommensurability" than a stage in an historical process. In Lyotard's view, incommensurability defines the experience and practices of postmodernist discourse. In opposition to modernism's utopian dream to create a universal life-experience and language based on Reason's rule, postmodernism announces that incommensurability (persistent difference) between languages, experiences, histories, and discourses cannot and should not be overcome. Incommensurability is the basis for "nontotalizing" experiences and practices. Thus, the postmodern condition defies the "totalizing" logic and politics implicit in the modernist metanarratives of the liberating effects of reason and of historical necessity.

Like Lyotard, Michel Foucault (1973) thinks that to go "beyond mod-

ernism" is to reject the great unifying metanarratives of the Enlightenment. Foucault's assault on what he calls "the modern episteme" sheds
additional light on the theory of the postmodern.[8] Foucault claims that,
contrary to popular liberal views, the horrors of the totalitarian state, the
maintenance of economic exploitation and political oppression, and the
disempowerment of the many are not the result of a perversion of the
Enlightenment project. Rather, Foucault shows that the "humanism" of
the modern episteme — the story of Man's victory over Nature through
the progressive spread of Reason and Truth — is the discursive ground
for all forms of exploitation, oppression, and disempowerment in post-
Enlightenment Western civilization. Exploitation, dominance, and disen-
franchisement are not anomalies in our culture. They do not represent
the absence of reason waiting to be overcome by the progressive unfolding of rationality.

Instead, the desire to know Man, to control him for the purposes of
efficiency and utility through this increased knowledge, produces the
notorious exercises of power in the modern age. In a seeming paradox,
Foucault shows that enlightened politics, built upon the foundation of
reason and knowledge, are contiguous with the most brutal demonstra-
tions of power and control. Thus, the reformer's desire for liberation
through the application of "humane" knowledge to human behavior and
political action is seen by Foucault to be a common condition of existence
for the "socialist humanism" of Stalin, the "futurism" of Hitler, and
economic exploitation in the capitalist factory. Since knowledge produced
by the "human sciences" has been directed toward watching, confining,
disciplining, and affecting — if reforming — the body of the prisoner,
mental patient, and worker, there is only a difference in degree between
the power and oppression effected by the prison reformer, the psychiat-
rist, the social worker, and the exterminator.

The concepts of incommensurability and anti-humanism ("the death of
Man," as Foucault puts it), represent the central terms of postmodernism. Complementing these terms are senses of the fragmentary, the
discontinuous, the uncertain, excess, reproducibility, the playful, the paradoxical, and "decentering." Postmodern discourse values these senses
and mirrors them. Incommensurability and anti-humanism, *understood
in the light of these senses*, allows postmodern discourse to oppose or
escape the primary conceptual values of modernist discourse. Such
values include the ideas of totality, the universality of reason, epistemological truth, efficiency and utility, originality, communication based on
rational knowledge, continuity, formalism, essentialism, and the centrality
of Man.

It may help to unravel the preceding statements with an example in contemporary economics. The contrast between modernism and post-modernism can make sense of current economic debates over epistemology and the procedures of scientific verification.

Postmodern Epistemology

Richard Rorty (1979), Jacques Derrida (1976), Louis Althusser (Althusser and Balibar 1970), Lyotard (1984), and Foucault (1972, 1973), and in economics, Donald McCloskey (1985), Arjo Klamer (1987), and Stephen Resnick and Richard Wolff (1987), have all put forward criticisms of modernist epistemological positions. Their criticisms suggest, albeit in different ways, the contours of a postmodern epistemology. These authors criticize modernist epistemologies, certainly the post-Enlightenment empiricist and rationalist theories of knowledge (and their recent variations, including positivism), for treating discourse as a "mirror of nature." Many of them also criticize rationalism, empiricism, and their offspring for positing a subject/object relation as the point of departure for knowledge. These two positions are closely related.

The subject/object opposition as the starting point for modernist epistemology implies the classical question of philosophy, "how do we know what we know?" How does Man extract knowledge from the "real world" of objects, which exists in epistemological discourse either in the form of the subject's concepts (rationalism) or as sensual things to be experienced and only then known (empiricism)? Epistemological truth is the idea that knowledge, rationally appropriated from the objects themselves (whether in "thought" or "reality"), can be "adequate" to the object it seeks to know. Knowledge exists only when the discourse the subject creates about the object adequately appropriates truth. Truth is contained as the *essence* of the objects of discourse. Knowing is the process by which a potentially omniscient, rational subject can extract the essence of a thing — its truth — in the form of discourse about it.

Since knowledge can be communicated between subjects, no knowledge-producing discourse is permanently incommensurate with any other. The basis of knowledge is the possibility that *any* rational subject can extract truth from the world of objects according to communicable methods. Discursive opacity can always be broken down as long as correct procedures for extracting truths ("abstraction") can be taught and learned. In post-Enlightenment epistemologies, the idea that knowledge mirrors nature, that it captures the essence or truth of things, is at once joined to a humanism that asserts the *possibility* of knowledge in Man's capacity to reason and communicate.

Positivism is a post-Enlightenment epistemology. Positivism blends empiricism and rationalism but goes further than both by postulating the necessary language through which scientific propositions must be posed if they are to be meaningful (i.e., potentially verifiable or falsifiable). This language is a formal language, borrowed for the most part from symbolic logic and other axiomatic systems. Although early positivists held out the possibility of discovering and employing an "object language" that would correspond perfectly to the objects of scientific investigation, recent positivist approaches abandon this search in favor of the language of universal logic. Thus, the formalism that characterizes positivist approaches in the sciences and in economics is founded on the premise that in the language of analytic logic, one can find the basic discursive principles of truth, clarity, consistency, elegance, and noncontradiction. Like other modernisms, positivist epistemology sees itself as having discovered the underlying formal principles of a scientific language and the correct protocols — the necessary technological means — of scientific method.

Positivism treats scientific discourse as "a mirror of nature," and it begins from the premise that there is a significant, necessary difference between the subject and object of knowledge. Its contribution to epistemology is the view that just as we can discover the essential truths of the object world, we can also discover the essential truths regarding the discursive appropriation and expression of these "real" truths. Positivism concerns itself with the unique and universal ways through which truths must be represented in discourse. In this regard, positivist epistemology, like other modernist practice, is a theory and practice of the formal representation of essences.

The response of Rorty and others to post-Enlightenment epistemologies is varied but unified in rejection. This common rejection suggests the terms of postmodern epistemology. First, Rorty and others reject the notion that scientific discourse is a "mirror of nature." No relation of adequacy exists between knowledge-producing discourses and their objects. As Althusser puts it, knowledge is a matter of the concrete "knowledge effects" that are *produced* by certain types of discourse. If "knowledge effects" are discursively produced, then we must pay more attention to the "play" of linguistic "signs" or "graphemes" (Derrida), the "rules of discursive formation" (Foucault) or the modes of knowledge production (Althusser) to see how discourses emerge as knowledges. On a related point, Foucault advises us that there is no "depth," no essences, to be discovered by discourse. Foucault stresses that the notion of representation that structures the "modern episteme" is one of essentialism. To Foucault, Althusser, and others, essentialism has ideological and political consequences that are deplorable (see Amariglio 1987, 1988).

Derrida, Foucault, and others reject the central contrasts that define modern epistemological discourse, such as subject/object, appearance/ reality, thought/being, mind/body, concrete/abstract, and theory/practice. These contrasts are essentialist and also promote a hierarchy of actions and effects beginning with the presumption of Man's unique position in "his" world and ending with the notion that rational behavior is a privileged mode of human existence. The social hierarchies that stem from such contrasts make possible the modern "technologies of power" that Foucault and others have documented.

For *some* of these theorists (McCloskey may be an important exception), the subject of knowledge is a fiction, a historically determined discursive "fact" whose existence has made empiricism and rationalism possible. But this fact is rapidly passing out of existence as a new idea begins to take hold: that subjectivity is transitory, decentered, and fragmented rather than structured as a totality and experienced as a universal condition. Most postmodern discourse questions the identity of the "I", whose a priori existence is the hallmark of both subjectivist and scientific approaches to knowledge. In postmodern discourse, every "I" is shown to be nothing more than a shifting and often contradictory series of subject positions and identities that result from the interaction of myriad discursive and nondiscursive processes.

Postmodern epistemologists stress the discursive nature of truth. Truth (or truths, to be exact) is not only transitory, it is discourse-specific. As Althusser argues, each scientific discourse has its own rules of verification.[9] These rules are not universal (there is no universal scientific method), nor are they easily transferable to other discourses, nor can there exist a universal, formal language (a mathematics, for example) that can be "neutrally" applied to every discourse regardless of the distinct conditions of its production. There are no methodological prescriptions that would guarantee the transdiscursive use of the same observation techniques and logical conjectures. Truths and discourses are "different" and discontinuous (synchronically and diachronically). At the very least, they are historically determinate.

Postmodern theorists portray discourse as inherently unstable and fragmentary. Thus, the "meanings" that emerge from discursive practices are themselves the result of the arbitrary play of discursive elements. Meanings are not fixed in any way, since the play of these elements guarantees nothing but paradoxes, surprises, and the undecidability of concepts and arguments. Efforts to postulate the "rules of formation" of discursive statements show the diversity of determinate conditions that, combined in different ways, produce ambiguity in meaning. Not only is it impossible to "fix" meaning, it is also impossible to "fix" the unique and irreversible lines of its causation. As Wolff and Resnick (1987) argue, following Althusser, discourse is "overdetermined," by which they mean that there is a multiplicity of intereffective determinations for meanings. Overdetermination, as an epistemological position, implies a "surplus" or "excess" of determinants for knowledge. But it also implies that there are no essential causes for knowledge and no guaranteed results.

The implications of these postmodern positions for debates in the philosophy and methodology of economics have only begun to be traced, but McCloskey, Klamer, and Wolff and Resnick have at least inaugurated this effort.

McCloskey calls attention to the scientism that informs discussions of economic analytic procedures and econometric practice. McCloskey's writings are noteworthy because they show that the way economic theory and econometrics "work" is through the use of particular figures of speech and rhetorical strategies. For example, McCloskey (1985) points out that John Muth's 1961 article is loaded with scientistic linguistic baggage. Yet, the scientific metaphors Muth uses are necessary for persuading other economists of the veracity of his arguments. McCloskey translates Muth's arguments into nonscientistic prose and in the process shows that Muth's propositions are conventional in their appeal to familiar metaphors in economic theory. Additionally, McCloskey judges Muth's few gestures toward econometric verification of his points to be inconclusive. Thus, McCloskey reveals the reasonable rhetorical structure of Muth's presentation while cutting through Muth's formalist posturing and the obligatory nod toward scientific experimentation.

At one level, McCloskey's discussion is subversive. It suggests that there is no necessity for economic arguments to be presented in a formal language nor for economic persuasion to hinge on adherence to epistemologically approved empirical procedures. To the contrary, McCloskey deconstructs the modernist language Muth uses to signify scientific operations. McCloskey achieves this deconstruction by showing that metaphor and other figures of speech are all that is persuasive even in the most formal of languages and strictest of scientific methods.

McCloskey's subversion ends here. It is remarkable that McCloskey's questioning of modernism and its effects ceases with discursive presentation. McCloskey's "rhetoric of economics" stresses only the form of argumentation and leaves completely untouched the "content" of economic theory. Thus, McCloskey neglects to pursue his criticism of modernism in the conceptual frameworks — and not just rhetorical structures — of the major schools of economic thought. McCloskey avoids the effect modernism has had on the concepts and approaches of the dominant neoclassical economic theory.

Hence, McCloskey does not subject to the same deconstructive analysis the modernist conception of economic rationality. As one sign of his neglect, McCloskey concludes that Muth's rational expectations argument makes perfect sense, despite the fact that rational expectations from Muth to Robert Lucas and Thomas Sargent prioritizes the existence of the unified, totalizing rationality of an unfragmented subject in the face of uncertainty. While McCloskey derides modernism in epistemology, he applauds it in neoclassical theory.

Klamer's work on economic persuasion is similar to McCloskey's, with these important differences. Klamer sees that modernism in economics goes far beyond the positivist formalism of economic methodologists. Klamer shows that from Samuelson, Hicks, and Keynes to the "new classical economists," we can discern several of the more important modernist themes: belief in the universality of formal principles; a preference for axiomatic language; reliance on the "myth" of unified subjectivity; and a choice of machine-oriented metaphors. Unlike McCloskey, Klamer notes the centrality of the rationality principle for modernism in economics. Favoring "anthropological" approaches, Klamer concludes that rationality is "unrealistic." He does not challenge the idea of a unified subjectivity. Instead, he is satisfied to point out the cultural determinations of subjectivity and the limits to rationality that such determinations impose. Unlike many of the other postmodernist theorists, Klamer does not call into question the primacy and composition of the "I."

Resnick and Wolff's contribution is of a different order. In *Knowledge and Class* (1987), they set forth what they regard as a distinct Marxist position in epistemology. They share with other postmodern advocates the rejection of epistemological essentialism and theoretical humanism. More pertinent here is their insistence on the irreducible differences between neoclassical/Keynesian and Marxian conceptual frameworks. From epistemological premises and "entry points," to the detailed concepts and methodological procedures, Wolff and Resnick (1987) find little in common between Marxian and neoclassical economic thought. Unlike positivists, however, they do not regard the existence of difference as a sign of the persistence of unscientific ideas and methods. For them, differences in theory cannot be overcome by more and better transdiscursive scientific practice. In a postmodernist spirit, Wolff and Resnick posit differences between neoclassical and Marxian economic discourses and believe that these differences can (but need not) persist through scientific practice.

Resnick and Wolff's, McCloskey's, and Klamer's criticisms of economic modernism have stayed mostly at the level of epistemologies and discursive structures. Now, however, the neoclassical and Keynesian discussions of uncertainty must be investigated to illuminate a postmodern moment at the core of modernist economic discourse. On the one hand, it can be shown that the threat of uncertainty to economic modernism consists of its potential to deconstruct the views of knowledge and subjectivity upon which it is based. On the other hand, it can be suggested that a postmodern ("discursive") approach to knowledge and subjectivity is consistent with uncertainty's more "nihilistic" interpretations and is, thereby, productive of alternative economic discourses.

Uncertainty and the Economic Modernism of Frank Knight

In 1921, Frank Knight published his classic work, *Risk, Uncertainty, and Profit*. This text is contemporaneous with the ascendancy of modernist movements in the arts and sciences. Knight's work, too, bears the birthmarks of modernism. His text stands out as an influential treatment of one of the more problematic concepts of modernism: uncertainty.

Knight was not the first economist to write on uncertainty. He was following a well-established tradition (like Irving Fisher before him) in attempting to relate probability and statistical theory to leading issues in economic discourse. According to Claude Menard (1980), however, some of the most notable "mathematical" economists of the nineteenth century had balked at the application of probabilistic and statistical analysis to economic problems. Both Cournot and Walras, while expertly conversant with statistical theory, were unenthusiastic about its use in economic analyses of individual rational choice and market equilibrium. Walras, for example, preferred analytic geometry and calculus for presenting the effects of market choices at the margin. In Menard's view, Walras's reticence to embrace statistical theory signified the economics discipline's commitment to notions of certainty and invariant laws. Only when economics experienced a change in its "vision inspired by the statistical equilibrium suggested by thermodynamics" did economists embrace the sensibilities of "variety, of probability, of approximations" (Menard 1980, p. 541). Knight was one of the first to assert that the application of probabilistic and statistical theory to rational choice was fundamental, if problematic.

Knight's modernist text left no doubt that a full account of rational behavior on the part of consumers and entrepreneurs depended on a delineation of the motives for and different types of choice taken in the absence of "certain" knowledge. Indeed, Knight solves one of the most pressing issues of economics to his satisfaction by showing profit to arise from a condition of "true uncertainty." The wide use Knight made of the concepts of risk and uncertainty has disturbed many later modernists, such as Kenneth Arrow (1971). Arrow faults Knight not only for basing his theory of profit on the existence of uncertainty but for overextending the use of concepts of risk and uncertainty to the point where the entire "free-enterprise system . . . arises as a reaction to the existence of uncertainty" (Arrow 1971, p. 7).

That Knight was a modernist should not be doubted. The first chapter of his text contains one of the more careful discussions before Robbins of "scientific" epistemological and methodological procedures. Although Knight's arguments about the unreality of assumptions and the separation of concrete prediction and abstract theorizing might give pause to positivists, Knight clearly enunciated his belief that the method of economics "is the scientific method" (1921, p. 8). Knight's constant comparison and recourse to physics throughout his text suggests his fascination — with reservations — with modernist conceptions of knowledge.

Knight is also the author of these sentiments: "The basis of a science of conduct must be fixed principles of action, enduring and stable motives. It is doubtful, however, whether this is fundamentally the character of human life. What men want . . . is to have interesting experiences. And . . . an important condition of our interest in things is an element of the unanticipated, of novelty, of surprise" (1921, p. 53–4). These sentiments do not contradict Knight's admiration for science. On the contrary, Knight poses this view for the twofold purpose of (1) establishing the challenge for science in coming to grips with the arbitrary and the unknown and (2) indicating that rational knowledge, too, finds its natural limits in humans' "preference" for chance and uncertainty.

Knight's procedure for handling the issue of uncertainty is exemplary. He sets out to show that uncertainty is a normal condition for human existence. This is true in part because the future cannot be known in advance with absolute certainty; but it is also true because humans prefer to structure their knowledge and "adaptations" not on past events but on expectations about the future. The "human condition" Knight presents is consonant with modernist culture: human beings are future oriented; they prefer to transcend time and space and leave the past and present behind. Knight stresses the inherent paradox in all of this: "We live only by knowing *something* about the future; while the problems of life, or of conduct at least, arise from the fact that we know so little" (1921, p. 200).

Knight sees the potential danger in opening up discourse to concepts of uncertainty. What is at stake, most of all, is rationality, not only of the economic agent, but of the economic scientist as well. Thus while Knight admits his sympathies with a type of "irrationalism" that questions the validity of logical principles, he concludes that "there is to my mind no question of understanding the world by any other method" (1921, p. 209). The threat to economic theory posed by "irrational" understandings of uncertainty requires a careful distinction between risk and uncertainty.

Knight differentiates between risk and uncertainty in the following way: Whereas a rational agent could approach risky situations either with an a priori calculation of probable outcomes or, for unique events, with a statistical estimate based on the accumulation of relevant data, true uncertainty means that neither probability nor statistical estimation can fully operate. For Knight, uncertainty marked the limits of probabilistic calculation, since truly uncertain outcomes were unmeasurable. However, Knight handles this problem of uncertainty by claiming that (1) agents facing true uncertainty do, indeed, make estimates of probable outcomes, (2) agents generally prefer uncertainty over certainty because of their interest in the unpredictable, and (3) despite this preference, agents seek to minimize uncertainty by finding ways, over time, to control the future through learning and other methods. Through these ways, agents transform uncertainty into a situation of probability or of statistical guess.

Knight's distinction between risk and uncertainty undermines potentially "nihilistic" understandings of uncertainty. Indeed, it is only with Keynes and G.L.S. Shackle that these more nihilistic understandings are given voice. Knight, however, has anticipated some of the subsequent debate among economic modernists in his text. Three other points are notable.

First, Knight anticipates Shackle's concern to ground the "experience" of uncertainty in subjectivity rather than in the natural world (cf. Simon, 1976 and Arrow, 1971 for similar statements). Though Knight often treats uncertainty as a "fact" of nature, he turns repeatedly to the subject's self-experience and self-consciousness to explain the peculiar ways agents respond to this "fact." Knight, therefore, presages Shackle's more detailed discussion of the critical function of uncertainty for the "freedom" of the subject. For if the world is truly uncertain and "indeterminate," then the subject will have meaningful choices open.

Second, in its response to the "real indifference" of risky and uncertain situations, the essence of rational subjectivity is affirmed. As Knight explains, real indifference means that "mind" is the only helpful guide to action. In encountering uncertainty, the "mind" — in contrast to emotion or instinctive reaction — manages the behavior of agents. As Arrow puts it, for Knight, "human consciousness itself would disappear in the absence of uncertainty" (1971, p. 1). Rather than signifying the limit to intellectuality, uncertainty confirms the hierarchy of mind over body.

Third, Knight asserts that the rational behavior of economic agents is necessarily of a different order from the reasoning of economic scientists. Knight says:

> The opinions upon which we act in everyday affairs and those which govern the decisions of responsible business managers . . . have little similarity with conclusions reached by exhaustive analysis and accurate measurement. The mental processes are entirely different in the two cases. . . . There is doubtless some analogy between the subconscious processes of "intuition" and the structure of logical deliberation, for the function of both is to anticipate the future and the possibility of prediction seems to rest upon the uniformity of nature. Hence there must be, in the one case as in the other, some sort and amount of analysis and synthesis; but the striking feature of the judging faculty is its liability to error. (1921, p. 230)

This statement anticipates the furor over rational expectations.

For some modernists, however, Knight's discussion is lacking in one critical respect. Knight's is not a formal presentation. As a result, the clarity normally won by a formal, rigorous language is sacrificed to often muddy and inconsistent prose. In Arrow's view, "Knight's analysis is so lacking in formal clarity that it is difficult to be sure" of his classification system regarding the differences between probabilities and statistical inferences (Arrow, 1971, 17). Arrow excoriates Knight for failing to give "a formal description of uncertainty situations" and for lacking "a rigorous proof" for some of his more important theorems (1971, 30). Thus, ironically, the absence of formal procedures calls Knight's modernist text into some question.

Knight's modernist approach to uncertainty marks the beginning of a long tradition in which the "nihilistic" (and I would say, postmodern) aspects of the concept of uncertainty have been avoided. The modernist way has been to "recuperate" uncertainty by treating it as negligible, or as a condition of existence for rationality, or in some cases, as instrumental certainty (if outcomes in the world are truly unforeseeable, what difference does it make to rational choice).

Uncertainty and Keynesian "Nihilism"

To a degree, Knight's modernist position on uncertainty was undermined by Keynes. Consider this famous quotation from Keynes's 1937 article in the *Quarterly Journal of Economics*:

> By "uncertain" knowledge . . . I do not mean merely to distinquish what is known for certain from what is only probable. The game of roulette is not

subject, in this sense, to uncertainty; nor is the prospect of a Victory bond being drawn. Or, again, the expectation of life is only slightly uncertain. Even the weather is moderately uncertain. The sense in which I am using the term is that in which the prospect of a European war is uncertain, or the price of copper and the rate of interest.... About these matters there is no scientific basis on which to form any calculable probability whatever. We simply do not know. Nevertheless, the necessity for action and for decision compels us as practical men to do our best to overlook this awkward fact and to behave exactly as we should if we had behind us a good Benthamite calculation of a series of prospective advantages and disadvantages, each multiplied by its appropriate probability, waiting to be summed. (pp. 213–214)

This quotation presages several subsequent debates over uncertainty and expectations, but more importantly, for modernist Keynesians this quotation is a source of embarrassment or of misunderstanding. The problem posed by Keynes's statements, as Shackle has pointed out, is the limitations to economic knowledge and rational behavior. From one point of view, Keynes's statements are seen as "nihilistic." Later in the 1937 article Keynes adds:

a practical theory of the future ... has certain marked characteristics ... based on so flimsy a foundation, it is subject to sudden and violent changes. The practice of calmness and immobility, of certainty and security, suddenly breaks down. New hopes will, without warning, take charge of human conduct. The forces of disillusion may suddenly impose a new conventional basis of valuation. All these pretty, polite techniques, made for a well-panelled Board Room and a nicely regulated market, are liable to collapse. At all times the vague panic fears and equally vague and unreasoned hopes are not really lulled, and lie but a little way below the surface. (pp. 214–215)

The two quotations taken together nicely indicate the ambiguity of the place of uncertainty in economic modernist discourse. For on the one hand, they convey that the barriers to knowledge and rational behavior are impenetrable. And, they convey the idea that the nearly inevitable reaction to these limits borders on the impotent (we shake our heads and sigh "We simply do not know") or on the apocalyptic. On the other hand, the quotations suggest that in the face of uncertainty we will reason calmly, albeit in less than ideal circumstances, since reason we must. Uncertainty must be dealt with through *some* form of reason so as to "save our faces as rational, economic men" (Keynes, 1937, p. 214).

The modernist and nihilistic (postmodern) implications of Keynes's statements are neatly summarized in recent articles by Alan Coddington (1976, 1982) and Tony Lawson (1985). Coddington (1976) distinguishes between three schools of interpretation of Keynes's "revolution": "fundamentalist," "hydraulic," and "reconstituted reductionist" Keynesianism. Fundamentalist Keynesians interpret Keynes's work as an all-out attack on the choice-theoretic "reductionism" of his neoclassical predecessors. Their interpretation turns on the degree of importance Keynes attached to the notion of uncertainty. For fundamentalists, the 1937 article deciphers the meaning of the Keynesian revolution.

In this article, "as against the clearly specified and stable objectives and constraints required by reductionist theorizing, Keynes emphasises that the basis of choice lies in vague, uncertain, and shifting circumstances" (Coddington 1976, p. 1260). Since the foundations of rational choice are challenged, reductionism is called into question. Thus, says Coddington, "for the fundamentalist ... Keynes's ideas require the rethinking and reconstruction of the whole body of reductionist theory: its choice-theoretic basis and the equilibrium theory of market that rests on it" (1976, p. 1261). The fundamentalist readings of equilibrium in this context "would have nihilistic consequences for the entire corpus of economic theory and in particular for its applicability" (1976, p. 1261). The nihilism of such "subjectivist" readings would require that fundamentalists "spend a good deal of time and energy in trying to convince those who engage in macroeconomics, econometric model building, mathematical economics, general equilibrium theory, and so on, of the folly of their ways. But, that task accomplished, there would be nothing left but for the whole profession to shut up shop" (Coddington 1982, p. 486).

With an almost visible sigh of relief, Coddington concludes that fundamentalist thought "reaches a purist and impractical conclusion that is in marked contrast to Keynes's own highly eclectic approach to economic theory" (1976, p. 1261). Coddington declares that fundamentalist Keynsianism (he mentions only Joan Robinson and Shackle) "sees Keynes's own ideas as a *first step* in a thorough-going revision of economic theory. Accordingly, it sees what Keynes did *constructively* as merely a makeshift, an improvisation, a stop-gap" (1976, pp. 1261–1262).

For Coddington, fundamentalism "does not provide any sort of determinate theory or model of how the economy functions at the aggregate level; it does not enable one to make any definite prediction about the likely effects of alternative policies or circumstances. On the contrary, it is a viewing point from which such constructions would appear as rather desperate makeshifts of transient applicability" (1976, pp. 1262–1263). Fundamentalism, then, is an economic modernist's nightmare. It defies the criteria for scientific knowledge because it resists the formalism of model-building and sees the limits to knowledge as constitutive of economic science itself. It builds uncertainty and its effects into the very structure of economic discourse.

As Coddington puts it, "to stress the basis of all economic activity in more or less uncertain expectations is precisely to emphasize the openness and incompleteness of economic theorizing and explanation. It does not itself provide any kind of fixed mechanism according to which the unfolding of events takes place; but it does show how one would set about constructing a narrative of events" (1976, p. 1263). Perhaps this is why some, like John Eatwell and Murray Milgate, have visceral reactions to the fundamentalist readings of Keynes. To Eatwell and Milgate,

> the appeal to unknowable imperfections — uncertainty, disappointed expectations, "conjectures" and the like — serves to deprive economic analysis of all definite content, thus reducing the discussion of economic policy to the status of guesswork and negating the single most important achievement of economic theory during the past two hundred years — namely that the market mechanism is governed by systematic, objective forces. (1983, p. 279)

If fundamentalists emphasize openness, incompleteness, etc., then they come close to fulfilling Lyotard's definition of postmodern science. Making uncertainty a *principle* of economic discourse leads the fundamentalists, in this interpretation, to theorize the evolution of economic theory according to uncertainty and its effects. If Coddington's portrayal is right (I have my doubts), then fundamentalists advocate substantively postmodern positions for epistemology and causality. Finally, in this view, the discursive practices of fundamentalists, in which "narrative" displaces formalist science, are much like those preferred by Lyotard, Derrida, McCloskey, and others. In these respects, fundamentalist Keynesianism may represent a postmodern position in economic discourse.

Coddington is not sanguine about fundamentalist Keynesianism. Yet, he finds nothing subversive about its idea of uncertainty. This is because he regards this idea as either destructive of economic theory (and therefore to be ignored) or innocuous. If uncertainty is to have meaning, its proper scope must be defined. One problem, for example, is to what aggregates of economic activity and policy does uncertainty apply? As Coddington points out, Keynes stressed the uncertainty of expectations in certain realms (investment decsions) but not in others (consumption).

To define its scope as other than all-embracing means to admit, as did Keynes, that some "expectations" are more uncertain than others. If this is admitted, then the sharp distinction between certainty and uncertainty, or between knowledge and ignorance, collapses. Where possible, people will behave according to a "reasonable" conception of correct foresight, one that acknowledges margins of error. People will use the best information available (and will not concern themselves with an unattainable certainty) to provide themselves with reasonable grounds for their actions. Only the irrational will refuse to respond to systematic errors in foresight.

Lawson disputes Coddington's accounts of uncertainty in Keynes's own writings, though he shares Coddington's concern to avoid the nihilistic readings of uncertainty. To distance himself from Coddington's accusation that Keynes "flirted with subjectivism," Lawson begins his article by declaring uncertainty to be "a pervasive fact of life" (1985, p. 909). In contrast to Coddington's reading, Lawson contends that Keynes's use of uncertainty is far from being either innocuous or destructive of economic reasoning, though in his article, he is at greater pains to prove the latter than the former contention. In this vein, Lawson alleges that Keynes's writings on uncertainty allow for a "'research program' incorporating . . . a view of rational behavior under uncertainty" (p. 909).

Lawson denies the nihilistic connotations of Keynes's concept of uncertainty. His defense of Keynes is mostly modernist.[10] First, he shows that in *A Treatise on Probability* Keynes indicated belief in the existence of "certain" knowledge: "Keynes interprets certainty (of rational belief) as requiring not only 'complete confidence in a belief' but also 'the correctness of this belief'. Moreover in Keynes' account such certainty corresponds to knowledge. Keynes, however, *does* consider that knowledge and thus certainty *are* obtainable" (p. 911).

From *A Treatise on Probability* to the 1937 article, Keynes differentiates uncertainty from the improbable. Improbability, which is measurable, is distinct in kind from unmeasurable and indeterminate uncertainty. However, no matter how pervasive a fact of life uncertainty may be, it does not hegemonize human thought and action. Lawson argues that, according to Keynes, what humans are uncertain about is the *future* outcomes of all currently possible decisions. Clearly, then, if people have information and knowledge about *present* practices and their outcomes, there is a large part of their cognitive experience that relies on certainty and probability. Since they are "knowledgeable of certain 'facts' of the existing situation, and of ways of getting by in the absence of definite calculable knowledge of the results of all possible current actions," people use particular conventions to determine their actions (p. 916). Conventional knowledge is acquired partly through partaking in practical activities, through life-experience.

Keynes did not challenge directly the presumption that economic analysis can be built upon some conception of rational behavior. On the contrary, Keynes upheld the notion of a "meaningful subject" as a prime source of economic practice. Uncertainty does not undermine such a notion. Indeed, much like Knight and Shackle, Keynes's integration of uncertainty into analysis "presupposes notions such as *intention* and *deliberation* and allows the assumption that individuals have the *power* to choose" (Lawson 1985, p. 919). Although uncertainty may constrain choices, people use "good reasons" to choose. Lawson concludes, "it is only in as far as knowledge and reason guide action that people are free to discern alternative possibilities and to frame purposes" (p. 919).

Lawson tries to forestall comparisons of Keynes with the neoclassicals. He asserts that the fact subjects come to have knowledge through practice means that neither the subject nor the social practices within which he/she is inscribed are the primary presupposition for knowledge and action. Keynes is no "subjectivist," since he sees the "good reasons" behind subjects' choices and locates these choices in the interaction between subjectivity and social institutions. However, Lawson's determination to find a place for the rational behavior of unfragmented subjects in Keynes's discussions of uncertainty can be linked, if tentatively, to the modernist fear that without a specified and exalted place for rationality, economic theory is impossible.

Uncertainty as a Postmodern Construct: The Case of Shackle

For postmodernism, uncertainty is neither a "fact" existing outside of discourse nor is it a construct of the subject's mind. These two poles define precisely the modernist epistemological dilemma. Postmodernism treats uncertainty as a discursive construction, one that has no relation of adequacy to a given object world and no starting point in the inviolable unity of subjective consciousness. Discourse and its objects are material, "overdetermined," and social. Thus, uncertainty is "true" and functional within specific discursive formations and according to the rules of combination and interaction that constitute such formations.

This is to say, uncertainty is itself only experienced cognitively through discourse. It has no meaningful existence for us (we feel neither certain nor uncertain regarding outcomes of our acts) outside of the discourses that create such meanings. We may ascribe to uncertainty an ontological existence (though it is difficult to describe it in a manner akin to the existence of "objects"), but "proof" of such existence and its meaningful implications reside within discourse and not independent of it. Postmodern epistemology implies that uncertainty be treated as a "fact" of some (but not other) discourses. In this regard, uncertainty is a fact like every other concept: it is historically determined and discursively grounded. Postmodern epistemology stresses that there is no transdiscursive "truth" for uncertainty, and it posits that there may be some discourses (and social formations) within which uncertainty and certainty *simply do not exist* (not unlike the situation of societies described by anthropologists for which there may be no concepts of individuality or freedom).

It must be added that the discursive production of uncertainty is not restricted to the question of knowledge. Since discourse encompasses many more forms than knowledge, it may be the case that we may not "know" uncertainty but experience it anyway. Yet, this experience is also discursive insofar as it is "meaningful." Thus, the claim that there is some transcendent materiality to uncertainty outside of knowledge is countered by postmodernism, which stresses the plurality of discursive forms and the discursivity of all meaningful experiences. However, where uncertainty does exist as a discursive fact for formal knowledges, it need not imply the limit to theory and discourse, as in modernist positions. A postmodern approach to uncertainty avoids the epistemological dilemma of modernist economics wherein, as Coddington and Lawson suggest, uncertainty is either nihilistic and destructive of theory or translatable into familiar epistemological and methodological assumptions.

Uncertainty can pose unsettling, postmodern problems for modernist neoclassicals and Keynesians. Shackle's work on uncertainty shows that the twin achievements of modernism, the discovery of the essential principles of time and space and the demonstration of the primacy of reason, are instrumentally incompatible. His discussion tends toward postmodernism. In the end, however, Shackle upholds economic modernism.

Shackle's modernism consists mainly of his preservation of neoclassical theory's "entry point." Neoclassical analysis begins with a theory of subjective preference that expresses the knowledge subjects possess and their creative desires. Shackle does not question choice-oriented subjectivity as the starting point for theory. In Shackle's work (like Knight's), creative impulses and freedom to choose result from the subject's perception of uncertainty. Far from replacing unified subjectivity with a notion of fragmented, decentered, socially-constituted agency, Shackle sees uncertainty as a necessary condition for a subject's escape from determinacy and his/her leap into purposeful action. Although reason (in the sense of full knowledge or probability) may not be effective, a form of rationality does emerge as the sole basis upon which economic actions take place.

But Shackle's postmodernist tendencies are evidenced in his attacks on the formalism of economic theory, the reduction of uncertainty to probability (and, therefore, to "certainty-equivalents"), and the treatment of time and reason as complementary. In regard to the formalism of modernist economic thought, Shackle says, "economics has virtually turned imprecision itself into a science: economics, the science of the quantification of the unquantifiable and the aggregation of the incompatible" (1972, p. 360). For Shackle, formalism is wholly inappropriate for an analysis of situations involving uncertainty (which seem to be the majority of circumstances) because it starts from the premise that agents and theorists make decisions with certain (or probable) knowledge.

On this score, Shackle resorts to empiricism, for he accuses formalism of being unable to perceive correctly the essential vagueness of agents' thoughts and the impenetrability of the future. This has led some, like Macro Magnani (1983, p. 249), to accuse Shackle of criticizing neoclassical theory for its lack of realism and of remaining hostile to scientific abstraction. If, as Shackle states, the world is perceived as "imprecise," then one captures the truth about that world through similarly "imprecise" discourse. As Coddington points out, Shackle is not licensing "muddled or slipshod or woolly thought" (1975, p. 158). Rather, Shackle's view "leads to the seemingly paradoxical . . . idea that carefully imprecise concepts can give a more *accurate* expression of the economic world than precise ones" (Coddington 1975, p. 158). Thus, in standing modernism on its head, Shackle wants economic science to acknowledge "the manifoldness, the richness and the detailed particular variants and individual facets of humanity, rather than dismissing them as the contingent outcomes of some original and essential principles which it is the real purposes of science to identify" (1972, p. 29). This acknowledgment will bring about greater rigor and clarity and will reflect reality better than most formal models.

As Brian Kantor notes, "Shackle's attempts to abandon strict logic has not found many friends in the economics profession" (1979, p. 1428). Yet, Shackle's critique of formalism is restricted mostly to the models and empirical methods of the neoclassical-Keynesian synthesis. In the spirit of modernist aesthetics, Shackle chooses to formulate his own contributions in an axiomatic system. Shackle explains: "it became fashionable in the 1950's to set out deductive arguments about human conduct in the strict form of numbered axioms and theorems. This method . . . has a beauty and incisiveness, and offers safeguards against loose reasoning; which amply justify it" (1961, p. 79).

If Shackle finds fault with the "mechanistic" metaphors of formal economic models, such as general equilibrium schemas, it is because they promote a deterministic veiw. Such metaphors obliterate the possibility of subjects' decisions. General equilibrium, in particular, excludes uncertainty, because "it assumes that economic man knows all he needs to know, can feed his tastes alone into a mental computer and obtain unambiguous directions about what to do to secure their maximum satisfaction" (1966, p. 9). Man is not like a computer, nor is the "economic cosmos" like a machine. Here, Shackle counters one facet of modernist culture (the metaphor of the machine) with another — the primacy of individual subjectivity.

General equilibrium models are not adverse, these days, to incorporating ideas of "incomplete information" into their formal structure. But, for Shackle, this move "betrays a still arrogant assumption of ultimate, unlimited human power," since "to speak of 'incomplete information' suggests that there is such a thing as 'complete information', *known to be such*" (1966, p. 9). Modernist economic discourse cannot cope with such a problem because "how, in science's name, does one find out how much there is yet to be discovered?" (1966, p. 9). The discernible limits to modernist knowledge cannot themselves be theorized.

This is the sense, then, of Shackle's treatment of uncertainty. Since we cannot know what we do not know, we must concern ourselves with the creative process — decision-taking — whereby imagination, and not Reason, rules. Decisions are taken as a creative act in the face of uncertainty. These acts reflect subjects' desires to pursue paths that will bring about an outcome they feel to be possible. They neither know with certainty outcomes of their actions, nor do they rule out alternative possible paths, which they can rank order in terms of preference. Most importantly, they do not view the set of possible paths to be complete. Or rather, they remain in doubt about the possibility or impossibility about actions and their outcomes. In this sense, probability is not true uncertainty, since the probability calculus stipulates that the set of mutually exclusive paths is complete (sums up to unity).

Thus, there is no clear separation between the possible and the impossible, but there are degrees of possibility, giving rise, when an act brings about a result that was anticipated or not, to degrees of "potential surprise." Shackle's possibility calculus shows both the necessity and openendedness of subjective decision-taking. The existence of uncertainty forces us to imagine the possible paths for altering our circumstances or anticipating their alteration. However, these paths are not simply "probable," for if that were true, we would be little removed from the world of determinacy (we would know in advance all the options available to us). As Paul Davidson comments, "replacing the concept of certainty by the concept of a known probability distribution merely replaces the assumption of perfect foreknowledge by the assumption that economic agents possess actuarial knowledge" (1983, p. 161). For Shackle, "knowledge and uncertainty are mutually exclusive" (1961, p. 60).

The concept of uncertainty must not imply the powerlessness of subjectivity. "If history is determinate," Shackle tells us, "[the subject] cannot alter its predestinate course." But, equally, "if history is anarchy and randomness, he cannot modify this randomness nor mitigate the orderlessness of events" (1966, p. 86). Uncertainty must be understood, therefore, as "bounded uncertainty."

Bounded uncertainty does not overturn the idea that there is a natural order in the world. What it does suggest is the difficulty in going from subjective, cognitive experience to knowledge and foresight about events. As with most modernist epistemologists, Shackle preserves the duality of a natural order and the knowing subject. Unlike them, however, he posits an incommensurability that stems from Man's natural limitations and, more importantly, from the fact that in creative actions, Man makes history (thus changing the world's order). Reason and time are forever out of sync because historical time — as subjective, lived experience — can exist only when creative acts take place. And, creative acts take place only when certain knowledge is impossible. Subjectivism is potentially destructive, in this way, of modernist epistemology, but can achieve that destruction only by upholding other key elements of that epistemology, the subject/object distinction and the "centering" of the subject. Hence, Shackle's antimodernism does not translate into postmodernism.

Uncertainty and Postmodern Epistemology

There is an overlap between postmodern epistemology and the postmodern moments in Knight's, Keynes's, and Shackle's treatments of uncertainty in economic thought. Postmodern theories of knowledge posit the persistent differences among knowledge-producing discourses. As a result, they see the existence of sciences rather than Science, methods rather than Method, logics rather than Logic, and so on.

Knight, Keynes, and Shackle deal with a related incommensurability, the one between knowledge of the present and expectations of the future. In discussing uncertainty, they each entertain the possibility that there may be no limit to the mutually exclusive anticipations subjects hold about the future. Disinclined to call such anticipations "knowledges," they treat uncertainty as representing the limtits to knowledge (but not to rationality). The plurality of expectations is not mirrored by a plurality of knowledges about the present, though Knight and Shackle do ponder the idea that present knowledge, too, may have multiple determinations and interpretations. The explosiveness of their concept of uncertainty consists of the threat to modernist pretensions to know the unknowable, the future; its presumed nihilism lies in the possibility that such knowledge may be impossible.

The modernist "recuperation" of uncertainty can be seen in Knight's and the others' discussions. They each avoid the aporia of modernism, its inability to theorize the unknowable, by resorting to the primacy of the subject and to a modified notion of rational behavior. Thus, *subjects* can *know* the present, if incompletely. This knowledge and the "information" we acquire about the future (once it becomes present) provide a basis for rational action and an object for standard economic analysis.

Knight and the others defuse the nihilism of uncertainty by assuring theorists that there is (limited) basis for rational choice and scientific analysis. The expectations of subjects may be "wild"; subjects may be of multiple minds and have contradictory apprehensions and hopes in regard to the future, but they are practical and rational in making choices in regard to the present. Uncertainty is "bounded" by bringing present knowledge to bear on the future. Postmodern epistemological notions, then, may apply to the future, but have no particular relevance to knowledge of the past and present. This explains the meaning of "information" and "learning" in modernist economic discourse. There is information to be learned: it is assimilable by the unified, rational mind and "exists" in the form of objective truth. It is transferable (a key assumption for it to be bought and sold) from subject to subject and can be acted upon uniformly, so that there is a one-to-one mapping of information and activity sets (i.e., *this* "knowledge," if held, will produce *these* actions). With information and learning, with knowledge-surrogates and certainty-equivalents, we are back in the world of modernist epistemology.

A thoroughly postmodern epistemology implies a rejection of all modernist concepts of rationality and subjectivity. In the case of uncertainty, it is legitimate to ask whether its nihilism would be disrupted if economists believed that there are multiple "knowledges"; that subjectivity is discursively constructed; that the "subject" is decentered (any "I" is comprised of multiple "I"'s); that the objects of knowledge are produced within discourse and do not lie outside of that discourse (making the idea of acquiring information without adopting the perspective of the discourse that produced it absurd); and so on. Indeed, the true nihilism of uncertainty lies not in its application to an unknown future but to a presumably known past and present. Uncertainty has the power to deconstruct any economic discourse that starts from the modernist "entry points" of rationality and subjectivity, but only if the postmodern moments of uncertainty are allowed more freedom to operate within that discourse.

Of course, this has not been the trajectory of recent mainstream economic discourse. A brief look at the idea of "rational expectations" will show that modernism has revenged itself on uncertainty's postmodern moments, thus "recuperating" it for analytical purposes.

Modernism's Revenge: Rational Expectations

While uncertainty unleashes a postmodern reaction to knowledge and rationality, modernist economists have sought consiously to counter this reaction and its effects. Muth states, for example, that "it is sometimes argued that the assumption of rationality in economics leads to theories inconsistent with, or inadequate to explain, observed phenomena, especially changes over time (e.g., Simon). Our hypothesis is based on exactly the opposite point of view: that dynamic economic models do not assume enough rationality" (1961, p. 316). If a postmodernist interpretation of uncertainty proposes the extension of its nihilistic effects on rationality and knowledge to present behavior, modernists push back the other way by extending the traditional neoclassical understandings of these concepts to expectations about the future.

The "new classical economists" were aware of the potential nihilism of the Knight/Keynes/Shackle view of uncertainty. What they criticized is precisely the turn to modernism to which Keynes and his followers were led in order to prevent the destruction of economic theory "immanent" in uncertainty. It is valid to ask why we would assume that unified subjectivity (which is necessary for a notion of "self-interest") and rational behavior regarding all "present" concerns are inapplicable to expected outcomes of future occurrences. Why would we expect subjectivity and rationality to fall apart in confronting the unknown? In accordance with the time-honored mainstream tradition in economics of positing the eternality and universality of rational choice, new classical economists asked why we should discard this view in discussing expectations. As Maddock and Carter say: "The rational expectations hypothesis, in itself, should not be provocative to economists. It merely brings expectations within the scope of individual maximizing behavior" and "provides a way of incorporating expectations which is consistent with the orthodox economic theorizing" (1982, p. 49). Perhaps the great modernist synthesizers, Samuelson and Hicks, and not Lucas and Sargent, should be the main targets of criticism.

Rational expectations makes possible a sharp division between modernist and postmodernist moments of mainstream economic discourse. Rational expectations highlights different positions on knowledge and subjectivity. It does so by supposing the essential identity, under competitive market conditions, between expert knowledge (economic science) and subjective knowledge, at least in regard to expectations. And it does so by employing the "entry point" of neoclassical economic discourse, the economic rationality of subjects.

The rational expectations approach shows that if economic agents are self-interested, then they will make every effort, over time, to acquire information that bears upon outcomes that can affect their economic well-being. According to Mark Willes, "irrationality is unnecessarily expensive — it is more expensive than using the available information efficiently" (1981, p. 86). If markets are competitive, knowledge is transferable, and information is not withheld or hoarded, subjects will try to supply themselves with information that could make anticipated events less uncertain. As Klamer puts it, "rational expectations . . . assume[s] that individuals do not leave any opportunity unused to improve their decisions" (1984, p. 14). More importantly, there is no reason to believe that the information subjects acquire (through learning, purchase, or gift) is of a different consistency than the information economic scientists produce in their forecasts. If scientists' information is better at predicting future outcomes than subjective expectations independently formulated, economic agents will have the necessary incentive (since they fear being "fooled" and hope to make some pecuniary gain) to acquire like information in forming their expectations. In particular, if policy rules and their effects are known by theorists, as long as these rules and knowledge of their effects are made available (through markets or otherwise), self-interested, rational subjects will have an interest in and should be able to use such information.

New classicals and their interpreters stress that rational expectations does not imply the omniscience of either subjects or scientists. It does not imply that scientists and economic agents make no errors in their predictions and subjective anticipations. Indeed, one defense of rational expectations is that rationality, as new classicals define it, does not require either full or certain knowledge for forecasters or for expectant buyers and sellers. Rational expectations does imply, however, that if errors are systematically biased, then both scientists *and* agents will have reasons to take this into account in their next forecast and formation of expectations. Uncertainty is understood, in this case, to be a matter of either predictable outcomes or complete randomness. If predictions can be made, tested, and adjusted through a probability calculus, then uncertainty can be faced by rational behavior. If, however, deviations from predictions (errors) are "random shocks," then uncertainty can be practically ignored in forming expectations and forecasting economic trends.

This defense, though adequate to some criticisms, is no response to the nihilistic versions of uncertainty nor to postmodern epistemology. Postmodernism explodes the "specularity" of subjectivity and scientific knowledge not by preserving the pristine difference between the two, but by breaking the mirror. The mirror is broken by postmodernism's emphasis on the discursive constitution of subjects *and* knowledge and on irreducible differences, where they exist, among knowledges.

For now, however, the modernism of rational expectations has prevailed in mainstream discussions of uncertainty and expectations. In the rational expectations debates, only the Post Keynesians seem to have insisted on the more nihilistic senses of Keynes's and Shackle's discussions of uncertainty and expectations (this is especially true of the Post Keynesian notion of the "heterogeneity of expectations"). However, Post Keynesianism's crude empiricism (see, for example, Eichner 1983) and committed humanism are inscribed within modernist discourse and seem far away indeed from postmodern epistemology and theory.

Nevertheless, as my previous discussion should suggest, the elaboration of uncertainty within modernist economic discourse has produced change in the concept of economic knowledge. If Lyotard is right, then as the meaning of knowledge changes and the discursive production of the "unknown" continues, postmodernism will have taken hold, even in the midst of economic modernism.

Notes

[1] A voluminous literature on modernism and postmodernism now exists. For the uninitiated, a good place to start is with Jencks (1984), the essays in Foster (1983), Lyotard (1984), Jameson (1984), and Hutcheon (1986–87). Hutcheon's essay appears in a special issue of *Cultural Critique* devoted to the modernist/postmodernist contrast.

[2] For the importance of "parody" to postmodern art, architecture, and theory, see Jameson (1984), Jencks (1984), and Hutcheon (1986–87).

[3] The discussion that follows is indebted to the work of Arjo Klamer (1987). However, my descriptions of modernism and postmodernism differ from his in important ways and lead me, at times, to alternative conclusions.

[4] Readers should note that my use of the term "Man" is wholly ironic and meant to

draw attention to one of the critical "political" conditions of existence (theoretical and cultural gender bias or "sexism") for post-Enlightenment thought and to "theoretical humanism," which I reject.

[5] Peter Bürger (1984) presents a thoughtful analysis of the uneasy relationship between artistic avant-garde movements and the "high modernism" of the 1920s and 1930s.

[6] See Mirowski (1981) for this "imitation" in the nineteenth century.

[7] My discussion here parallels but does not entirely overlap Klamer's (1987) seven "characteristics for modernism."

[8] See Amariglio (1988) for an extended discussion of Foucault on this matter and on the issues that follow.

[9] A full treatment of Althusser's notion of "science" is in Amariglio (1987).

[10] I share much of Lawson's interest in a nonpositivist, "interactionist" notion of knowledge and respect his use of Marx to argue for it. Yet, I think he does not go far enough in this direction.

References

Althusser, L. and Balibar, E. 1970. *Reading Capital*. London: Verso.

Amariglio, J. 1987. "Marxism Against Economic Science: Althusser's Legacy." In Paul Zarembka, ed. *Research in Political Economy*, Vol. 10. Greenwich, Conn.: JAI Press.

——. Winter 1988. "The Body, Economic Discourse, and Power: An Economist's Introduction to Foucault." *History of Political Economy* 20(4):583–613.

Arrow, K. 1971. *Essays in the Theory of Risk-Bearing*. Chicago: Markham.

Bürger, P. 1984. *Theory of the Avant-Garde*. Trans. by M. Shaw. Foreword by J. Schulte-Sasse. Minneapolis: University of Minnesota Press.

Coddington, A. June 1975. "Creaking Semaphore and Beyond: A Consideration of Shackle's 'Epistemics and Economics'." *British J. Philosophy of Science* 26(2):151–163.

——. December 1976. "Keynesian Economics: The Search for First Principles." *Journal of Economic Literature* 14:1258–1273.

——. June 1982. "Deficient Foresight: A Troublesome Theme in Keynesian Economics." *American Economic Review* 72(3):480–487.

Davidson, P. 1981. "Post Keynesian Economics." In D. Bell and I. Kristol, eds. *The Crisis in Economic Theory*. New York: Basic Books. Pp. 151–73.

Derrida, J. 1976. *Of Grammatology*. Trans. by Gayatri Chakravorty Spivak. Baltimore: Johns Hopkins University Press.

Eatwell, J. and Milgate, M. 1983. "Unemployment and the Market Equilibrium." In J. Eatwell and M. Milgate, eds. *Keynes's Economics and the Theory of Value and Distribution*. Oxford: Oxford University Press. Pp. 260–280.

Eichner, A., ed. 1983. *Why Economics Is not yet a Science*. Armonk, New York: M.E. Sharpe.

Foster, H., ed. 1983. *The Anti-Aesthetic: Essays on Postmodern Culture*. Port Townsend, Washington: Bay Press.

Foucault, M. 1972. *The Archaeology of Knowledge*. Trans. by A.M. Sheridan Smith. New York: Harper & Row.

———. 1973. *The Order of Things*. New York: Vintage.

Hutcheon, L. Winter 1986–1987. "The Politics of Postmodernism: Parody and History." *Cultural Critique* 5:179–207.

Jameson, F. 1984. "Postmodernism, or the Cultural Logic of Late Capitalism." *New Left Review* 146:53–92.

Jencks, C. 1984. *The Language of Post-Modern Architecture*. 4th ed. New York: Rizzoli.

Kantor, B. December 1979. "Rational Expectations and Economic Thought." *Journal of Economic Literature* 17:1422–1441.

Kern, S. 1983. *The Culture of Time and Space, 1880–1918*. Cambridge, Mass.: Harvard University Press.

Keynes, J.M. February 1937. "The General Theory of Employment." *Quarterly Journal of Economics* 51(2):209–223.

Klamer, A. 1984. *Conversations with Economists*. Totowa, New Jersey: Rowman and Allanheld.

———. 1987. "The Advent of Modernism." Unpublished paper.

Knight, F. 1921. *Risk, Uncertainty, and Profit*. Boston: Houghton Mifflin Co.

Lawson, T. December 1985. "Uncertainty and Economic Analysis." *Economic Journal* 95:909–927.

Lyotard, J.-F. 1984. *The Postmodern Condition: A Report on Knowledge*. Trans. by G. Bennington and B. Massumi. Foreword by F. Jameson. Minneapolis: University of Minnesota Press.

McCloskey, D. 1985. *The Rhetoric of Economics*. Madison: University of Wisconsin Press.

Maddock, R. and Carter, M. March 1982. "A Child's Guide to Rational Expectations." *Journal of Economic Literature* 20:39–51.

Magnani, M. 1983. "'Keynesian Fundamentalism': A Critique." In J. Eatwell and M. Milgate, eds. *Keynes's Economics and the Theory of Value and Distribution*. Oxford: Oxford University Press. Pp. 247–259.

Menard, C. Winter 1980. "Three Forms of Resistance to Statistics: Say, Cournot, Walras." *History of Political Economy* 12(4):524–541.

Mirowski, P. 1981. "Physics and the 'Marginalist Revolution'." *Cambridge Journal of Economics* 8:361–379.

Muth, J. July 1961. "Rational Expectations and the Theory of Price Movements." *Econometrica* 29:315–335.

Resnick, S. and Wolff, R. 1987. *Knowledge and Class: A Marxian Critique of Political Economy*. Chicago: University of Chicago Press.

Rorty, R. 1979. *Philosophy and the Mirror of Nature*. Princeton: Princeton University Press.

Shackle, G.L.S. 1961. *Decision, Order, and Time in Human Affairs*. Cambridge: Cambridge University Press.

———. 1966. *The Nature of Economic Thought: Selected Papers 1955–64*. Cambridge: Cambridge University Press.

——. 1972. *Epistemics and Economics*. Cambridge: Cambridge University Press.

Simon, H. 1976. "From Substantive to Procedural Rationality." In Spiro Latsis, ed. *Method and Appraisal in Economics*. Cambridge: Cambridge University Press. Pp. 129–148.

Willes, M. 1981. "'Rational Expectations' as a Counterrevolution." In D. Bell and I. Kristol, ed. *The Crisis In Economic Theory*. New York: Basic Books. Pp. 81–96.

Wolff, R. and Resnick, S. 1987. *Economics: Marxian versus Neoclassical*. Baltimore: Johns Hopkins University Press.

COMMENT BY PAUL WENDT

Jack Amariglio holds two theses that should interest all of us in metalevel studies of economic science. First, he holds the modernist thesis:

(M) Mainstream economics is modernist.

The modernist thesis is not so much demonstrated in his chapter as it is supposed; the chapter is an illustrative example of the work one may do based on this supposition. Second, he argues for the immanence thesis:

(I) Postmodernism is immanent in modernist economics.

Although the immanence thesis is interesting in its own right, it is "subversive" in conjunction with the modernist thesis, for together the theses imply that mainstream economics includes "concepts" that " 'deconstruct' the very modernism they are thought to reflect" and that it "can 'undo itself' in its own elaboration."

Amariglio's principal argument for the immanence thesis is a case study of theories of uncertainty and expectations. He demonstrates that there are "postmodern moments" in the work of Frank Knight, John Maynard Keynes, and G.L.S. Schackle. He also asserts that Knight, Keynes, and Shackle are modernist economists, so that their postmodern moments establish immanence. Finally, Amariglio deals briefly with the rational expectations program, which he holds to be "modernism's revenge" in the theory of uncertainty and expectations. This may be contested on the grounds that a nonmodernist reflexive move is the heart of the rational expectations critique of macroeconomic policy, but it will not be discussed here (see note 5).

Regarding the demonstration of immanence by consideration of Knight, Keynes, and Shackle, I am in all three cases unconvinced. More pertinent, I believe that Amariglio's audience will generally be unconvinced, so that the burden of proof remains on him. Briefly, Knight, Keynes, and Shackle are poor cases to establish that postmodernism is immanent in modernist economics because they are outside the modernist conversation themselves, *non*modernist or even *anti*modernist, if not *post*modernist. In order to make the terms more useful, modernism and the -modernisms will be discussed in the next section.

The immanence thesis is clearly expressed by Amariglio, and its significance is probably clear to the reader: there is a dialectical contradiction in modernist economics. The modernist thesis (M) is not so transparent, but it is a thesis of the highest importance to the history, sociology, and philosophy of economics, so a section is devoted to its clarification and to suggestions for its test.

Amariglio is an advocate as well as a theorist of postmodernism. Throughout, he calls for a postmodernist turn, or two: one in economic theory and one in metalevel studies of economics; that is, in studies of both business and science.[1] There is some disparity between his call for discourse studies and his own example; indeed, the modernist and immanence theses may be improved especially by closer attention to discourse, first in their formulation and second in their demonstration. To treat business and science as "discourse" is evidently central to Amariglio's postmodernism, but the nature of discourse studies, per se, is not closely examined, as it must be. I will begin the work in a discourse on discourse in the fourth section of this comment.

Modernism and the -Modernisms

Amariglio's concept of modernism is not McCloskey's; it is much closer to Klamer's. McCloskey (1985, p. 5) prefers 'modernism' to 'positivism' "[t]o emphasize its pervasiveness in modern thinking well beyond science," but his modernism is principally an epistemology founded on an understanding of science. "It is the attitude that the only real knowledge is, in common parlance, 'scientific.'" Although his modernism includes architects, musicians, and politicians, McCloskey takes epistemologists and philosophers of science as paradigms. For Amariglio and Klamer (1987), on the other hand, twentieth century 'modern' art is also a paradigm of modernism, and perhaps the most important one. This is also the approach of at least one of Amariglio's principal postmodernist theorists (Jameson 1984).

Amariglio pays some attention to characterizing modernism and postmodernism, but both are left ill-defined. Apparently definitive statements are scattered rather than collected in one place, or the terms in the whole are used diversely (see notes 8 and 9). Briefly, the matters that seem in most urgent need of attention are (1) the relative focus of the modernist project on philosophy, science, and art and (2) the relative significance for modernism of the seventeenth, eighteenth, and twentieth centuries.[2]

Perhaps it is most useful to present one concept of modernism and to raise questions in the course of that presentation for all who speak of modernism and the -modernisms. The metaphor of the machine is modernist; on that we all agree. Here are three of its implications, which can be taken as the definitive elements of modernism.

Foundationalism. The machine is composed of parts, and Man as its maker knows its parts and understands that it works the way it does because of the way it is composed. Modernist science views the object of study as a machine, and so values analysis into components as a method. Foundationalism includes analysis into purely logical components, too, which is undertaken by the method of axiom and proof. More broadly, it includes formalization and mathematization of both our conception of the world and our presentation of scientific knowledge, although this conflation is historically contingent and logically unnecessary.

Foundationalism is evident in the formalism of twentieth century philosophy and art.[3] Similarly, Samuelson's *Foundations of Economic Analysis* (1974) is aptly titled: the work is foundationalist, indeed modernist. However, foundationalism is also evident in Galileo and DesCartes; their mathematization of the world is one of the paradigmatic foundationalist achievements. Since modern art is by all accounts a twentieth century phenomenon and Galileo and DesCartes and seventeenth century philosophers, I question taking modern art as an example in terms of which to understand modernism generally.

Objectivism. The machine is an object separate from Man as its maker and when the machine is put in use it operates on its own. Modernist science takes the world to be a machine — without a maker, perhaps, but a machine separate from Man as the metaphor implies. Thus modernism holds the subject/object distinction: the subject of knowledge (the scientist) and object of knowledge (the world) are separate. This is one aspect of objectivism, which also includes methodological value placed on a particular relation between subject and object: the subject knows the object by passive sense-perception only; there is no interaction. As a corollary, objectivism implies that introspection and participation can produce no knowledge, so that feelings, meanings, and conventions are outside the scope of science.[4]

Control. The machine serves a purpose; it is the instrument in Man's control of the world. As such, it is strictly controlled by Man; at least, this supposed aspect metaphorically informs modernism. Modernist science seeks not merely to know, but also to control the object of knowledge by the use of knowledge. So, the modernist ideal comprehends not only fitting and predicting facts, but especially controlling facts. The value placed on control makes technology integral to modernist science, and so the engineer is a central figure in the modernist tradition (as for Hayek 1952, part 2). Just as the modernist project should consider Newton,

Bentham, and Mendel, it should consider the military engineer, the social engineer, and the genetic engineer.[5]

Control, as Man's triumph over Nature, is celebrated in twentieth century "modern" art and architecture and constitutes "the 'humanism' of the modern episteme." Certainly, control of the macroeconomy by economic policy was the raison d'être of macroeconomic theory for many of the -Keynesians, including both Samuelson and some non-neoclassical Keynesians; similarly for Pigou and microeconomic welfare theory. Yet, the scientific interest in control was expressed by Bacon four centuries ago, and our paradigms should be relative ancients: the turn of the nineteenth century social scientists Bentham and Saint-Simon, and their nineteenth century followers.[6] Again I am troubled by the status of twentieth century art as paradigmatic for modernism.

I recommend stopping here, with foundationalism, objectivism, and control, but two other elements of Amariglio's concept of modernism are crucial to his case studies: universality and rationality. It may seem unfair to deny him these; if so, I hope that my discussion will at least stimulate careful attention to universality and rationality in reaction. This will be important in the book Amariglio plans with Klamer (Amariglio 1988, 601n).

Universalism.   Universalism as a value means that science seeks knowledge comprehensive in scope, and interprets its results as comprehensive.

It is not commonly recognized that "universal" is relative: it means true (or right, beautiful, rational, etc) throughout some domain taken for granted. For the historian or philosopher of economics it is always pertinent to ask, and rarely easy to answer: in what domain, under what conditions? For Amariglio, what is universal transcends history, culture, time, and space. So the internationality of the "international style" in architecture is universality; the style transcends cultures and geographic locations. This is a start, but it still leaves universality fatally unspecified.

For example, is it antimodernist in a neoclassical economist to reject Becker's (1968, 1981) expansionist program in the social sciences, which argues that economic laws (the marginal equations of individual optimization, the price=cost equation, and Pareto optimality) are true of marriage, childbearing, and crime? I seek a concept of modernism that leaves assent to and dissent from Becker's program incidental to modernism, so that a follower of Samuelson (1947) or Debreu (1959) *within the traditionally defined scope of economics* may be a full-fledged modernist.

There are several kinds of comprehensiveness, several relativist senses of "universal." Modernist science may value a more comprehensive law in each sense, but claims to universality in the sense of the logical universe do not exist in actual discourse. Since the term "universality" suggests the latter, it is a misnomer for the value placed on comprehensiveness. Perhaps our concept of modernism should not include any comprehensiveness claim at all. Indeed, it seems in keeping with modernist formalism that no specific stance on the empirical scope of the formal theory is mandated.

Rationality. No concept of rationality follows from the metaphor of the machine; on the contrary, the machine is nonrational and suggests modeling Man and Society in terms of determined *mechanical* behavior.

Amariglio does include some rationality thesis among the elements of modernism, and it is crucial to his case studies. My main complaint against including it is that to make modeling in terms of rational behavior a definitive element of modernist social science is to strike out many theories I wish to include. Consider "hydraulic Keynesianism." Along the lines of the mechanical metaphor, it is the nonrational model of the hydraulic Keynesians that is most clearly modernist among the works of the three schools of Keynesians distinguished by Coddington (1976). Such psychological constants as the marginal propensity to consume and the convergence coefficient in adaptive expectations are nonrational; they are posits that serve to close a formal mathematical model tractably. Coddington is right that hydraulic Keynesianism is "radically inconsistent with reductionism" and "is a scheme in which there is only one agency making deliberate acts of choice; that one agency is 'the government'" (1976, 1265). Amariglio recognizes the modernism of the hydraulic Keynesian moves himself, if I catch his allusion to "the turn to modernism to which Keynes and his followers were led in order to prevent the destruction of economic theory 'immanent' in uncertainty."

The hydraulic Keynesian models constructed of nonrational psychological constants are not the only instances that should be considered carefully before we follow Amariglio in making rationality definitive of modernist social science. In one piece, Becker (1962) argues that the laws established by neoclassical theory do not depend on rationality; under a number of alternative specifications of habitual or random behavior, the laws follow from constraints alone. Alchian (1950) also argues that the neoclassical laws do not depend on rationality; rather, they follow from sufficient variation plus a process of competition as natural selection.

Do we wish to strike Alchian, Becker, and the hydraulic Keynesians out of bounds as nonmodernist, on the grounds that they do not model the economy in terms of individual rationality? I do not wish to do so, and Amariglio and others working on the modernist project should at least consider these cases seriously. The theories of Alchian and others discussed here are non-*neoclassical* because they do not model the economy in terms of individual maximization. Tentatively, one of the strengths of the *modernist* project might be that it can see these theories as modernist, hence legitimate in mainstream economics despite being non-neoclassical. In pursuit of that possibility, perhaps our concept of modernism should not include modeling in terms of individual rationality.

Modernism: Foundationalism, Objectivism, and Control

For purposes of discussion, I suggest that we take modernism to be an intellectual position composed of or movement that advances foundationalism, objectivism, and control, as these are sketched here, and take universality and rationality to be incidental. This concept of modernism sticks close to the metaphor of the machine, for universality and rationality are the two components of Amariglio's modernism that are not mechanical.[7]

Nonmodernism, Antimodernism, and Postmodernism

Before discussing postmodernism, it is useful to introduce nonmodernism and antimodernism. "Nonmodernism" is a contraction for "not modernism," so nonmodernism comprehends all intellectual positions and movements other than modernism. In contrast, antimodernism is characterized by deliberate critical rejection of elements of modernism. Nonmodernism strictly includes antimodernism, and includes other nonmodernisms (which may overlap), such as postmodernism. Neither the nonmodernist nor the antimodernist necessarily holds a concept of modernism, but the antimodernist conceives of some element of modernism and deliberately, critically, rejects it.

For economic examples, I suggest that Marx, Veblen, Schumpeter, Knight, Mises, Hayek, Galbraith, Kirzner, and Shackle are nonmodernist, and that the partial truth of Amariglio's modernist thesis explains why they are all outsiders, recognized by mainstream economists as irregulars. For an example likely to be more controversial, McCloskey argues that until at least the 1950s the Chicago school was a nonmodernist one, which he refers to as "Good Old Chicago" (Klamer and

McCloskey 1988, pp. 11–15). For a final example, "fundamentalist Keynesians" interpret Keynes as a nonmodernist, and possibly a postmodernist (Coddington 1976; Amariglio, this chapter).

Klamer and McCloskey are antimodernists themselves, as is Amariglio. I judge that Veblen, Knight, Mises, Hayek, Kirzner, and Shackle from the list above are all antimodernists. Of these Knight, Hayek, and Shackle are important for Amariglio's theses and supporting case studies: Knight and Shackle because they are the subjects of two of the cases; Hayek because he is Shackle's dissertation supervisor and with Keynes is Shackle's foremost acknowledged intellectual creditor (Shackle 1972, acknowledgment). Discourse studies care about such things. Also, Hayek's 1942–1944 "Scientism in the Study of Society" and 1941 "Counter-Revolution of Science" are such deliberate and famous examples of antimodernism that the modernist project should cut its eye teeth on his example. Neither Amariglio nor I hope to see Knight, Hayek, or Shackle judged *post*modernist; at the least, testing by Hayek will enforce clarification of postmodernism, to distinguish it clearly from Hayek's antimodernism.

The reader may wonder just what postmodernism is. What distinguishes postmodernism among all the possible nonmodernist positions? What distinguishes postmodernist discourse study from discourse study in general? In what sense will the postmodernist project(s) have "nihilistic" implications?[8]

The reader will not find a clear answer in Amariglio's chapter. Although the term (and the movement) does receive some explicit attention, Amariglio does not consistently use any particular definition.[9] Fortunately, he recurrently heralds what postmodernism will bring, and attending to the heralded fruit I have constructed the following list of items. (Since I am uneasy about what postmodernism supposes or posits, as opposed to what it demonstrates or what are its characteristic results, I use "involves" here as a noncommittal verb. This needs work in the book.)

Postmodernism:

1. Involves *multiple knowledges* or discourses, with *incommensurability* and *persistent* or *irreducible differences* among them.
2. Involves the *discursive production of subjects*, which *decenters the individual*. This is the specifically postmodernist version of *antihumanism*.
3. Involves the *discursive production of knowledge*. Involves the

historically determined, the *discourse-specific*, and the *socially constituted*. Denies the *natural order*, in favor of knowledge or its object as *discursively produced/constructed/grounded/formed/constituted*.

4. Is antimodernist in all respects.
5. Involves *narrative*.
6. Involves the following topics of twentieth century mathematics and natural science: *fracta, catastrophes, discontinuity, chaos* and *relativity*.
7. Rejects individual *intention, deliberation*, and *power to choose*.
8. Involves the *fragmented individual* or *subject*, who is of *multiple minds*.
9. Involves *irrationality, contradiction*, the *arbitrary, play*, and *surprise*.
10. Involves knowledge or discourse as *unstable, everchanging, desperate makeshifts of transient applicability*.
11. Involves the *unmeasurable*, the *unknowable, guesswork*. Rejects *content* and system or the *systematic*.
12. *Deconstructs modernism* or *modernist discourse*. Involves the *destruction of economic theory and reasoning*.

Here I judge that items 1 and 2 distinguish the specifically postmodernist among discourse studies; 3 is an insight fundamental to all discourse studies; 4 and 5 are also nonmodernist positions more general than postmodern; 6 provides postmodernism with some hard scientific sanction, but plays no other role; 7 and 8 together deconstruct a common concept of individual rationality, 7 being certainly more general than postmodernist and 8 probably postmodernist; and 9 through 12 are postmodernist positions that involve nihilism. I propose that:

1. *Postmodernism is an antimodernist program that calls for discourse studies and is distinguished further by items 1 and 2 and 8 through 12 above.*
2. Items 9 through 12 above constitute postmodernism's "involvement" with nihilism.

The Modernist Thesis

Some concept of modernism is taken for granted here, but it need not be my own suggestion, outlined in the previous section. The focus here is on a way of discussing the economics discipline that should characterize all discourse studies, postmodernist or otherwise. It involves a sociological turn that is empirical in the sense of accepting actual economists and their discourse as tests.

Some version of the modernist thesis (*M*) is a supposition of Amariglio's chapter, but he does not attend to its formulation. It is important to identify the source of confusion and the stakes. "Mainstream economics" is one term taken for granted by Amariglio and "neoclassical" is another. Such usage is common and often a minor nuisance; however, it is crucial for Amariglio. I can best explain why in the course of offering my own suggestions.

Mainstream economics is what we mean when we speak generally of economics — when we speak of *the* economics discipline on the unexamined supposition or the as-if assumption that there is *one*. In our talk about economics we need such a concept. I propose that we define "mainstream economics" in sociological terms: it is a group of economists who can and do recognize each other as regular members. (Without good reason to do otherwise, we should use "current," "dominant," "standard," "orthodox," and "traditional" as synonyms for "mainstream" — and better yet, do without so much elegant variation.)

Appreciation that economics is discourse informs this definition. Discourse is social, so we who study it must be concerned with how economists recognize each other as regular members, and should conceive of economics primarily in terms of groups that do recognize each other and do communicate. Thus, what we mean by saying that Amariglio's own chapter is not mainstream is that economists would not generally recognize it. On this interpretation, the meaning of the modernist thesis is:

(*M'*) *Economists generally recognize each other as regulars by the criterion of common modernism.*

Neoclassical economics may *in fact* be mainstream, but we should not *define* it to be so. For purpose of discussion here, consider it defined in terms of a common economic theory, the marginal and subjective utility theory of value (utility theory, for short). This is a superfical characterization of neoclassical economics, but the point is simply that neoclassicsm is not related by definition to the mainstream or to modernism. On the suggested interpretation, what we mean by saying that Amariglio's own chapter is not neoclassical is that it does not build on utility theory.

Along these lines, common casual use of "mainstream" and "neoclassical" as synonyms may not vicious. Rather, it may aptly express a widely held view that *the economics discipline* is in fact unified by a *common economic theory*, utility theory. That is, it may be widely held that:

> *(N) Mainstream economics is neoclassical,*

or, as I have suggested we understand these terms:

> *(N') Economists generally recognize each other as regulars by the criterion of common marginal, subjective utility theory.*

For Amariglio, in contrast to the commoners, such casual use is vicious, because it remains unclear whether his modernist thesis *(M)* is advanced in opposition to the thesis *(N)*. Does he intend this strong modernist thesis:

> *(M_s) Mainstream economics is modernist, as opposed to neoclassical.*

I believe this is Amariglio's intention, but the strong interpretation is only indirectly supported by his paper. The evidence is his use without comment of terms "neoclassical and Keynesian," "neoclassical/Keynesian," and "modernist Keynesian," and his citation without comment of the modernist (but surely nonneoclassical) Milgate and Eatwell in support of general claims about economic scientists.

Let me recount what is at stake for studies of economic science. Certain theoretical economic tenets constitute the discipline of economics — the mainstream — as conceived by most historical and philosophical studies. So economic tenets, such as the equation of marginal subjective utility and value, have been privileged criteria in our discourse on economic science. The modernist thesis as I interpret it here is a proposal that aspects of modernism — such as the metaphor of the machine and the values placed on foundationalism, objectivism, and control — should be privileged instead. According to the modernist thesis, *it is principally the modernism, not the neoclassicsm, that constitutes what is mainstream in economics*. So the hallmark of mainstreamness in economics is nothing specific to economics; rather, it is an epistemological and methodological position (or a cultural condition, per Jameson 1984). So interpreted, the modernist thesis is an important one for the history and philosophy of economics. The thesis should be refined and tested, and I have some specific suggestions for testing here.

Perhaps the modernist thesis can explain the relative isolation of Veblen, Schumpeter, Knight, Mises, Hayek, Galbraith, Kirzner, and

Shackle. Many young economists find their work interesting, yet they have few followers among the fully-fledged. To consider these cases more closely is to test the modernist thesis, and I expect that here the test will be confirming. Utility theory, for example, does not distinguish this group, nor does a position on laissez-faire or the business cycle; what these eight share is common nonmodernism.

Conversely, there are some examples of non-neoclassical modernism to test the modernist thesis in form (M_s): for example, analytical Marxism, by Roemer (1982) and others; and the reswitching critique of neoclassism, by Robinson (1953–1954), Sraffa (1960) and others. It seems to me that analytical Marxism and the reswitching critique are modernist — indeed, appropriate paradigms of modernist economic science, not to mention more clearcut as examples than are Amariglio's Knight, Keynes, and Shackle. Do we find that their nonneoclassical modernism is mainstream?

Amariglio is well-placed to deal seriously with the example of Roemer's analytical Marxism as a test case. Roemer recently debated Amariglio and others concerning the appropriate direction for Marxian economics and the crux of their debate was modernism, advocated by Roemer and criticized by his opponents (Roemer et al. 1988). The modernist thesis implies that Roemer is mainstream and prepares us to see that he is a regular participant in mainstream conversations, despite his Marxism, because he is modernist and modernism is the foundation of the mainstream. I do not know the reception of Roemer sufficiently well to make a judgment regarding this test, but Amariglio probably does and I urge the exercise upon him.

Regarding the reswitching critique, Amariglio does not mention it, but two Cambridge economists appear in a cameo role. True to his modernist thesis, Amariglio cites Murray Milgate and John Eatwell (1983) without further comment as "some" who "have visceral reactions to the fundamentalist readings of Keynes," in support of which he quotes their expression of modernist values against the fundamentalist Keynesian "appeal to unknowable imperfections" and rejection of "systematic forces." Well done as a demonstration that the modernism of Keynes is controversial, and so that some economists care about modernist values, but for me the example turns against the modernist thesis itself, for Eatwell and Milgate are evidently not mainstream. Why not?

What project in the recent history of economic thought is more clearly modernist than the British program in the Cambridge capital controversy? The British Cambridge apparently followed all the modernist rules, yet lost. Sraffa's (1960) contribution is as spare and formal as

Mondrian's painting (for which, see Klamer 1987), clearly styled foremost by values of foundationalism and objectivism. Following Sraffa, the lacuna in neoclassical capital theory could be demonstrated without resort to durable plant and the uncertain future, a strikingly minimalist demonstration of the problem of time in economics, without a hint of postmodernism or attendant nihilism. Yet the British Cambridge lost, while Samuelson (1962) spoke of "parables." Why?

Offering one possible explanation in oral debate at the 1987 History of Economics Society Conference, McCloskey used this defeat of the British Cambridge in the capital controversy as proof of his own thesis that neoclassical economic practice is not in fact modernist — although its "official methodology" is modernist (McCloskey 1985, ch. 1). That is, the episode is a test that shows Amariglio's modernist thesis to be false.

Whatever the explanation of the episode, it is clear that neoclassical economics is not thoroughly modernist, for the victorious "parables" are a nonmodernist moment. Further, the Sraffian position has certainly been excluded from the *mainstream,* whether or not we identify that with the neoclassical; so mainstream economics, too, is not *thoroughly* modernist.

Discourse on Discourse

Amariglio calls for a postmodernist turn in economics, and in metalevel studies of economics. His postmodernism is informed by the constituting insight of discourse studies, the discursive insight (*DI*) for short:

> (*DI*) *Social phenomena are constucted discursively; i.e., through communicative social interaction.*

One version of this discursive insight is postmodernist item 3 mentioned earlier in this comment, but postmodernism includes the more specific theses on discourse, items 1 and 2, so discourse studies are not necessarily postmodernist. Evidently, more careful attention to discourse is needed in future programmatic pieces by the postmodernists, merely to clarify the nature of the program advanced. Modernism and postmodernism aside, all who study economic science should still take the discursive insight seriously, since economic theory is an example of a social phenomenon.

Discourse may be a method of study, may be an object of study, or may inform a study more loosely. Discourse is a method of study when the researcher deliberately engages members of the group studied (say, economists) in interactive discourse; the interview is an example (e.g.,

Klamer 1984). Such engagement by interview is not passive sense-observation, so it is contrary to modernist objectivism. Discourse is an object of study when the researcher observes or models verbal inter-action, whether or not as a participant. Insofar as the researcher is a participant, discourse is also the method and the study is nonmodernist, but insofar as the researcher is not a participant the subject/object distinction may be preserved and the study may be modernist. An example of modernist discourse study would be counting male-female and female-male transitions in a videotape-recorded discussion. Finally, the discursive insight (*DI*) may otherwise inform a study. For example, a text might seem to be an isolated object, its nature neither social nor discursive. But the discursive insight supports heuristic maxims such as "Every author has an audience" and so fosters the imaginative reconstruction of authorial suppositions and tactics. More generally, it supports the thesis that theories are socially and historically contingent.

Amariglio provides an example of discourse-informed study of the history of theories of uncertainty and expectations, but it is a short piece insufficient to serve as a paradigm for the program advanced. Unfortunately, there is not space to establish paradigms here, but I can consider one study briefly. Arjo Klamer's (1984) discourse study is well-known to those who study economic science but outside economics another and better study is accessible to us: *Opening Pandora's Box*, the discourse study of a specialty in biochemistry by G. Nigel Gilbert and Michael Mulkay (1984).

Gilbert and Mulkay focus more consistently than Klamer on scientists' discourse as the object of study, as opposed to scientists' action and belief (see also Mulkay 1981). Their study also goes further than Klamer's in theoretical interpretation of the discourse, beyond its mere report; Klamer evidently imagines an audience rather narrowly interested in quotation from the macroeconomists rather than in his interpretations. Like Klamer's study, *Opening Pandora's Box* is empirical, in the sense that Gilbert and Mulkay are guided by observer's values common in the empirical tradition, values constructed in the course of a four century conversation that includes the modernist champions. Like Klamer's, Gilbert and Mulkay's study is realist in attitude toward its scientists; relativist in attitude toward objects of its scientists' studies.

Like Klamer (1984, pp. vii, x), Gilbert and Mulkay begin with a prefatory statement regarding the observed fact of diversity.

It gradually became clear that we needed to employ rather different methodological assumptions and forms of analysis from those that we had been used to

in order to make any sociological sense of these data [the interview trans-
cripts]. We had to learn how to deal with variability in our accounts, in a way
that recognised that the variability was not just a methodological nuisance, but
was an intrinsic feature which we needed to exploit in our analysis. 'Pandora's
Box' is our metaphor for the conflicting voices that spoke to us. We shall show
that, nevertheless, we have been able to find order in their diversity. (p. vii)

Note that the last sentence points to reducibility of differences (cf. postmodernist item 1) and to systematic content (cf. item 11), in contrast to
Amariglio's postmodernist nihilism. The promise is not empty, for the
book is full of interesting findings. The claim that there is system, order,
or regularity in scientists' discourse despite their disagreements and differences, recurs in Gilbert and Mulkay and is convincingly established by
their arguments. Diversity of discourse need not have generally nihilistic
implications, and for Gilbert and Mulkay it does not.

After establishing that their scientists resort *systematically* to two different "reportoires of social accounting" — the "empiricist" and the
"contingent" — in different discursive settings (ch. 3), Gilbert and Mulkay deal serially with five more specific kinds of discursive activity:
accounting for scientific error, claiming that "the truth will out," constructing consensus, illustrating by pictures, and joking. It will be most
useful here to consider their results on "constructing and deconstructing
consensus" (ch. 6) and note in passing that Amariglio and others in the
modernist project should consider visual illustrations.[10]

Consensus (like diversity) is of the highest importance to all historians
and philosophers of economics, for some claims regarding consensus are
fundamental to our favored concepts of classical and neoclassical economics, if not to Marxian, Austrian, Chicago, and modernist economics,
too. Gilbert and Mulkay's discussion begins with a criticism of common
approaches, to take consensus in science entirely for granted or to rely
naively on scientists' reports (pp. 118–120). They provide an alternative
analysis that must strike a chord in anyone who has thought seriously
about neoclassical economics, or conversed with economists in terms of
"neoclassical."

In our interviews, almost every scientist clearly operated with at least two
versions of chemiosmotic theory. On the one hand, chemiosmosis was depicted
as a theory dealing in some detail with the processes involved in oxidative and
photosynthetic phosphorylation.... On the other hand, there was a highly
simplified, basic version of chemiosmosis. (p. 130)

Each scientist is able to resort systematically to different versions.

> [S]upposedly the same theory is interpreted in idiosyncratic terms as covering only those phenomena with which the speaker himself is centrally concerned and as composed only of those theoretical claims which he takes as validated....
>
> ... the speakers clearly alter the meaning of such terms as 'chemiosmotic theory' and 'Spencer's hypothesis' as they proceed.... we can observe these speakers sustaining an appearance of consensus in their discourse through the subtle deployment of various versions of a theory which is said to be generally accepted. (p. 133)

Is this postmodernist on the grounds that it shows scientists to be of "multiple minds" (cf. item 8)? It may be so, but Gilbert and Mulkay identify persistent regualarity here, rather than arbitrary play (cf. items 9 through 11). Discourse analysis is not doomed to nihilism.

Conclusion

I support Amariglio's call for discourse studies of economic science, such as studies of the Cambridge reswitching debate as discourse. It seems clear that there will be more discourse studies of economic science, and likely that there will be a transformation within the fields of history, sociology, and philosophy of economics. Many who study economic science have now browsed in those aisles of the library and found them interesting, and we already have some example studies (Klamer 1984, 1987; McCloskey 1985; this book).

I also support the call for discourse studies of business, such as studies of saving as discourse, although this call has not been discussed here. Amariglio's immanence thesis (I) is pertinent, for it asserts that there is a tendency to postmodernism already latent in modernist economics. As I am unconvinced of the immanence thesis, I am unconvinced that there will be more discourse studies of business, much less a transformation of mainstream economics. Amariglio suggests that in calling for discourse studies he can be midwife to a discursive turn in economic science; I hold that it is only the doctors, not the patients, who are pregnant.

I do not support the call for specifically postmodernist discourse studies, or the "nihilism" that postmodernism evidently implies for Amariglio. First, "postmodernism" and "nihilism" do not receive from Amariglio the care and attention necessary to support a programmatic call. Second, I hope for discourse studies that raise new questions but suspect that Amariglio's programmatic postmodernism insists on the answers in advance. So, his program implies "nihilism" in the sense of "destruction of economic theory," and insists on "persistent differences" among discourses and the "fragmentary" nature of discourse and of the individual. Those embarking on discourse studies may be prepared for such results, or even programmatically motivated by their prospect, but postmodernism as Amariglio describes it begs the questions.

Discourse studies should be empirical as well as philosophical. Testing is appropriate, in the sense of confronting an analysis with actual examples. So Amariglio considers Knight, Keynes, and Shackle — tests I contest — and so I have made suggestions for other tests of his modernist and immanence theses. I look forward to seeing the results.

Notes

[1] "Economics" and its cognates confuse the matter here, so it is useful to use "business" for "the economy"; "science" or "economic science" for "economics." Amariglio uses "economic agents" and "economic scientists" for which "businessmen" and "economists" (or "scientists") are shorter.

Amariglio calls for a postmodernist turn in studies of business as well as studies of science, but in this paper he is concerned principally with economists' discourse; it is a metalevel study that speaks directly to the concerns of the history and philosophy of economics (as is Amariglio 1988).

[2] Also please attend to the relation of modernism to "scientism" as it is used by Hayek 1952, part 1; Knight 1956, essay 10; McCloskey 1985, 8, *passim*; and Amariglio — in the last two cases as a synonym for "modernism" (?).

[3] I owe the point on art to Klamer's audio-visual presentation of his (1987).

[4] One contradiction in mainstream neoclassical economics may seem immediate from the attribution of objectivism, since neoclassical economics is commonly said to be "subjectivist." The subjectivism of "the subjective theory of value," however, is in mainstream neoclassism an *ontological* thesis unattended by subjectivist *method* or by knowledge claims about subjective utility.

[5] One contradiction in modernist science is in the tension between passive sense-perception and active control. There may be another, also bearing on control, *depending on the force within modernism of the reflexive move* that insists people as objects of knowledge have the problem-solving or creative capacities they have as subjects of knowledge. Amariglio makes some good points on this in discussions of Shackle and rational expectations.

Reflexivity and self-reference need attention in the booklength version. For starters, the reflexive move probably depends on the universalism and rationality elements of Amariglio's modernism, which I question.

[6] For Bentham as a paradigmatic modernist, see Foucault (1975) and Hutchison (1956). Hutchison includes a review of the literature on Bentham and control, albeit those reviewed participate in the liberal tradition in which liberalism and control are conceived to be opposite (contrast Foucault). For Saint-Simon as a paradigmatic modernist, see Hayek (1952, part 2).

[7] Note too that this makes "modernism" a synonym of "scientism" when it is applied to the social sciences. See note 2.

[8] Amariglio often relates postmodernism to "the nihilism of uncertainty," rather than to nihilism per se. Once, postmodernism avoids nihilism, so that the "nihilism" of uncertainty is merely that uncertainty can deconstruct *some* economic theories — modernist ones. There is no doubt that Amariglio celebrates "nihilism," but one is left to doubt whether post-modernism is in fact generally nihilistic.

[9] For example, Klamer qualifies as a postmodernist despite that "unlike many of the other postmodernist theorists, Klamer does not call into question the primacy and composition of the 'I'." Elsewhere, such failures would disqualify him as a postmodernist, as they disqualify Shackle.

Note that Klamer disavows postmodernism (Klamer and McCloskey 1988, 13).

[10] Pictures! Discourse studies should not be limited in scope to verbal communication but should include the visual. Pictures play a large part in the public face of the economics profession, located in the introductory college course. Further, if the new requirement that we go to the gallery as well as to the library and the laboratory is to be fruitful, one may expect the fruit especially in analysis of scientists' use of visual media.

Gilbert and Mulkay's discussion of scientific illustration has more general implications concerning the roles of fiction and reality in science (ch. 7).

References

Alchian, Armen. 1950. "Uncertainty, Evolution, and Economic Theory." *Journal of Political Economy* 58:211–221.

Amariglio, J. 1988. "The Body, Economic Discourse, and Power: an Economist's Introduction to Foucault." *History of Political Economy* 20:583–613.

Becker, Gary. 1962. "Irrational Behavior and Economic Theory." *Journal of Political Economy* 70:1–13.

——. 1968. "Crime and Punishment: an Economic Approach." *Journal of Political Economy* 76:169–217.

——. 1981. *A Treatise on the Family*. Cambridge and London: Harvard University Press.

Coddington, Alan. 1976. "Keynesian Economics: the Search for First Principles." *Journal of Economic Literature* 14:1258–1273.

Debreu, Gerard. 1959. *Theory of Value*. New Haven: Yale University Press.

Foucault, Michel. 1975. *Discipline and Punish*. Translated by Alan Sheridan. New York: Random House, Vintage Books Edition, 1979.

Gilbert, G. Nigel and Mulkay Michael. 1984. *Opening Pandora's Box: A Sociological Analysis of Scientists' Discourse*. Cambridge: Cambridge University Press.

Hayek, Friedrich A. 1952. *The Counter-Revolution in Science: Studies in the Abuse of Reason*. Glencoe, IL: Free Press. [Cited articles 1941–1944.]

Hutchison, T.W. 1956. "Bentham as an Economist." *Economic Journal* 66:288–306.

Jameson, Frederic. 1984. "Postmodernism, or the Cultural Logic of Late Capita-
lism." *New Left Review* 146:53–92.
Klamer, Arjo. 1984. *Conversations with Economists*. Totowa, NJ: Rowman
and Allanheld.
———. 1987. "The Advent of Modernism." Paper presented at the Interpretive
Economics Conference, Wellesley, MA, June.
Klamer, Arjo and McCloskey Donald. 1988. "The Rhetoric of Disagreement."
Paper presented at the 101st annual meeting of the American Economics
Association, New York, December.
Knight, Frank. 1956. *On the History and Method of Economics: Selected Essays*.
Chicago and London: University of Chicago Press. [Cited essays 1940–1947.]
McCloskey, Donald. 1985. *The Rhetoric of Economics*. Madison: University of
Wisconsin Press.
Milgate, Murray and Eatwell John. 1983. "Unemployment and the Market
Equilibrium." In their *Keynes's Economics and the Theory of Value and Dis-
tribution*. New York: Oxford University Press. Pp. 260–280.
Mulkay, Michael. 1981. "Action and Belief or Scientific Discourse?" *Philosophy
of the Social Sciences* 11:163–71.
Roemer, John. 1982. *A General Theory of Exploitation and Class*. Cambridge:
Harvard University Press.
Roemer, John et al. 1988. "Marx and Analytical Marxism." Session at the 101st
annual meeting of the American Economics Association, New York,
December.
Samuelson, Paul. 1947. *Foundations of Economic Analysis*. Cambridge: Harvard
University Press.
———. 1962. "Parable and Realism in Capital Theory: the Surrogate
Production Function." *Review of Economics Studies* 29:193–207.
Shackle, G.L.S. 1972. *Epistemics and Economics*. Cambridge: Cambridge Uni-
versity Press.
Sraffa, Piero. 1960. *Production of Commodities by Means of Commodities*.
Cambridge: Cambridge University Press.

3 A HERMENEUTIC APPROACH TO ECONOMICS: IF ECONOMICS IS NOT SCIENCE, AND IF IT IS NOT MERELY MATHEMATICS, THEN WHAT COULD IT BE?

Raymond Benton, Jr.

The rising interest of sociologists, anthropologists, psychologists, political scientists, and even now and then a rogue economist in the analysis of symbol systems poses — implicitly anyway, explicitly sometimes — the question of the realtionship of such systems to what goes on in the world....

— Clifford Geertz. 1983. "Blurred Genres: The Refiguration of Social Thought." *Local Knowledge: Further Essays in Interpretive Anthropology.* New York: Basic Books, p. 35.

An earlier version of this paper was presented before the faculty and graduate students of the School of Business, Queen's University, Kingston, Ontario, Canada, during the summer of 1988, while the author was a Visiting Summer Research Scholar. I would like to thank Queen's University for the opportunity to present these ideas, for the ensuing discussion that helped to clarify many of the points, and for the time to work on the revision of this paper.

From its inception, economics has been considered a science. For almost as long it has been under siege for clinging to what Arnold M. Rose once called "a prescientific psychology and sociology under which it happened to grow up" (1954, p. 209). The major critique is that economists fail to consider the context in which people live their lives.

For example, Michael S. McPherson (1983) recently noted that economists tend to explain society as the product of individual choice. Economists accept that choice stems from preferences, which are personal and private phenomena. Nothing more needs to be said; nothing more can be said. McPherson insists, however, that wants and preferences are in major part a reflection of the cultural and social phenomena that precede the individual.

> It is the cultural and social milieu that in large measure endows goods and activities with meaning and presents people with the matrix of constraints and opportunities within which they develop themselves.... People form their ends as well as their beliefs about effective means to ends in cultural contexts. (1983, p. 107)

Even Ludwig von Mises acknowledged "society is — logically or historically — antecedent to the individual," which is to say, the individual person "is born into a socially organized environment." Von Mises maintains, however, that society "exist[s] nowhere else than in the actions of individual men," but then adds, human action must always be comprehended "as meaningful and purposeful behavior" (1949, p. 142).

Methodological individualism gets in the way of accepting the full implications of otherwise admitting that something *is* logically and historically prior to the individual person. Methodological individualism does not accept that human thought and feeling is thoroughly social, "social in its origins, social in its function, social in its forms, social in its applications" (Geertz, 1973, p. 360). McPherson's "cultural and social milieu" and Von Mises' "socially organized environment" is the source of individual meaning and purpose. Von Mises does not acknowledge, as does McPherson, that wants and preferences, knowledge and belief, sense and sentiments, are public phenomena. To von Mises meaning and purpose are private, personal phenomena; to McPherson they are public and social.

But even McPherson misses that economics is part of that cultural milieu that in large measure endows goods and activities with meaning. Economics, generally considered a science, is culture. It is culture in the sense that it is an "effort to provide a coherent set of answers to the existentialist situations that confront all human beings in the passage of their lives" (Bell, 1976, p. 12).

The study of culture, the accumulated totality of ordered systms of symbols and meanings, is the study of the machinery individuals and groups of individuals employ to orient themselves in a world otherwise opaque. The point of a semeiotic approach to culture is to aid anthropologists in gaining access to the conceptual world in which their subjects live. The point of a hermeneutic approach to economics is to aid ourselves in gaining access to the conceptual world in which we, ourselves, live. The analytical task is to delve into the meaning of economics, to delve into the manner in which it provides a set of general, yet distinctive, answers to the existential situations that confront people in the passage of their lives.

The first section of this chapter reviews our image of the relationships between science and other knowldege systems. The second section reviews, briefly, the status of economics as a science. The third and fourth sections consider economics from the perspecive of a nonscientific knowledge system — from the perspective of religion as a cultural system. The argument is that economics is first and foremost a system for the creation and inculcation of meaning and purpose and that economic laws, such as the laws of supply and demand, are not laws that govern behavior but rules that govern practice. Economics provides the terms and expressions and ordinary language that *we* use to give meaning to *our* world of daily life as we confront it, act in it, and live through it.

Scientific and NonScientific Cultural Knowledge Systems

> *. . . it is only when we have clearly recognized art as a mode of knowledge parallel to but distinct from other modes by which man arrives at an understanding of his environment that we can begin to appreciate its significance.*

> — Herbert Read. 1967. *Art and Society*. Fourth edition.
> London: Faber and Faber, p. 7.

> *. . . what men know or think about the external world or about themselves, their concepts and even the subjective qualities of their sense perceptions are to Science never ultimate reality, data to be accpeted. . . . The concepts which men actually employ, the way in which they see nature, is to the scientist necessarily a provisional affair . . .*

> — F.A. Hayek. 1955. *The Counter-Revolution of Science*.
> London: Free Press of Glencoe, p. 22.

There are several modes of knowledge by which people arrive at an understanding of their environment. Science, one perspective among perspectives, is privileged at the top of the knowledge hierarchy. Although science itself is in a state of disarray, there still remains a consensus as to its defining characteristics. Those characteristics emerge most clearly when it is placed against other perspectives in terms of which people experience their world (Geertz, 1973, pp. 111–112; Richter, 1972).

The world of everyday knowledge accepts the world as pretty much what it seems to be and combines that acceptance with a pragmatic motive, "the wish to act upon the world so as to bend it to one's practical purpose, to master it, or if that proves unworkable to adjust to it" (Geertz, 1973, p. 111). The world of everyday life, itself, is a cultural product, for it is framed in terms of the symbolic conceptions of "stubborn fact" handed down from generation to generation. As Kenneth Boulding once noted, "We do not perceive out sense data raw; they are mediated through a highly learned process of interpretation and acceptance" (1956). There are no such things as brute facts, even at the most rudimentary level. There are only interpretations.

In the aesthetic perspective such naive realism and practical interest is avoided. To grasp the world aesthetically is to manufacture a deliberate untruth, to disengage from belief, so as to penetrate into deeper truths. "The reading of literature requires a willing suspension of disbelief," D.G. Kehl notes, because the belletrist is a fabricator, "presenting heightened truth through the openly acknowledged illusion of art" (1983, p. 34).

The religious perspective moves beyond the realities of everyday life to wider ones that correct and complete them. Emphasis is not action on these wider realities but acceptance of them, faith in them. The religious perspective questions the realities of everyday life in terms of what it takes to be wider, nonhypothetical truths.

Lastly, to grasp the world scientifically is to suspend the naive realism of everyday knowledge and the practical motive not in favor of a disengagement and illusion, nor in favor of larger realities beyond them, but in favor of disinterested observation, deliberate and institutionalized doubt, and systematic inquiry in terms of abstract conceptions rather than the concrete conception of everyday knowledge.

All knowledge systems are recognized as ways of coming to terms with the world, as ways of interpreting and giving meaning, objective conceptual form, to the world as experienced. They all tend to develop and maintain some degree of internal coherence, logical consistency, and mutual reinforcement among the propositions of the system. All tend toward developing and maintaining factual plausibility — compatibility with accepted facts and a capacity to explain those facts that the system is expected to explain.

Science as a form of knowledge is distinctively European in origin and particularly Western in its orientations. It claims universality because the processes of nature are presumed to be everywhere the same regardless of whatever local nonscientific knowledge systems may have been historically created to explain whatever it is that the people who created them think they ordinarily experience in the course of their everyday lives. It claims superiority because it not only believes that there exists such an external world independent of the perceiving subject but that that world operates "according to general laws which remain largely hidden under ordinary observation circumstances" (Richter, 1972, p. 2). The goal of science as a form of knowledge is to capture those processes, natural or social, and relate them in abstract symbolic form, often the form of mathematics: from a mathematics professor I once learned, "The universe is ordered and highly structured. Mathematics, the primary language of this universe, is also ordered and structured."

Although as a form of knowledge science shares much with all other forms of knowledge, it is considered drastically different from them. Scientific constructs are supposed to be more powerful because they are subject to more rigorous and critical verification procedures than are the constructs in other forms of knowledge. The rules of evidence applied to scientific knowledge either do not apply or are not applied to other forms of knowledge. In the rules of scientific procedure, "testability" means that the knowledge system provides a basis for accurately predicting observable outcomes, not merely for formulating plausible retrospective explanations. Those outcomes must be testable in practice and not just in principle because it is in terms of the accuracy of the predictions that a scientific proposition is evaluated. Traditional cultural knowledge systems are not scientific because they typically cannot be tested against situations that have not yet occurred. Hence they cannot be refuted.

All of this implies a hierarchy of knowledge systems that elevates science, and the scientist, to a status and position of privilege and prestige as the arbitrator of "truth." Anthropologist Claude Levi-Strauss evidenced as much when he distingusihed between an observer's model (what he termed "science") and a participant's (or "home-grown") model. Levi-Strauss did not belittle home-grown models. He wrote, "each [society] has its own theoreticians whose contributions deserve the same attention as that which the anthropologist gives to colleagues" (1953:527). The thrust of Levi-Strauss' position was clear, however: the scientist (anthropologist) may find information provided by native theoreticians useful but he or she cannot expect to obtain an adequate understanding of the phenomenon under study merely by accepting their observations and explanations. This same relationship is exhibited by Richter:

> Sociologists generally assume that they cannot expect to obtain an adequate understanding of a social phenomenon merely by accepting the observations and intuitive interpretations of sociologically unskilled participants.... Thus, sociologists do not accept primitive people as experts on primitive society, or ordinary Americans as experts on American society, even though such participants may provide information about their respective societies which sociological experts will find useful. (Richter, 1972, p. 9)

Science, in our world, is more than a method by which knowledge is gathered and organized. By its privileged position it arbitrates between the real and the unreal; it dictates what is possible; it suggests what can be done. George C. Lodge was on target when he wrote, "Science is indeed the religion of today" (Lodge, 1976, p. 314). Nowhere is that more true than in the case of economics.

Economics as Science

> *Euclidean geometry was once styled the science of space, but calling it a science did not make it one.... Economics is often defined as the science of the distribution of scarce resources, but calling it a science does not make it one.*
>
> — Alexander Rosenberg. 1983. "If Economics Isn't Science, What is It? *The Philosophical Forum* 14 (Spring–Summer):309.

As a science economics shares the general goals of science and is subject to scientific standards of verification. Science, traditionally speaking, seeks to understand the universal processes, natural and social, in terms of which life must, of necessity, be lived. It seeks to symbolically formulate the general laws of nature, laws which remain largely hidden to ordinary observation. To the economist this means grasping the regularities of "the economic process" by formulating economic laws, laws of the economy that govern man's behavior. The standard of verification is the accuracy of the predictions that the theory generates.

Although economists have been very busy formulating such laws there remains some question as to their success. Philosopher Alexander Rosenberg, in *Microeconomic Laws: A Philosophical Analysis* (Rosenberg,

1976), argued that economic theory is a conceptually coherent body of causal general claims that stand a chance of being laws. More recently Rosenberg (1983), referring to himself as an erstwhile apologist of economists, has revised even this hesitant conclusion. He now writes that economists have failed to find any such laws that have improved their ability to predict, say, consumer behavior, any better than Adam Smith could have two hundred years ago (Rosenberg, 1983, p. 301).

Rosenberg now suggests that we give up the notion that economics any longer has the aims or makes the claims of an empirical science of human behavior. Rather,

> we should view it as a branch of mathematics, one devoted to examining the formal properties of a set of assumptions about the transitivity of abstract relations: axioms that implicitly define a technical notion of "rationality," just as geometry examines the formal properties of abstract points and lines. (Rosenberg, 1983, p. 311)[1]

Douglas Hands' (1984) reply to Rosenberg was that he failed to demonstrate his claims. But Hands offered little more in rebuttal. Of his own arguments Hands wrote that they "are not sufficient to 'prove' that general equilibrium theory is 'something more' than mathematics," and concluded,

> There is no doubt that the nature of abstract economic theory is a thorny philosophical issue without a currently foreseeable neat and easy solution. (p. 501)

Befitting a descipline that has failed to formulate any general laws, economics has a poor predictive track record, the scientific standard for verification. Whereas economists were once confronted with explaining their assumptions, they are now confronted with explaining why economic theory does not predict very well.[2]

Writing in 1965, Adolph Lowe noted that during the 1940s and the 1950s theoretical economics had moved in the direction of scientific exactitude. But consistent as this development may appear, he wrote,

> it poses a puzzle when we try to evaluate the results of these sophisticated procedures by the only relevant yardstick — their correspondence with observable facts. To put it bluntly, our ability to explain and to predict has not improved in proportion to the exactitude of the methods applied. (1965, p. 5–6)

Similarly, Wilbur and Harrison (1978) noted that it is somewhat problematic why prediction of economic phenomena has been consistently lacking over the years given that standard economists place so much weight on the ability to predict as the means of verifying the truth of a theory. More recently, Brady (1986) has written that Friedman's own work consists of a long series of failed forecast:

> A comparison of Friedman's forecasts with experience leads one to reject his theories, as presently formulated, using his own method of appraisal.... Although he has failed to predict future events, his predictions of the *past* have been successful. This, however, strikes the author as a desperate last ditch attempt to save a failed theory. (pp. 845–846, 848)

And, finally, Donald McCloskey (1984, 1985, 1988), a critic of economic methodology but not of economics, points out that although economists have set up a very tight methodological structure, they fail to adhere to it when making their arguments in favor of economic reasoning. And for good reason: the empirical support, even for the most basic and fundamental of economic principles, the Law of Demand (1984; 1985, pp. 57–62), is not too persuasive. This is critically important because supply and demand provides the framework into which all other economic arguments must be made to fit. McCloskey comments that if economists stuck to the empirical arguments they may not believe as stridently as they do in the Law of Demand. But does the economist doubt the Law? "Certainly not. Belief in the Law of Demand is the distinguishing mark of the economist . . . Economists believe it ardently" (1985, p. 59). Economists must maintain their own persuasion, and they must persuade others, of the validity of the Law of Demand as well as other laws in economics. They do so by other, nonpositivist rhetorical devices. Economists, it turns out, are rhetoricians just like everybody else — only they are unaware of it.

We are, therefore, left with a very central question: if economics is not a science, and if it not merely mathematics, then what is it? To answer this question we must delve into the meaning of economics. To do that we must approach economics not as a scientific knowledge system but as a nonscientific knowledge system.

On Codes and Conduct

> *Material production is essentially social. Humans are not genetically endowed with the physiology or mentality to enable them to survive, much less prosper, on their own. Group interaction in the form of a division of labour is thus required, with the character and complexity of the rules differing with specific cultures and types of production.*

— Len Doyal and Ian Gough. (1986) "Human Needs and Strategies for Social Change," In Paul Ekins eds. *The Living Economy: A New Economics in the Making*, London and New York: Routledge & Kegan Paul.

From the standpoint of evolution, it seems plausible to say that ideology is a substitute for instinct. The animals seem to know what to do; we have to be taught.

— Joan Robinson. (1962) *Economic Philosophy*. London: C.A. Watts & Co. Ltd., p. 4.

In a market economy the spontaneous and free action of innumerable persons results in an ordered and efficient use of resources and human effort and an ordered flow of the goods and services required by people as biological and social beings. The mystery has always been how the market does this, how it orchestrates production and distribution without a conductor. This is the binding mystery that holds and enchants the American mind and to which economics is a liturgical expression. The reification of the market (Barber, 1977) causes the economist to miss a very significant point necessary for understanding the role of economics and of economic laws.

What must be realized is that social living requires some acceptance of and compliance with fixed rules of conduct. Random behavior in any society does not result in social coherence; it results in tension, confusion, and conflict. In order for a coherent social economy to materialize, human behavior must be patterned behavior, patterned according to a set or sets of rules accepted and instituted by society. Such patterning renders human behavior meaningful and purposeful — purposeful to the actor and meaningful to others.

This can be readily illustrated by considering a society such as that of the Trobriand Islands. Among the Trobriand Islanders production and distribution were coordianted by as many as six different social institutions, some of them kinship based. In one, those living in interior villages that did not have fishing rights would, at harvest time, bring quantities of yams to those living in seaside villages. Every man would set his yams in front of his partner's house. Soon after, the men of the lagoon village would give notice to the inland people that they were going out on a fishing expedition. By the time they returned, the people from the inland village had arrived on the beach. The haul of fish was taken directly from the canoes and carried to the inland village. It was all systematic, predictable, and coordianted because it was carried out in accordance with specific rules of conduct.

Another sphere of exchange existed in which a man gave as much as three quarters of his crops as annual contributions of food to his sister's husband (or, lacking that, to his mother's husband) and as tribute to a chief. The man's sister's husband, in turn, gave his crops to his sister's husband. Thus, a man and his family was largely dependent for subsistence not on himself but on his wife's brother. Such exchanges were not the manifestation of random behavior. It was the result of patterned behavior, behavior pattern after specific rules of conduct.

These were not the only patterns of production and distribution among the Trobriand Islanders. They serve, however, to illustrate that exchanges must take place and with a certain degree of certainty and predictability if there is to be both biological and social coherence and continuity. Among the Trobriand Islanders there was coherence and continuity because the exchanges did, in fact, take place and with a reasonable degree of predictability. They took place because most of the Trobriand Islanders, most of the time, followed the rules for conducting the exchanges that were part of their society. Certainly there was nonconforming behavior; every society has not only nonconforming behavior but customary ways of not following custom as well. But on the average, that nonconforming behavior was insufficient to threaten the stability of the society.

Just as the social economy of the Trobriand Islands did not result from central administrative command, neither was it a result of unpatterned random action. It was a system of interlocking *patterned* actions, indeed several such patternings. Predictable patterns of social interaction emerge only when most of the people most of the time adhere, willfully, to a set of fixed rules; if the adherence is not willful then some system of power and authority, ultimately backed up by sanction, will emerge to ensure that the rules will be taught, learned, and correctly followed.

The West is so tied up in its myth of liberation that "free choice" and "individual action" is often understood as free, noncompulsory, unpatterned action. Teleology, hierarchy, and tradition are constraints left behind with the passing of the medieval world. But modernism, of necessity, has its traditions, too, even if it does not call them that. It is necessary to repeat, if only for emphasis, that obedience to fixed rules of conduct is the price that must be paid to live in a social economy. Only if people know that their actions will elicit from others adequate reactions will a coherent social economy take shape. Such certainty results only when the rules for conduct are followed by most of the people most of the time.

In order to grasp the real meaning and significance of economics and of economic laws, we must consider them not as symbolic expressions of natural laws or natural processes nor even as the representation of statistical regularities, but as a specific set of rules appropriate for a specific mode of production and distribution found in a particular society. The laws of supply and demand provide a particular people, living in a particular era, with a distinctive directive for their economic decisions. To the members of a commerical exchange economy, the standard that organizes production and distribution and assures the society's continuity and success is provided by the Law of Supply and Demand.

A decision, for example, to acquire a hat in the market is not in itself sufficient to bring forth action from others, even if one possesses purchasing power. Some hatter has to be interested in selling a hat. But all the hatters in the market are fully entitled to refuse, as are the owners of the productive factors whose services have to be enlisted if any hats are to be supplied at all. If all the hatters adopted the medieval ideal of aiming at a customary standard only, at ceasing production when they have "had enough," they may disregard any additional demand and increase neither prices not production, as the Law says they will. When buyers' preferences and sellers' incentives are influenced not by money considerations alone but by all sorts of personal, national, racial, and other discriminations, and when such preferences are motivated by the injunction "enough is best" rather than "as much as possible," then even physically homogeneous goods and equal money offers will lose their economic equality and interchangeability. If that were to happen then the process of provisioning through the market would cease to function, and the social economy would become either disorganized or, more likely, organized and integrated through some other institutionalization of social code.

The general acceptance of some standardized pattern of behavior was a primary condition for commercial exchange to historically develop into an economic system and to become a predominant means of economic provisioning. The Law of Supply and Demand is the formulation of such a social code. It defines a line of economic behavior that brings the actions of discrete individuals into agreement, and thus contains an imperative rather than a description of empirical facts. It should be formulated in terms somewhat like following: "If commerical exchange is to be an effective instrument for want satisfaction, sellers should raise prices when buyers increase their demand," and so on, for its various propositions (Lowe, 1942, pp. 439–440). In this way the Law of Supply and Demand acts as the beacon from which human action takes its bearings. Only in this way does the price system act as the signal system conveying the inforamtion that economists insist it conveys.

Obedience to fixed rules of conduct is the price to be paid for living in a social economy. But people are not born with an understanding of theories and practices relevant to the modes of production and reproduction in their society, nor are they necessarily predisposed to accept the particular system of allocation and distribution that characterize it. Such understanding and acceptance has to be learned. The mere existence of a set or sets of rules will not guarantee they will be taught, learned, and correctly followed. They must also be meaningful beyond the mere coordination of economic provisioning. They must provide, as well, coherent answers to the existentialist situations that confront the people in their world of daily life as they confront it, act in it, and live through it.

Economics as a Secular Religion

> *When religion ceased to be a political force, politics became a substitute religion.*
>
> — Lewis Mumford. 1973. *The Condition of Man.* New York: Harcourt Brace Jovanovich, (orig. 1944), p. 197.

> *So one meaning of "secular" is roughly "nontraditionally religious.*
>
> — Ninian Smart. 1983. *Worldviews: Crosscultural explanations of Cultural Beliefs.* New York: Charles Scribner and Sons.

> *Economics, rather than being paired with Newtonian physics, as is so often and . . . so fevently done, deserved to be ranked alongside Chritsianity as one of the great spiritual forces . . .*
>
> — Harvey C. Bunke. 1964. "Economics, Affluence, and Existentialism. *Quarterly Review of Economics and Business* 4(2):9.

The defining proposition of the following is that the universe in which man must, of necessity, live has no moral direction, no logic, no purpose, no order, no meaning, in and of itself, either in the sweep of history or in the daily course of events. "We labor under a number of delusions," anthropologist Edward Hall wrote, "one of which is that life makes sense" (Hall, 1977, p. 11). It is a delusion we cannot do without, however, for man cannot live in a world he cannot understand, a world without empirical regularity, without emotional coherence, without individual and social justice.

If there is to be meaning and purpose in this world man must create it. Traditionally that has been the role of religion. In the modern world that task has fallen, significantly, on the shoulders of the economist. To see how traditional economics has done this we must first look at the nature of the existentialist challenges that threaten to break in upon man.

There are at least three points where events threaten to lack not just interpretations but *interpretability*: at the limits of our analytical capabilities, at the limits of our powers of endurance, and at the limits of our moral insight. Each, if severe enough or prolonged enough radically challenges the proposition that life is comprehensible and that we can, by taking thought, orient ourselves effectively within it (Geertz, 1973, pp. 87–125). These are the existentialist challenges with which any religion, however primitive, must attempt somehow to cope.

The Limits of Our Analytical Capabilities

Economics provides a very important, and certainly the most widely used, background against which we cast the wider world of our experience. The Laws of Supply and Demand, for example, are uttered, and often, with an air of authority and unquestioned, indeed unquestionable, truth. They convey a sense of the really real in the sense of an implicit understanding that this is how things are and the way things have been.

Such understandings are certainly part of formal instruction in economics. They are, as well, part of our informal education, the enculturation, socialization, or indoctrination that our children go through as they become civilized, that is cultured, beings. Parents complain that things cost so much, or so much more than they did before, and they often do so in the company of children. But they do not just complain, wondering in dumb astonishment. They also explain, and they explain in accordance with what they, themselves, have been taught. It is not so much an act of "explaining" as it is an act of convincing oneself, and others if they are listening, that things are explainable within the accepted scheme of things.

When a parent explains about the high level of prices the child will hear an elementary presentation of the Law of Supply and Demand. Some people, the story holds, want something but are unable for various reasons to provide it to themselves so they "pay" others for it. Others are able and willing to make the item in question and will do so "for a price." If a lot of people want something but few people make it then the "price" will be higher than it would be if a lot of people made it and few people wanted it. This because the "demand" is greater than the "supply". If the "supply" were greater than the "demand" the buyers could pick and choose so that they got what they wanted and at the cheapest price. Since all those making the item will want to sell it (certainly they do not need for themselves all that they make) each will vie with the other sellers for the buyers' favor. The price that the buyer pays will fall. But since, generally, demand outpaces supply (we "know" that it does and we "know" why), the amount wanted generally exceeds the amount available. Consequently prices are high or higher than they used to be. The explanation may be extended to include something about government spending or about unions demanding higher wages. Higher wages drive the cost of making things up and therefore things cost more.

Although the details may vary[3] the story is, in its essence, always the same. Similar stories are woven around other laws, other principles, and other fundamentals in economics — such as the law of increasing (or decreasing) returns and its corollary, the economies of scale. They all serve to ascribe meaning, objective conceptual form, to the situations that people face in the passage of their lives. They serve, in the present case, to explain "the economy."

The Limits of Our Powers of Endurance

Economics not only provides a framework for interpreting what is, it also provides a framework for enduring situations of emotional stress.

Social arrangements are not without problems. They are seemingly riddled with contradictions and inconsistencies that must be resolved if life and its inevitable pain and suffering is to be endurable. Since social friction is experienced as personal insecurity people must have an interpretation of their lives such that the conflicts are settled, the unbearable features are eliminated or otherwise understood, and the meaningfulness and purposefulness of life is preserved.

Economics is no less at work here than it is in the more cognitive aspects of meaning. How is this magic worked? Anthropologist Mary Douglas has suggested that one way of dealing with such situations is by projecting them into a sort of mythical fairy-tale world where the salient social contradictions are stated and restated "in more and more modified fashion, until in the final statement the contradictions are resolved, or so modified and masked as to be eliminated" (Douglas, 1967, p. 57).

Walter Weisskopf (1949, 1950, 1951, 1955) has shown how certain central ideas common to traditional economics, ideas that have long been recognized as untenable, can be understood as means of fulfilling the kinds of psychological pressures referred to above. Concepts like perfect knowledge, which human beings do not possess, or equilibrium, which admittedly is never reached, or economic rationality, which, as generally recognized, is not the only motive of human behavior. From a strictly scientific point of view it is unintelligible why these and other concepts are retained in spite of their admitted insufficiency on strictly scientific grounds. But if looked at in the light of the anxiety-avoiding function of thought such intellectual concepts become meaningful.

Thought constructs eliminate or settle conflicts, in part, through the abstracting process. We extract from the innumerable stimuli in the real world certain elements with which we then build a model, an explicit metaphor. The abstracting process itself is not what is important. What is important is what is left behind, what is abstracted *out*. Some elements of the real world are "conveniently" left out and thereby not recognized. It is difficult to "see" things in the real world that are not "in" the model by which that reality is grasped. But, as well, some things are included — *added* — to the "abstracted" model which are not, and are knowingly not, found in reality. While leaving some things behind for theoretical convenience may seem suspicious, inserting other things not found in the real world should seem unnecessary. That is, unless doing so performed some unsuspected function.

In both cases the abstracting process serves to deny the multitude of conflicting experiences, to deny that we live in a bewildering, incomprehensible, and troubled world. In economics the process results in a mythical fairy-tale world of perfect competition in which things are, as we say, "perfect."

Further, the idea of an autonomous economic system functioning separately from social and political factors certainly acts as an anxiety-reducing mechanism. By abstracting out the purely economic phenomena many of the troublemaking features of our social system are both identified and left behind. Psychologically, the emphasis on rationality and decision making excludes the irrational, the erratic, and the capricious. Sociologically, those collective phenomena that impinge on the individual, as well as the facts of social stratification and class conflict are removed. Politically, the drive for power is ameliorated while the stubborn fact that economic relationships imply at least the potential for power of man over man is excluded. In short, the more repugnant features of our economic and social system, and the chief elements that create social conflict and evoke criticism, are left out of the picture.[4] If doubts remain about the palliative effect of this type of model building one need only consider a model of the economic process in which all of these troublemaking features are reintroduced.[5] As Weisskopf noted, "it is easier to arrive at a well ordered picture of reality if large parts of it are ignored" (Weisskopf, 1949, p. 307).

When the well-ordered picture is used, in turn, as the model, the metaphor, through which experience is interpreted the empirical aspects of life take on a semblance of well-orderness as well. Wish fulfilling intellectual imagery, as Weisskopf termed it, substitutes for the unbearable facts of life by filtering many of them out in the process of interpretation. What cannot be seen does not exist and what does not exist cannot be troublesome.

Equilibrium, the distinction between the long run and the short run, and other concepts embodied in traditional economic expressions, all function in an anxiety-reducing capacity.[6] Justified or not, merchants and manufacturers have always been among the highly criticized. Even Adam Smith (1937) had short words for them.[7] He noted, "People of the same trade seldom meet together, even for merriment and diversion, but the conversation ends in a conspiracy against the public." And he warned against the generally antisocial political proposals of those "who live by profit."

> The interest of the dealers in any particular branch of trade or manufacture is always in some respects different from, and even opposite to, that of the public... The proposal of any new law or regulation of commerce which comes from this order ought always to be listened to with great precaution.... It comes from an order of men, whose interest is never exactly the same with that of the public, who have generally an interest to deceive and even to oppress the public, and who accordingly have, upon many occasions, both deceived and oppressed it. (Smith, 1937, p. 250)

Equilibrium, a central construct in traditional economics, is a modern embodiment, in somewhat diluted form, of the older concept of the harmony of interests. The equilibrium concept eliminates the risk-taking entrepreneurs and their profits. But only a formidable array of admittedly artificial "abstractions," including complete rationality, perfect knowledge, perfect intercommunication, perfect mobility in space, no cooperation, no collusion, and more, make it possible to attain equilibrium. Under such conditions profits would be absent because omniscience, perfect rationality, and perfect intercommunication removes all uncertainly. Profit and entrepreneurship exist because of the uncertainty created by the absence of these things. What remains is, in the long run, a profitless economy and without those "who live by profit."

Not all conflict and suffering can be eliminated merely by excising it from thought. In fact, no society denies altogether that life occasionally hurts. Some situations of conflict and suffering do remain and they are, in fact, often celebrated. It is not that people must know how to avoid suffering; they must know how to suffer: how to accept it and how to endure it. Here, again, economics plays a vital role.

The image presented by economics is heroic. But it is a double-edged sword. A perfectly competitive economy may be as nearly a perfect system as can be envisioned but it is, also, nothing less than the socialization of insecurity and economic helplessness. A perfectly competitive economy requires nothing less of people than continuous exertion, an inhuman amount of flux and mobility, the renunciation of all human ties with other people and with habituations, as well as a hostile competitive attitude toward others.[8] All such stances are contrary to human inclination. As a result they embody elements of pain and suffering, even if that pain is only occasionally physical.

People do, on occasion and sometimes frequently, experience insecurity and economic helplessness. How are they, or those around them, supposed to feel? What kinds of moods are they supposed to have? What is the tailor or the corner grocer supposed to feel when suddenly unable to support themselves and their families because their customers no longer stop by? The very thought is enough to threaten one's sense of security. When it in fact happens it can be devastating. Without having any real "facts," however, the tailor or the corner grocer "knows" what has happened and each "know" how to feel about it. Customers, always in need of clothing and food, have gone elsewhere. Someplace, somewhere, there is somebody providing a better product at the same price or the same product at a cheaper price. It is nothing personal; there are no personal bonds involved. Don't brood but persevere, work harder, and set your nose to the grindstone. That is the message that economics relates.

And it is only what any right thinking person would feel. The victims are, as we say, "victims of progress", victims of the unyielding Law of Supply and Demand. And although we may momentarily forget there are those who will remind us: "as much as some would like to repeal the laws of supply and demand, it can't be done" (Grayson, 1973, p. 107). Although one may be angry, and one may even momentarily experience a loss of self-control bordering on fury, one does not (at least the reasonable person does not) feel indignation, that anger or scorn that results from perceived injustice or meanness. What else is it that we mean when we counsel our friends, neighbors, and acquaintances to be "realistic" than to accept the dictates of reality, the dictates of "the market." When times are tough, believers look to something greater than themselves and their perceived oppressors to see them through. The traditionally religious look to and even blame God; the nontraditionally religious look to and even blame "the market."

To anyone out of work, to anyone who has suddenly discovered his or her lifetime efforts gone or hard-learned trade rendered obsolete, to anyone who has suddenly lost a means of livelihood, the experience can be distressing. Economic theory presents a specific and concrete image of such suffering that relates back to the Law of Supply and Demand in such a way that the suffering is seen as natural, realistic, and, given the unalterable structure of reality, sometimes unavoidable. Some suffering thus becomes part of the human condition. The image, as long as it is embraced, is strong and powerful, strong and powerful enough to resist the challenge of emotional meaninglessness raised by such intense pain.

The Limits of Our Moral Insight

The distance is short between the problem of suffering and the problem of morality. If suffering is severe enough it usually, though not always, seems morally undeserved as well, particularly to the sufferer. Where bafflement, bewilderment and confusion is the problem of making sense out of the sometimes strange and opaque events that are part of the world, and suffering is the problem of making sense out of intense, relentless, and stubborn pain, evil is the problem of making sense out of the perplexing and seemingly inexplicable lack of righteousness, equity, and fairness that also appears, on the surface, to be part of the world.

The problem here centers on the gap between the way things are and the way things ought to be if conceptions of right and wrong make sense. It is the gap between what we deem various individuals deserve and what we see that they in fact get that causes the problem. "[T]o be just," MacIntyre points out, "is to give each person what each deserves" (MacIntyre, 1984, p. 152). Justice in the world is important because it ameliorates the hurt that is in the world.

Nowhere does the lack of justice threaten a society more than in the distribution of the spoils of effort. The problem is to come up with a definition of justice that is acceptable to all and with means of achieving it. One such concept of justice, one that goes far back in history beyond the emergence of economic theory, is that people should receive in accordance with what they produce: payment in accordance with product, reward in relation to effort. The contemporary institutionalization of this value judgement, it will surprise no one to learn, is "the market."

This brings us back to the issue of prices and the subject of employment. In conventional economics employment has been used as the main means of income distribution and the wages of labor is the "price" on the market. Hence prices and wages are inexorably linked to the issue of justice.

The labor theory of value in the writings of the classical economists was an attempt to discover an ethical justification in prices by relating them to the amount of work, labor, and effort that went into the item produced. The marginal productivity theory of wages and factor prices — the application of the Law of Supply and Demand to "human capital" and natural resources, eventually replaced the labor theory of value. In either case the effort was to affirm that in a market economy, in an economy ruled by the Law of Supply and Demand, every factor unit receives a reward proportional to its productive contribution.

To Adam Smith labor was accepted as the main foundation and determinant of economic value. The price at which a commodity actually sells, the market price, has a tendency, he explained, to gravitate around a natural price. If effective demand exceeds supply, market prices will be higher than natural prices but this will be temporary as the surplus value, in the form of profit, attracts additional quantities of the commodity to be offered. The effect of this, and of the reverse, would be to turn the market price back toward the natural price.

Why is it not enough to say that sometimes prices are up, sometimes they are down, and always they are on the move. Why posit a metaphysical nonentity toward which they are moving? It is because Smith's natural price is that price that covers all the costs of production, the amount that gives due reward to all productive factors in the form of rent, wages, and profit. It is that price which indicates what a thing is actually worth. In terms of an older vocabulary, the natural price is the "just" price.

The matter is complicated, of course, inasmuch as the market price for any one commodity tends toward its natural price only as the rent, wages, and profits that make it up tend toward their respective natural prices. If all components would settle at or near their natural prices and if when the price of any commodity were neither more nor less than what is sufficient to pay them, the commodity would then be sold "for what may be called its natural price, . . . precisely for what it is worth" (Smith, 1937. p. 55).

Smith devotes much time in *The Wealth of Nations* to show what the different parts of the natural price are. In each case the component is traced back to productive labor. The interpretation is, then, that market prices and incomes correspond, ultimately, to effort expanded. Payment is made in accordance with product. Though the medium of the natural price, actual prices are shown to be ethically justified according to the accepted principle of justice.

Philosophically, the marginal productivity theory of factor prices shifts from an objective basis to a subjective basis, but the ideal of the original is maintained: factor prices correspond to effort, rewards are commensurate with sacrifice. The ultimate interpretation is that in the world as it should be, and as it could be if at the moment it is not like that, actual prices and incomes would be ethically just: they would be based either on labor effort expended (the labor theory of value) or on one's contribution as valued by the consumer (the marginal productivity approach).

A persistent irritation in the economy today is the differential between the lowest paid corporate members and the average of the top executive group. Just exactly how top executive salaries are determined is also some cause for alarm to some people (Williams, 1985; Bennett, 1988). That differential is an irritation because it invites the question, On what basis is this spread justified? Some look at the corporation and the kind of work being done and claim that the original rationale, the market, becomes less relevant for the determination of the relative differences between "grades" of labor and persons (Lodge, 1976). Since the original rationale won't do, "because human beings want and need a clear rationale for the differences in reward among them, some principle of social justice for social distinctions will have to be articulated" (Bell, 1971, p. 25) But the faithful are not discouraged. They respond, as did Robert Topel of the University of Chicago's business school:

> I am of the opinion, until proven otherwise, that the market is competitive. Competition is going to dictate what people make. The best measure we have of the value of what someone produces is what he was paid. (Bennett, 1988, p. 1)

This is, of course, a tautology: one is paid according to what one produces, and the best measure of the value of what one produces is what one is paid. The inner logic of traditional economics concludes that the well off are well off because they are productive and that the poor are poor because they are not. No other conclusion is permitted. It all sets the mind to rest or spurs it to action: the well off see themselves as deserving — they must be, they are well off — and the poor see only that they must work harder.

Economic reasoning cannot deny the undeniable — that there is *inequality* in the world. What it denies is that such inequality represents an *inequity*. Among the faithful, belief is strong that "Adam Smith's invisible hand, guided by supply and demand in the labor market, equitably signs everybody's paycheck" (Bennett 1988, p. 1).

Summary

The story that economics tells is that the price-setting market is comprehensible, the problems and difficulties experienced are sufferable, and they are sufferable because they are, above all else, just. In short, life has empirical regularity: it is, at times of suffering, sufferable, and the intractable moral paradoxes experienced everyday are a mirage.

The effect of all this is to deny what common sense and day-to-day observation might otherwise hold: that life is meaningless. The model provided by economic theory does it, and it does it all.

The laws of physics can never be more than principles of *explanation*, since we cannot escape from their dominance. The laws of the market, as Lowe recognized, are better conceived as principles at once of explanation and *action*, because though we can evade them we "should" not. We should not evade them because if we do society will not turn out as imagined. The Law of Supply and Demand "does not *describe* what an individual member of the market actually *does*, nor does it *predict* what he *will* do. It *prescribes* what he *should* do" (Lowe, 1942, p. 45). The Law of Supply and Demand is the metaphor we live by; it is the metaphor with which we interpret our experiences, give expression to our feelings, and by which we guide our action.

Conclusion

> *We should not be surprised or disappointed that the generalizations and maxims of the best social science share certain characteristic of their predecessors — the proverbs of folk societies, the generalizations of jurists, the maxims of Machiavelli.*
>
> — Alasdair MacIntyre. 1984. *After Virtue*. Second edition. Notre Dame, Ind: University of Notre Dame Press, p. 105.

The epigram at the beginning of this article refers to a fundamental debate raging in the social science community (Geetz, 1983, pp. 19–35). That debate is not just over its methods, but its aims. Seemingly, what is wanted today is the anatomization of thought not the manipulation of behavior. The move is toward conceiving of social and economic life as organized in terms of symbols and symbol systems whose meaning must be grasped if we are to understand what the relationship is between such symbols and symbol systems and what goes on in the rest of the world. The movement is toward an interpretive explanation of what the usual objects of social-scientific interest — institutions, action, images, customs — mean to those whose institutions, actions, customs, and so on they are.

What is required of the investigator is a systematic unpacking of the conceptual world in which the people live. Anthropological myth to the contrary notwithstanding, anthropologists do not grasp the conceptual worlds of other people through some inner correspondence of spirit with their informants (Geertz, 1983, pp. 55–70). They do so by placing the day-to-day concepts the people have fashioned for themselves in illuminating connection with the concepts the theorists have fashioned to capture the general features of social life.

In this regard economics presents a particular challenge. It represents both the concepts that economists have fashioned to capture the general features of economic life and the concepts that we, ourselves, use naturally and effortlessly to define what we and our fellows see, feel, think, imagine, and so on. An interpretive explanation of economic theory — requires that it be placed in illuminating connection with the concepts theorists other than economists have fashioned for other purposes. I have chosen to juxtapose economics with religion as a cultural system — knowing full well that ordinary economists do not like to think of themselves as theologians. My conviction is firm that to do so will illuminate the meanings embodied in the concepts and symbols, symbols such as the Marshallian Cross, that make up economics proper. Then, and only then, can we inquire into the relationship, or lack of relationship, between economics and what goes on in the world.

Notes

[1] Rosenberg's argument resembles that of Janos Kornai's in *Anti-Equilibrium* (1971). Kornai distinguishes between a real science, the fundamental task of which is to explain reality, and a decision theory, a logical mathematical science. Kornai argues that economics should be a real science but because of a mistake made by the early classicists, a mistake sustained to the present time, it has been modeled after a logical-mathematical science. In its present form it is a decision theory, not a real theory.

[2] Milton Friedman's essay "The Methodology of Positive Economics" (1953) remains the immediate philosophical justification for much of the contemporary approach to economics research. At the time that Friedman wrote this essay, much overt criticism of economics centered on its assumptions. Friedman wrote, "the belief that a theory can be tested

by the realism of its assumptions independently of the accuracy of its predictions is widespread and the source of much of the pernnial criticism of economic theory as unrealistic" (p. 41). Friedman argued that such criticism was "largely irrelevant" because a science is not to be judged "by the realism of its assumptions." adding that it "cannot be tested by comparing its assumptions directly with 'reality'" (pp. 4, 41). A science, he wrote, can only be judged "by the precision, scope, and conformity with experience of the predictions it yields" (pp. 41).

In his essay, Friedman did not say that the underlying assumptions are irrelevant, although some of his more eager followers have, and do. But neither did Friedman say anything to prevent such a notion from becoming widespread. Consequently, a belief has developed in economics that the test of a theory lies in the accuracy of its predictions irrespective of the realism of its assumptions. Friedman could have simply stated that the predictability of a theory is what counts, but that predictability could possibly be improved if the assumptions underlying that theory were made more realistic. The realism of the assumptions would not then be the test of a theory, but neither would they be irrelevant. Such a proposition is consistent with what he did say. To have made it explicit would not have served to direct attention away from the underlying assumptions of the theory, which is what was needed to protect it as a non-scientific knowledge system. Indeed, it may have more intensely focused attention on them.

[3] This is the story that I heard from my father while driving to my aunt's house when I was about 12 or 13 years old. I remember the occasion because later in the day, when the conversation turned to why things cost so much I explained to the "men." My father immediately remarked: "I didn't think you were listening." I may not have been, but I learned my lesson for the day anyway.

[4] Things like modern corporations, which continue to be excluded from the basic image of the economy projected by economics despite the fact that they have been around for nearly a century and have come to dominate both the political and the economic landscape.

[5] Business schools emerged and evolved in explicit juxtaposition with these troublemaking features — particularly the large corporation — yet have been successful, themselves, in shielding them from open criticism by those who study business and management. How that is done is treated in Benton (1987).

[6] "[t]he long-run," Weisskopf noted "plays a role similar to the belief in life after death in many religions. Its role is one of a compensatory fantasy gratification. What we are lacking now is promised to us, in the one case after death, in the other in the long run" (Weisskopf, 1955;219).

[7] The Austrians have a more congenial view of the risk-taking entrepreneur than does conventional economics. Appropriately, they have no use for concept of equibrium. Their analogous concept is the concept of spontaneous order.

[8] In *Capitalism and Freedom* (1962) Milton Friedman asked what it is we mean by "free" as modifying "enterprise." He made it clear that we are free to compete not free to cooperate.

References

Barber, Bernard. 1977. "Absolutization of the Market: Some Notes on How We Got From There to Here." In Gerald Dworkin, Gordon Berman, and Peter G. Brown, ed. *Markets and Morals*. Washington: Hemisphere Publishing Corporation.

Bell, Daniel. 1971. "The Corporation and Society in the 1970s." *The Public Interest* 24 (Summer):5–32.
——. 1976. *The Cultural Contradiction of Capitalism*. New York: Basic Books.
Bennett, Amanda. 1988. "Corporate Chiefs' Pay Far Outpaces Inflation and the Gains of Staffs." *The Wall Street Journal*, Monday, March 28th, pp. 1, 6.
Benton, Raymond, Jr. 1987. "The Practical Domain of Marketing: The Notion of A 'Free' Enterprise Market Economy as a Guise for Institutionalized Marketing Power." *The American Journal of Economics and Sociology* 46 (October):415–430.
Boulding, Kenneth. 1956. *The Image: Knowledge in Life and Society*. Ann Arbor: The University of Michigan Press.
Brady, Michael Emmett. 1986. "A Note of Milton Friedman's Application of his 'Methodology of Positive Economics;" *Journal of Economic Issues* 20 (September):845–851.
Bunke, Harvey C. 1964. "Economics, Affluence and Existentialism." *Quarterly Review of Economics and Business* 4(2):9–16.
Douglas, Mary. 1967. "The Meaning of Myth." In Edmund Leach, ed. *The Structural Study of Myth and Totemism*. London: Tavistock Publications.
Doyal, Len and Gough Ian. 1986. "Human Needs and Strategies for Social Change." In Paul Ekins, ed. *The Living Economy: A New Economics in the Making*. London and New York: Routledge & Kegan Paul.
Friedman, Milton. 1962. *Capitalism and Freedom*. Chicago: University of Chicago Press.
Geertz, Clifford. 1973. *The Interpretation of Cultures*. New York: Basic Books.
——. 1983. *Local Knowledge: Further Essays in Interpretive Anthropology*. New York: Basic Books.
Grayson, C. Jackson. 1973. "Let's Get Back to the Competitive Market System." *Harvard Business Review* 51 (Nov–Dec):103–112.
Hall, Edward T. 1977. *Beyond Culture*. Garden City, New York: Anchor Books.
Hands, Douglas W. 1984. "What Economics Is Not: An Economist's Response to Rosenberg." *Philosophy of Science* 51:495–503.
Hayek, F.A. 1955. *The Counter-Revolution of Science*. London: The Free Press of Glencoe.
Kehl, D.G. 1983. "How to Read an Ad: Learning to Read Between the Lies." *English Journal* 72 (October):32–38.
Kornai, Janos. 1971. *Anti-Equilibrium: On Economic Systems Theory and the Tasks of Research*. Amsterdam and London: North-Holland Publishing Company.
Levi-Strauss, Claude. 1953. Social Structure. In A.L. Kroeber, ed. *Anthropology Today*, Chicago: University of Chicago Press. Pp. 524–553.
Lodge, George C. 1976. *The New American Ideology*. New York: Alfred A. Knopf.
Lowe, Adolf. 1942. "A Reconsideration of the Law of Supply and Demand." *Social Research* 9(4):431–457.
——. 1965. *On Economic Knowledge*. New York: Harper and Row.

MacIntyre, Alasdair. 1984. *After Virtue: A Study in Moral Theory*. Second edition. Notre Dame, Indiana: University of Notre Dame Press.

McCloskey, Donald M. 1984. "The Literary Character of Economics." *Daedalus* 113 (Summer):97–119.

——. 1985. *The Rhetoric of Economics*. Madison: University of Wisconsin Press.

——. 1988. "The Limits of Expertise: If You're So Smart, Why Ain't You Rich?" *American Scholar* 57 (Summer):393–407.

Mises, Ludwig von. 1949. *Human Action — A Treatise on Economics*. New Haven, Conn.: Yale University Press.

Mumford, Lewis. 1973 (orig. 1944). *The Condition of Man*. New York: Harcourt Brace Jovanovich.

Read, Herbert. 1967. *Art and Society*, Fourth edition. London: Faber and Faber.

Ritcher, Maurice N., Jr. 1972. *Science as a Cultural Process*. Cambridge, Mass: Schenkman Publishing Company.

Robinson, Joan. 1962. *Economic Philosophy*. London: C.A. Watts and Co.

Rose, Arnold M. 1954. *Theory and Method in the Social Sciences*. Minneapolis: University of Minnesota Press.

Rosenberg, Alexander. 1983. "If Economics Isn't Science, What Is It?" *The Philosophical Forum* 14 (Spring–Summer):296–314.

——. 1976. *Microeconomic Laws: A Philosophical Analysis*. Pittsburgh: University of Pittsburgh Press.

Smart, Ninian. 1983. *Worldviews: Crosscultural Explanations of Cultural Beliefs*. New York: Charles Scribner and Sons.

Smith, Adam. 1937. *An Inquiry into the Nature and Causes of the Wealth of Nations*. New York: Modern Library.

Weisskopf, Walter A. 1949. "Psychological Aspects of Economic Thought." *Journal of Political Economics* 57:304–314.

——. 1950. "Individualism and Economic Theory." *American Journal of Economics and Sociology* 9 (April):317–333.

——. 1951. "Hidden Value Conflicts in Economic Thought." *Ethics* 61(3): 195–204.

——. 1955. *The Psychology of Economics*. Chicago: The University of Chicago Press.

Wilbur, Charles K. (with Robert S. Harrison). 1978. "The Methodological Basis of Institutional Economics." *Journal of Economic Issues* 12 (March):61–89.

Williams, Monci Jo. 1985. "Why Chief Executives' Pay Keeps Rising." *Fortune* (April 1):66–76.

COMMENT BY C. EDWARD ARRINGTON

Nothing is easier than to acquire the faults of one's opponents.

— Mary Midgley, *Wickedness*, p. 3

Like its own regard for the historicalness of understanding, hermeneutics is a term that is mediated by history — to understand the term today is to understand it very differently from its past. In the hands of Schleiermacher and Dilthey, it places our understanding in the prison house of history; it liquidates the interpreting self and demands a kind of objectivity that, like positivism, negates reflexivity. In the hands of Hans-Georg Gadamer and other contemporaries, it demands that we participate in history, that we mediate rather than reconstruct understanding. Hermeneutics from this view frees us to read history as an horizon of possibility, and to practice history — to make history — through critical engagement with the past, a critical engagement informed by our prejudices and our experience. In Gadamer's terms, "The real power of hermeneutical consciousness is our ability to see what is questionable" (1976, p. 13) and to *question* places us outside the pale of determinism, outside of an illusory objectivity, outside of historicism and into the flow of history, into our *effective* historical agency (see Habermas, Appendix, 1971; Gadamer, 1976, 1981; Bernstein, 1983).

In reading Benton's essay I get very little sense of the critical force of hermeneutics as it might illuminate either economics or religion. I do get a strong sense of determinism, a sense that hermeneutics can take over the role of the now suspect scientistic foundations of economics. I get a sense that while the positivistic *episteme* can no longer provide the metaphysical security for economic knowledge, one need not worry — historical determinism can fill the void. The order, the laws, the regimes of orthodox economics are not threatened in the slightest. There is no *critical* epistemic force to the chapter.

This is a serious problem for a discipline that is trying to make a turn toward discourse and hermeneutics. It is serious on two counts. First, if hermeneutics is to *do* something for economics it can not simply replace

---

I thank David Klemm for his detailed and thoughtful comments on an earlier draft of this essay.

scientism as a source of comfort. That would amount to simply replacing positivism with the force of positivism — in Habermas' terms, "A delusive philosophy of history . . . is only the obverse of deluded decisionism." That is a particularly dangerous epistemic move when one construes "economics" in the narrow and partisan way it is approached here ("the market," the "law" of supply and demand). Habermas continues, "Bureaucratically prescribed partisanship goes only too well with contemplatively misunderstood value freedom" (1971, p. 316).

A second and more important danger has to do with the moral force of Benton's essay. A determined world (historically determined or scientistically determined) leaves only one place for *critical* and transformative potential — a focus on the individual subject who, if uncomfortable with the world, if victimized by the world, must learn to accept, to obey, and to remediate herself or himself to avoid further victimization. This is the modernist morality that Nietzsche's invectives are directed against, and Benton's paper overflows with such modernism.

These are the two moments of Benton's essay — one epistemic and the other moral — that I want to redress here. I will not critique the essay so much as provide an alternative view on what hermeneutics and religion can offer economics *if* one turns away from determinism and toward critical participation in history. Before beginning, two caveats are in order. First, my critique is not directed at the intentions of the author; it is directed at the text. Second, I believe that the text has grossly misconstrued much about science, about hermeneutics, about religion, and about economics, even to the point where much of the essay is simply unintelligible to me. I will not comment upon those misconstruals in any complete way; I will only caution the reader about them. My task is not to play the role of the intellectual police. It is instead to suggest possibilities for very different stories about the triptych of hermeneutics, economics, and religion.

Hot and Cold Hermeneutics

At a broad and crude level, we can think of hermeneutics as the ongoing struggle toward understanding, toward "making sense" out of our knowledge and our lives. We might think of two kinds of hermeneuts and how they might approach the question of what it means to "make sense." Hermeneuts of the First Kind want some fixed foundations, some arche, out of which "sense-making" can proceed. Derrida speaks of such points of departure as "the center," and he reads the history of Western thought (what he calls the ontotheological tradition) as a series of substitutions of this or that "center":

> ... the entire history of the concept of structure ... must be thought of as a series of substitutions of center for center, as a linked chain of determinations of the center. Successively, and in a regulated fashion, the center receives different forms or names. The history of metaphysics, like the history of the West, is the history of these metaphors and metonymies. . . . It could be shown that all the names related to fundamentals, to principles, or to the center have always designated an invariable presence — *eidos, arche, telos, energeia, ousia* (essence, existence, substance, subject) *aletheia*, transcendentality, concious-ness, God, man, and so forth. (1978, pp. 279–280)

The goal here is to get closure, to build systems, above all else to stay away from dis-order, from dis-ease. If one center gets into trouble (as, say, God did in the seventeenth century), act immediately to replace it with another (say, "the laws of nature," human or otherwise). If positiv-ism can no longer fill the bill, then perhaps historical determinism will work. The important point is to retain order, to remember that the-law-is-the-law-is-the-law.

Hermeneuts Of The Second Kind don't care about some fixed founda-tion for knowledge. They see Hermeneuts Of The First Kind as neurotics suffering from what Bernstein calls the Cartesian Anxiety — the "longing for ultimate constraints, for a stable and reliable rock upon which we can secure our thought and action" (1983, p. 19). They see knowledge (whether philosophy or pea farming) as something that humans *invented*. The only "foundations" at work are pens and voices participating in what Rorty (1979) calls "The Conversation of Mankind." If things don't turn out so well, then *we*, not God, not the laws of the cosmos, not history, must bear the burden and try to find not only new and better ways of speaking and writing but also of *acting*.

This second tribe includes troublemakers like Socrates, Nietzsche, Kierkegaard, Heidegger, and Derrida (see Caputo, 1987). They think that life is difficult, and they want to stick with that difficulty. They think that we ought to be uncomfortable and keep our distance from the tranquilizing comfort of metaphysical foundations and "laws." They would agree with John Dewey (1922) when he argues that if the goal is comfort and order, the quickest way to achieve it is to go to sleep or die. They sense that what we are tyrannized by is not chaos but Order, the way in which, for example, the "laws of economics" all too easily become excuses for the horrors of economic *life*. John Caputo calls these "radical" hermeneuts, and their *ethos* look something like this:

> The point is to make life difficult, not impossible — to face up to the difference and difficulty which enter into what we think and do and hope for, not to grind them to a halt. Indeed, it is the claim of radical hermeneutics that we get the best results by yielding to the difficulty in "reason," "ethics," and "faith," not by trying to cover it over. Once we stop trying to prop up our beliefs, practices, and institutions on the metaphysics of presence, once we give up the idea that they are endowed with some sort of facile transparency, we find that they are not washed away but liberated, albeit in a way which makes the guardians of Beings and presence nervous. Far from abandoning us to the wolves, radical hermeneutics issues in far more reasonable and indeed less dangerous ideas of reason, ethics, and faith than those that metaphysics has been peddling for some time now. Curiously enough, the metaphysical desire to make things safe and secure has become consummately dangerous. (1987, p. 7)

Benton's text is Of The First Kind — of limits, of accepting those limits, of foundations, and of constraints. Here are a few examples, and I provide a Translation Of The Second Kind for each one:

Hermeneut 1: "[A]s much as some would like to repeal the laws of supply and demand, it can't be done." (p. 27)

Hermeneut 2: "The 'law' of supply and demand is a way of speaking about how humans relate to each other, how they treat each other. It has no imperative force. Of course it can be 'repealed.' We do it all the time (can a wealthy terrorist buy a nuclear weapon?). If you withhold food from the hungry because they cannot 'pay,' for example, the only 'law' at work is your own moral agency. The rhetoric of the 'law' is a palliative, and an insidious one at that."

Hermeneut 1: "History is handed down as 'stubborn fact' from generation to generation." (p. 5)

Hermeneut 2: "History is what other people chose to write down about their lives, the choices they made, what they thought about, how they built abodes, made love, and treated each other. It tells us something about who we are. *We* are not imprisoned by but responsible for transforming history by writing down similar things about ourselves. As an aside, it also tends to be written by aristocratic, elitist, wealthy, and smart white men."

Hermeneut 1:   "[O]bedience to fixed rules of conduct is the price that must be paid to live in a social economy."

Hermeneut 2:   "That tells me nothing about which rules one ought to obey. It tells me nothing about when to break them. It tells me nothing about what to do about bad law. Did you ever notice how the law is always referred back to God? Did you ever notice how someone (who?) signs for the law and signs in the name of 'the people?' Did you ever notice how often it is the 'laws' and the 'rules' that provide the most insidious examples of the horrors of history?"

Hermeneut 1:   "[I]t is not that people must know how to avoid suffering, they must know how to suffer: how to accept it and how to endure it." (p. 26)

Hermeneut 2:   "Pure unadulterated modernism. Focus on the subject/ victim. If we are not to 'avoid' suffering, then history is guaranteed to be a continuous suffering, an annuity-in-perpetuity. But I suppose that is what we mean by history as 'stubborn fact'."

Hermeneut 1:   [Advice to the Victim]. "It is nothing personal; there are no personal bonds involved. Don't brood but persevere, work harder, set your nose to the grindstone. That is the message that economics relates. And it is only what any right thinking person would feel. The victims are, as we say, the 'victims of progress.'"

Hermeneut 2:   "See above. That is precisely the point — there are no *personal* bonds involved because your modernism doesn't deal in 'persons,' only in objects and victims. That is why the liberation theologians speak of the Latin American poor as 'nonpersons,' those without the material well-being necessary to secure the minimal conditions of human dignity. Work harder at what? For whom? Under what conditions? But remember that I am not a 'right-thinking' person."

Hermeneut 1:   "Although one may be angry ... one does not (at least the reasonable person does not) feel indignation" (p. 27).

Hermeneut 2:   "See above. I am most assured that I am neither right-thinking nor reasonable. I certainly *do* feel indignation."

Hermeneut 1: "The laws of the market...are better conceived as principles at one of explanation and *action*, because though we can evade them we 'should' not. We should not evade them because if we do society will not turn out as imagined" (p. 33).

Hermeneut 2: "Where is the moral force of this 'should?' You just betrayed yourself. If we *can* evade them, then where is the force of *law*; what is it other than the choices and actions that we *invent* that provides the 'center?' Who is this 'we' anyway? Is *this* society, this *world* that we live in, the one that you imagined?"

If Benton wants to tell us that economics is grounded in the way that we talk with each other, write about each other, and act towards each other, then fine. If he wants to tell us that we learn from history, then fine. But those two points do not license the moral force of his arguments about "victims," and "coping," and the nature of reality as equivalent to an apologia for the "market" or "The Law of Supply and Demand." Admittedly, I am clearly a Hermeneut of The Second Kind, something of a fuzzy and confused Marxist, and one who prefers The Black Forest and Paris to The University of Chicago. Those are moral postures, not comments on "the nature of knowledge." But similar points, or something like them, can be found in plain, old, B-flat Amereican pragmatism, in Richard Rorty and in the Economist Don McCloskey. While sharing Benton's enthusiasm for market economics, McCloskey doesn't speak in terms of foundations, and laws, and historical determinism — he speaks about economics as a moral choice — how to deal with other people for the moment. He speaks critically; he knows that humans invented economics, and he knows that they can apply it as they see fit. He is also of The Second Kind.

Praxial Hermeneutics: Theology and Economics

There is an intimate relation between hermeneutics and *praxis*; in Gadamer's (1975) hands, hermeneutics stands as the heir to practical philosophy. In this sense, interpretation and understanding not only share the hermeneutical space with application but are inseparable from it. To interpret the world, to understand the world, is inextricably bound up with an obligation to act upon the world in a transformative way (see

Bernstein, 1983, p. 38). That awareness is nowhere more clear than in contemporary theology:

> Properly speaking, the so-called hermeneutic problem of theology is not the problem of how systematic theology stands in relation to history, but what is the relation between theory and practice, between understanding the faith and social practice. (Metz, 1969, p. 112)

Benton's essay draws upon religion as an analogical referent for economics. There are very odd claims to view economics as somehow hierarchically replacing religion as a "cultural" system. I dont't know what that could possibly mean, and I will pass on it. The problem that I do want to address is that the chapter never articulates what is meant by religion. I can only speculate on the sense of the term within the essay — religion stands, like economics, as "a system for the creation and inculcation of meaning and purpose." Benton does *explicitly* make a kind of eschatological move:

> The religious perspective moves beyond the realities of everyday life to wider ones that correct and complete them. Emphasis is not action on these wider realities but acceptance of them, faith in them. The religious perspective questions the realities of everyday life in terms of what it takes to be wider, nonhypothetical truths.

This is a heteronomic approach to religion, and it is difficult to discern how religion ought or ought not to stand with respect to practice (e.g., economics). On the one hand, religion moves "beyond the realities of everyday life to wider ones that correct and complete them." What does it *mean* to correct and complete practical realities here? While of course we do not act upon the "wider realities" (to the extent that we act at all, we always act *in* the world), do we *act* upon *our* reality — is it *that* action that "corrects and completes" or is no *action* necessary to correct and complete? What does it mean to *question* the realities of everyday life? Do we question and act or do we simply question?

My sense is that Benton never moves toward action, toward the hermeneutical relation of theory and social practice that Metz identifies as the central problematic of theology. Indeed, he never moves toward questioning. Religion, like economics, appears only as a palliative — as a "sense-making" discourse that resigns itself to a determined world.

Particularly in the Christian tradition, there has always been a salient theological imperative to act upon the world in a transformative way. Augustine is a good example. So is Christ. And the most important point about this imperative is that it is identical to the imperative of economics — the liberation of the human from the constraints of poverty. A praxial theology, like a praxial economics, only "makes sense" when it *makes* worlds, and theologians (if not economists) have taken that *praxis* seriously.

My task here is not to go into the massive literature that engages theology with economics. Rather, I want to point out some efforts of contemporary theology to understand what is going on in the world through the lens of the hermeneutical relation between theology and economics.

Market ideology and its metonym, the Law of Supply and Demand, are not "conceptual" apparati — they are the discursive structures that sustain incredibly powerful forces that shape lived experience throughout the globe. Given a praxis oriented toward liberation from poverty, many theologians have made a presumption *against* these forces. These are not radical Marxists; they include in their number even the pope:

> Analyzing this situation [poverty] more deeply, we discover that this poverty is not a passing phase. Instead it is the product of economic, social, and political situations and structures, though there are also other causes for the state of misery. In many instances this state of poverty within our countries finds its origin and support in mechanisms which, because they are impregnated with materialism rather than with any authentic humanism, create a situation on the international level where the rich get richer at the expense of the poor, who even get poorer. (Pope John Paul II, Opening Address to the Puebla Bishop's Conference, III, 3, cited in Guttierez, 1983, p. 133)

In the hands of liberation theologians like Gustavo Guttierez (1973; 1983), the "texts" of the Christian tradition are being interpreted as a *preferential option for the poor* — in a word, the hermeneutical interpretation of religious texts as an obligation to theological praxis understood as *economic* praxis. The preferential option for the poor stands in sharp contrast to the Law of Supply and Demand. That "Law" axiomatically makes a *presumption in favor of the wealthy* — the more one can supply or demand the more one partakes of the benefits of the law. One can certainly argue that the market also enhances the poor, one can be comfortable with economic "talk" to that effect, one can "make sense" out of one's own ideology and "conceptual" world that way.

But is that enough? I think not, and I believe that conclusion follows from hermeneutics. At least since Heidegger, hermeneutics has oriented itself toward human dwelling in the world, not toward epistemic assurances designed to make us comfortable in our concepts. Hermeneutics is an ontological project, not an epistemological one. If that is the case, then economics has not "supplanted" religion so much as "religion" offers an alternative economics (see above) — which presumption does one wish to make with regard to "what is going on in the world?" In any case, hermeneutics will not remain content if it is simply asked to serve an epistemic, ideological, and comforting role for market economists.

A Word on Justice

Benton makes two appeals with respect to justice. I want to comment on them very briefly. First, he states "The problem is to come up with a definition of justice that is acceptable to all and with means of achieving it." That is another modernist moment. We can and do define justice until the cows come home — there is no shortage of logically impeccable and *absolutely incommensurable* theories of justice available (see Mac-Intyre, 1984, 1988). Our problem is to *be* just — not to define justice. Adam Smith was well aware of that, and he never offerred the market as a "just" system (his appeal, like Aristotle's, was to the virtues, particularly self-command).

Benton also uses Alasdair MacIntyre to make an appeal to a justice-of-deserts. He then tells a story about how markets provide a justice-of-deserts. Here is what MacIntyre (who spends most of his time *attacking* "systems" of justice) has to say about that story:

> ...the tradition of the virtues is at variance with central features of the modern economic order and more especially its individualism, its acquisitiveness and its elevation of the values of the market to a central social place. (1984, p. 254)

MacIntyre also understands how a hermeneutical economics ought to be a *critical* encounter with history, and he has some good advice about where those who share Benton's ideology might begin such an encounter:

> The property-owners of the modern world are not the legitimate heirs of Lockean individuals who performed quasi-Lockean . . . acts of original acquisition; they are the inheritors of those who, for example, stole, and used violence to steal the common lands of England from the common people, vast tracts of North America from the American Indian, much of Ireland from the Irish, and Prussia from the original non-German Prussians. This is the historical reality ideologically concealed behind any Lockean thesis. (1984. p. 251)

"And What Is A Poor Boy To Do?"

There are two kinds of poverty — intellectual and material. Intellectual poverty is what economics (and other modernist disciplines) are experiencing as the postmodern condition of knowledge challenges us all (see Lyotard, 1984). That is the challenge of responding to the breakdown of the grand narratives of the Enlightenment that have sustained us for some three centuries. The urge is strong to scramble around and find some terms, like hermeneutics, that might jump in and keep us comfortable with our orthodox *epistemes*. But that is a false comfort.

The second kind of poverty is where economics and religion ought to do their *work*.

Which poverty claims us?

References

Bernstein, Richard. 1983. *Beyond Objectivism and Relativism: Science, Hermeneutics, and Praxis*. Philadelphia: University of Pennsylvania Press.

Caputo, John. 1987. *Radical Hermeneutics: Repetition, Deconstruction, and the Hermeneutic Project*. Bloomington, In: Indiana University Press.

Derrida, Jacques. 1978. *Writing and Difference* (transl. by Alan Bass). Chicago: The University of Chicago Press.

Dewey, John. 1983, text references to 1922. "The Good of Activity." In *John Dewey: The Middle Works, 1899–1924*. Vol. 14. Carbondale, IL: Southern Illinois University Press.

Gadamer, Hans-Georg. 1976. *Philosophical Hermeneutics* (transl. by David E. Linge). Berkeley: University of California Press.

Gadamer, Hans-Georg. 1981. *Reason in the Age of Science* (transl. by Frederick G. Lawrence). Cambridge, Mass.: MIT Press.

Guttierez, Gustavo. 1973. *A Theology of Liberation* (transl. by C. Inda and J. Eagleson). Maryknoll, NY: Orbis Books.

Habermas, Jürgen. 1971. *Knowledge and Human Interests* (transl. by Jeremy J. Shapiro). Boston: Beacon Press.

Lyotard, Jean-Francois. 1984. *The Postmodern Condition: A Report on Knowledge* (transl. by Geoff Bennington and Brian Massumi). Minneapolis, MN: University of Minnesota Press.

MacIntyre, Alasdair. 1984. *After Virtue*. second edition. South Bend, Ind: University of Notre Dame Press.

Metz, Johannes. 1969. *Theology of the World*. New York: Herder.

Midgley, Mary. 1984. *Wickedness: A Philosophical Essay* London: Routledge & Kegan Paul.

Rorty, Richard. 1979. *Philosophy and the Mirror of Nature* Princeton, NJ: Princeton University Press.

4 ECONOMICS AS IDEOLOGY

Robert Heilbroner

The first urgent issue in the philosophy of economics is the question of the intelligibility of a separate discipline devoted exclusively to the explication of an abstract concept called "the economy," separate from other categories of social phenomena, and separate from the relationships we attribute to the physical or non-human world. These are the fundamental issues that any coherent discipline of economic theory must address: it must carve up reality, and must have some claim to have carved artfully "at the joints"; it must have some resources to adjudicate boundary disputes with other disciplines, which requires a clear conception of its own theoretical object; it must nurture some epistemological conception of the economic actor and the economist and presumably reconcile them one with the other; and it must build bridges to the conceptions of power and efficacy within the context of the culture in which it is to subsist.

— Mirowski, 1987, p. 1003

I

I take Mirowski's brilliant summary as my charge, and I shall attempt to fulfill its demands by considering economics as ideology. Hence the first

101

order of business is to clarify what I mean by this troublesome word.[1] As
I have been at some pains to assert in my previous writings, I do not use
ideology in a pejorative sense, as an apologia offered on behalf of some
unannounced, usually political, interest, or as a description or explanation knowingly at variance with perceived reality. On the contrary, I
understand an ideology to be utterances in which the speaker deeply
believes — statements to which the "interests" themselves repair in
search of enlightenment. Ideologies in this sense are "social constructions of
reality" in Berger and Luckmann's (1966) terminology. They are conceptual frameworks by which order is imposed upon, and moral legitimacy
accorded to, the raw stuff out of which social understanding must be
forged (Heilbroner, 1973; 1985, Chapter 5; and 1988, Chapters 1 and 8.)

From this viewpoint, two questions come to the fore. One of them is,
of course, the content of the ideology of economics, or more accurately,
the varying contents of the various ideologies that can be perceived
in a retrospective consideration of economic thought. I shall return to
this matter in the pages to follow, but a prior issue must initially be
examined. This is the epistemological assumption from which the inquiry
proceeds, an assumption implicit in Mirowski's reference (at the beginning of this chapter) to the economy as an "abstract concept" whose
"intelligibility" is at stake. Such a reference is wholly discordant with a
conception of the economy as a direct, unchallengeable aspect of reality
whose recognition and description present no more difficulties than those
faced by the geographer who wishes to draw the rivers and mountain
chains of an unexplored land. The assertion that the economy is an
"abstract" rather than a concrete aspect of social reality, that it must be
"rendered intelligible" rather than being mentally appropriated in some
wholly unproblematic fashion, places the entire enterprise of economics
in an unaccustomed and disturbing perspective. It introduces an interpretational or hermeneutic element into a discipline that has always established objectivity as its norm, and substitutes a relationship of personal
involvement — even responsibility — for the stance of the detached
recorder of events.

This hermeneutic approach to economics can be described in a number
of vocabularies — for example, "rhetoric" or "discourse" — as well as in
that of ideology. Each brings to the fore particular aspects of the relationship of the observer and the observed. Whatever the preferred vocabulary, the general interpretational approach imposes a relationship of
self-scrutiny upon the inquirer different from that implicit in the idea of
economics as a "science." The economist who carries on inquiries in the
name of science is aware of obligations of truth-telling and openness of

method but not of those pertaining to the construction of the domain to which he directs his gaze. The self-perceived "scientific" economist regards his task as that of exploring data that thrust themselves on his attention as impersonally as the advent of natural events. To the contrary, the essence of the idea of economics as a "reading" of social reality brings into being the political and social interpretations and understandings of the inquirer who creates the very concepts on which inquiry will be focused. Once chosen, the concepts and categories of society may be subjected to the same kinds of critical, more or less disinterested treatment as that to which we subject nature, but the initial subjectively determined choice of the explananda sets the interpretational conception of economics sharply apart from that of a "science." Its innocence is forever gone.[2]

II

As I hope to show, the choice of "ideology" as the vocabulary for discussing the hermeneutic approach to economics has considerable strengths, but it has as well undeniable difficulties. The latter stem from a penumbra of meanings that accompany the word, in particular those having to do with ideology as a distortion of the truth. Let me therefore first attend to this question, which will otherwise nag at our inquiry.[3]

In my view (as, incidentally, also in Schumpeter's), ideology rarely takes the form of a knowing misrepresentation of social reality (Schumpeter, 1949). Even at their most exaggerated, the pronouncements of "ideologues" do not have the appearance of knowing deceptions. They are, rather, selective, or partial representations of the world, aimed at supporting views that can often be anchored in social reality with impressive empirical data or plausible generalizations. As such, they fall within the general field of rhetoric, taking that word to mean the art of persuasion. "The Rhetoricall [form of discourse]," says Adam Smith, ". . . endeavours by all means to perswade us; and for this purpose it magnifies all the arguments on the one side and diminishes or conceals those which might be brought on the [contrary] side. . . ." (Smith, 1983, p. 149). Such "ideological" arguments can be put forward in complete sincerity, as highlighting the essence of a complex reality rather than deliberately distorting it. As such, these exaggerations, to give them a kindly interpretation, are in no way peculiar to an approach to economics that places ideology as a particular kind of belief system at its core.

More interesting, although still of only peripheral importance for our inquiry, are views whose "ideological" character does not lie in any partial or slanted presentation of the known facts, but in oversights or indifference to logical slips within the argument — slips that are reasonably apparent to the skeptical intelligence. I instance the statement by Milton and Rose Friedman that the distribution of wealth may be "unfair," but that there are many instances of unfairnesses in life, such as the unequal distributions of talent. "The inheritance of property can be interfered with more readily than the inheritance of talent," the authors write. "But from the ethical point of view, is there any difference between the two?" (Friedman and Friedman, 1980, p. 136).

The answer, of course, is that there is the vast difference of a categorical distinction, in that inequalities of talent, like all "givens" of nature, represent variations of endowments to which the term "ethical" does not apply, whereas inequalities of wealth are social differences to which the realm of ethics is specifically addressed. Another such instance involves the response of Robert Lucas to the question of whether government might not be an instrument for the redress of social injustice. Lucas replies: "That wouldn't be anything like my view. I can't think of explaining the pharoahs as being in existence to resolve the social injustice in Egypt. I think they perpetrated most of the social injustice in Egypt" (Klamer, 1984, p. 52). The ideological element here does not reside in the validity of the historical judgment with respect to the political practices of the pharoahs. It rests, rather, in Lucas's selection of pharoahonic Egypt to illustrate the abstract question of government and justice, rather than, say, Lincolnian or Roosveltian America — these latter, of course, also "ideological" choices (Heilbroner, 1988, pp. 187, 188).

Such examples surely indicate that economists make utterances whose selective view of social reality can be readily discerned. Yet, as with the previous case of rhetorical exaggeration, I do not wish to be understood as claiming that such more or less readily identifiable carelessness of argument forms the basis of what I call the ideological nature of economic inquiry. This carelessness, too, is a form of rhetorical error, in which arguments intended to persuade are shown to rest on insecure foundations. Among such rhetorical mistakes are economic statements that can be shown to contain self-contradictory or internally inconsistent elements. An instance involves the widely held view that "the rational maximizing individual" constitutes an ultimate conceptual building block of the economy — a building block not resolvable into simpler conceptual units.[4] The "ideological" problem with this statement lies not in the terms "rational" or "maximizing," both of which are admittedly imprecise and easily used to advance a hidden agenda, but in the seemingly neutral reference to *the individual* as the basic element of social theory. The difficulty here is that the individual's initial economic action is generally assumed to be the allocation of its income among competing ends. Here the telltale word is *income*, which logically implies another individual from which the first has received an income — a consideration that reveals a social framework to be a necessary prior posit to the individual-centered analysis.

As a second instance I cite the common conceptual treatment of capital and land as factors of production in every respect isomorphic with labor, in that the returns to each can be depicted as the remuneration for the sale of its services. The conceptual illogic is that of using the possessive relationship to connote both physical and legal connectedness, so that no attention is paid to the fact that the contribution made to production by the possessor of labor power can never be detached from the laborer, as is always the case with the material resources possessed by an owner. The studied ignorance of this difference leads to the fallacy of misplaced analogy, unforgettably illustrated in Marx's depiction of M. le Capital and Mme. la Terre as living creatures in the Aesop's fable of classical political economy.

From our viewpoint, what is of interest here is that such concepts as monadic individuals and isomorphic factors of production continue to be embraced even after their internal difficulties have been revealed. There is no sign in the regnant economic view of an abandonment of these ideas although their self-contradictory or misspecified natures have long been known. This intellectual rigidity suggests the need to impute to the belief systems of economics a sociopolitical basis capable of explaining their resistance to, or insulation from, conceptual challenge. That is the intent of the vocabulary of *ideology* in the sense to which we now turn.

III

Ideology, as I shall employ the term, refers in the first instance to the frameworks of perception by which all societies organize and interpret their existence. Insofar as these frameworks inform their possessors that the natural world is peopled with spirits or is a grid of spacetime devoid of sentience, one can perhaps describe them in the neutral terminology of a "belief system."[5] But I deliberately choose the more abrasive term *ideology* to describe the construction of *social* reality — that is, the frameworks by which societies perceive and interpret the arrangements that order their lives. The word then serves as a flag, alerting us to the

inextricable elements of social power, position, and values that enter into
such explanations, whether these refer to the structure of family life, of
tribal mores, of national authority, or of "economic" intercourse. I put
the critical word into quotation marks, because, as we shall immediately
see, its extraction from the social totality is by no means a task that can
be carried out in the objective fashion by which we isolate elements from
a chemical compound.

Economics as ideology forces us to confront directly the questions
posed by Mirowski in my opening citation — namely the constitutive
basis of what we call the economy and of the pronouncements about it
that comprise economics. This requires us to locate that "abstract concept" within the larger conceptual entity of society, using as our guide
some identificatory method — some chemical stain, as it were — that will
make explicit the relationship between the elements we designate as "the
economy" and our own sociopolitical embeddedness within the very
structure we are trying to conceptualize.

I take as my starting point that this structure consists of the activities of
provisioning and of the means of coordinating these activities that can be
discovered in all societies. This initial posit rescues us from the sterile
argument as to whether economics is properly understood as the study of
the accumulation of wealth or the study of the logic of choice under the
constraints of scarcity. That lengthy debate has taken place without any
prior determination of what parts or aspects of the social totality are
properly defined as constituting the economy, a failure that leads to
frustration from both vantage points. (Heilbroner, 1988, p. 14, n. 1; see
also Lowe 1965, Chapter 1).

It should be immediately noted, however, that the economic realm
appears entirely differently in primitive and early tributary societies than
in capitalist ones. The difference is that the earlier forms of social organization utilize coordination mechanisms that are extensions of the larger,
more all-embracing orchestrating practices of the society — namely, the
duties and roles inculcated by socialization and reinforced by institutions
of reward and punishment: mechanisms that we subsume under the
general heading of "tradition" in primitive society (Polanyi uses the term
"reciprocity"), and "command" in stratified, state-dominated systems.

As a consequence, the boundaries of the economy in traditional and
command social formations are not clearly differentiated from the surrounding society, as they are in market or capitalist settings. The task of
understanding the structure of provisioning in the Trobriand Islands or
the Kalahari Desert is not different from that of perceiving or legitimating
the structure of family or communal life; or in the case of state systems,

of describing the discharge of organized social functions of a religious, military, or "tributary" kind. Therefore the sphere of life called the economy in pre-market or pre-capitalist societies presents no special problems, above all no problems of social legitimacy, other than those that apply to the social formation as a whole. It is because of this seamless application of social interpretation, not because of any unique classification of substantive tasks, that there exists no "economics" within such societies, although there certainly exist systems of social provisioning that can be called their economies.

The appearance of a realm to which the term economics attaches with unmistakeable clarity appears in history only when the activities of provisioning (always including their all-important coordination mechanisms) are largely — although never entirely — separated from the community below and the state above. Such a vast transfer of responsibility has taken place only once in history, with the rise of capitalism from the rubble of the Roman empire, although it is possible that we are witnessing the first stages of a similar process in the emergence of an "economy" within the state socialisms of China and the Soviet Union. This view "carves at the joints" that bind "the economy" to the community and the polity, and sets the stage for the interpretation of economics as the belief system by which this unclearly bounded, uncertainly located sphere of activities and control mechanisms is perceived and understood. I call this belief system *ideological* to emphasize that behind the often remote, abstract, and socially detached terms in which the economy is described lie the realities of provisioning activities and of means of coordinating these activities whose purpose is to sustain a given sociopolitical configuration. The specifically "ideological" aspect of economics consists in its normal depiction of these activities and means in terms that ignore or conceal the sociopolitical structure whence they spring and which they serve. "Economic categories," writes Marx in *The Poverty of Philosophy*, "are only the theoretical expression, the abstraction, of the social relations of production" (quoted in Mannheim, 1936, p. 57).

IV

Economics as ideology thus begins by challenging the sheer facticity of the economy. It changes the observer's view of the economy from that of a system to that of a regime. By system I mean a social structure whose connections and order-bestowing forces can be entirely analogized to the affectless interactions of the physical universe, and whose properties can be discussed in the "neutral" language of a science. By regime I mean a configuration organized around principles of social hierarchy and communal relationship, principles that can only be made intelligible in the languages of psychology and politics — that is, in the understanding of behavioral drives derived from the psychoanalytic study of the infant and child, and from generalizations as to historical social tendencies ("All power tends to corrupt . . ."). Donald McCloskey has subjected the widespread scientific model of economics to scathing criticism, largely because of economists' unawareness that the language of science *is* a rhetoric, despite — or more accurately — because of its austere style. (McCloskey, 1985). McCloskey's analysis does not, however, identify the particular aspects of reality that are blocked out by scientific metaphors and tropes. These are the political aspects to which an ideological approach pays special heed.

Ordinarily, we have no difficulty in perceiving bygone social formations as regimes and their belief systems as ideologies: "It is seemly," writes Ramon de Lull in the late thirteenth century, "that the men shall plow and dig and work hard, in order that the earth may yield the fruits from which the knight and his horse will live; and that the knight, who rides and does a lord's work, should get his wealth from the things on which his men are to spend much toil and fatigue" (*Cambridge Economic History*, 1966, I, p. 277).

It is more difficult but not impossible to perceive the same ideological content in more recent explanations. Alfred Marshall writes:

> It matters not for our immediate purpose whether the power over the enjoyment for which the person waits, was earned by him directly by labour . . . or was acquired by him from others by exchange or by inheritance, by legitimate trade or by unscrupulous forms of speculation . . . the only points with which we are now concerned are that the growth of wealth involves in general a deliberate waiting for pleasure which a person has rightly (or wrongly) the power of commanding in the immediate present . . . (Marshall, 1948, pp. 233–34).

The explanatory basis for the second belief system ("the growth of wealth involves . . . a deliberate waiting for pleasure . . .") seems very far removed from the first ("it is seemly . . ."), but both are in fact addressed to the same question: how shall the inequalities of social condition (wealth) be understood? De Lull tells us that these sociopolitical differences reflect some supra-social scheme of things; Marshall says they result from different capacities for waiting. Each statement satisfies the promptings of its author, but neither would satisfy those of the other. It is this entanglement of belief systems in the fundamental values of their sociopolitical settings that warrants their designation as ideologies.

Economics from this perspective is thus intrinsically normative in the sense of embodying, whether it will or not, the constitutive beliefs of its parent society. These constitutive beliefs, in turn, are intrinsically political, not merely from the self-justifying intentions of their spokesmen, but because societies themselves ineluctably presuppose structures of subordination and superordination, of cooperation and conflict-resolution, of the instantiation and the utilization of power. All systems of thought that describe or examine societies must contain their political character, knowingly and explicitly, or unknowingly and in disguise. Economics is not, and cannot be, an exception to this generalization, except insofar as it is unaware of the manner in which these order-bestowing ties permeate its own representations of social reality.

V

This brings us to the aspect of economics on which the ideological approach sheds its special light. It is the prevailing belief that modern economic society hangs together by means that eschew the ancient integrative mechanisms of communality and power. The relationship of exchange, freely entered into, relatively insulated from communal taboos and shielded from coercive force, appears to make the modern market-meshed economy a part of the social order from which political considerations can be excluded and accordingly a mode of analyzing society to which "ideology" cannot apply.

It is this aspect of the economic belief system that we must now examine. I have already noted a few instances where ideology of a "rhetorical" kind distorts the perception of economics. But the deepest aspect of ideology enters in another guise, namely the denial of any trace of political power in the orchestration mechanism of society — its price system. Insofar as the price system is recognized as an integrative mechanism — the invisible hand may be invisible but it remains a hand — the denial raises the interesting question of how the orchestration process achieves its end. The answer, as we know, is the reliance of the price system on the motives of self interest. This generalized motive allows society to achieve adequate provisioning by inducements and sanctions rather than by slavish routines or unwilling obedience.

Where is the ideological content in this statement based on empirical generalization and logical analysis? There are several answers. One is the manner in which the "adequacy" of the social provisioning is judged. It is certainly not by criteria external to the social order — that is, by the attainment of standards that have been previously determined after careful consideration of feasible alternatives as to the quantity, quality, and sharing of output. Rather, the adequacy of provisioning is principally judged by its success in maintaining the *existing* social order, more or less in conformity with its general configuration of incomes. Thus the satisfactoriness of the market mechanism is determined mainly from the vantage point of the regime that depends on it. This does not deny its material achievements but views them in a less self-congratulatory light — economic "growth," for example, becomes recognizable as the term given to commodification, and the importance accorded to the volume of product is perceived as obscuring attention to its distribution.

Of no less importance is the manner in which the economic celebration of market choice as freedom masks any recognition of its function as a medium for political power. At the simplest level this is nothing but the recognition that freedom, in a context of necessity, is a hollow term — Anatole France's equal right of the rich and poor to sleep under the bridges of Paris at night. But the political element of the exchange process has a more far-reaching aspect. This is the priority accorded to the rights of property in the division of the product to which labor and capital have each freely contributed — the first its labor power, the second its equipment. In this division, all residual income goes to the contributor of capital. This allocation of output makes mock of the equality of factors-as-agents on which the argument for the apolitical nature of the market is based. For if equality were in fact to prevail, the claims on surplus would be equal, or there would be no surplus, insofar as the factors' separate claims would exhaust the total product. The last is, of course, the assumption of marginal productivity analysis, which is tantamount to the assertion that we can have capitalism without profit, a proposition on a conceptual par with that of monarchy without kings.

Finally, the ideological content of economics is revealed in its uncritical acceptance of market behavior, especially in the acquiescence of individuals in the "determinations" of the price mechanism. These determinations do not merely confront marketers with the terms on which they may have access to output — namely, prices. The market also often confronts its participants with onerous life situations, such as separation from the means of livelihood, the necessity to perform unwanted kinds of work, or forced relocation. These determinations are also "willingly" obeyed.

In a word, as an ideology, economics ignores or does not perceive the political core function of the market system — i.e., its capacity to mobilize and allocate labor power for ends that are not those of the laborers themselves. Such dispensations and allocations of income and effort would be instantly recognized as political under the aegis of an imperial or a feudal regime. Only as the "workings" of the market are they stripped, not of their real sociopolitical function, but as their recognizability as such. Once again this criticism in no way denies the vast difference between the status of the "wage slave" and the real slave. It only insists that the freedom of the marketplace is a partial and not a complete freedom, and that the workings of the marketplace serve a regimatic purpose, not merely those of an abstractly conceived "efficiency."

VI

Thus ideology permeates — indeed, constitutes — our social vision. There is no escape from it in seeking to explain that portion of social reality we denote as "the economy," because of necessity the economy contains elements of the political order in its mechanisms of coordination. The belief system called economics reveals its ideological character when it portrays this mechanism as apolitical — that is, as devoid of elements that cause it to favor some groups over others.

As I have already said, such a view of economics arouses a deep unease. The assertion that our economic perceptions are perforce ideological suggests that we must apply a kind of political corrective to restore 20–20 vision to our social inquiry. Perhaps even more troubling, it implies that the guiding ideal of science, with its noble ambition of rising above wishful interpretations of reality, must give way to the insecure guidance of a foundationless relativism. I must address these concerns as best I can.

Let me begin with the fear that we may seek to overcome the distortions of ideology by grinding into our lenses a corrective — say a Marxian or perhaps Veblenian prescription to remedy our imperfect perceptions. It is of course true that Marx and Veblen have among their central objectives the removal of the ideological veil that conceals many political aspects of society, and it is difficult to emerge from a study of either without becoming aware of a political substratum beneath what would otherwise be considered value-free propositions or concepts. Yet that is far from claiming that a Marxian or Veblenian approach yields an ideology-free vision. Deep preconceptions about the political nature of society remain buried within the Marxian deconstruction of economics —

for instance, in its notions with regard to the true or false consciousness of the members of social classes; its belief in a scientific understanding that could replace the fetishism of bourgeois economic inquiry; in the capacity of that understanding to guide social praxis; and in the destination toward which the historic process may lead humankind. Similar political constructions of reality inform the Veblenian view, including its vision of the machine process as the great agency for social demystification, its perception of science as "evolutionary," and its faith in an "instinct of workmanship" to which humanity might turn as a great stabilizing force. Thus political norms and values are implicit within the critiques directed against conventional economics as well as in the object against which they are aimed.

Is an ideology-free economics then possible? The question moves us from the problem of ideology in its more "particular" form, to use Mannheim's term, to its widest and most generalized manifestation as part of the sociology of knowledge. Mannheim believed that we could indeed detect the falsities or self-delusions of ideology in the small, but he had no such hopes for "total" ideologies, where "the subject's whole mode of conceiving things [is] determined by his historical and social setting." There the problem might be mitigated by the practiced self-criticism of the ideologically aware observer but could never be entirely overcome (Mannheim, 1936, pp. 265–66; Berger and Luckmann, 1966, p. 9).

It is not to be expected that economics could be exempted from the cultural vulnerability that affects all systems of beliefs, and insofar as it is concerned with questions of contribution and reward, it is inherently subject to the moral and political values of its parental social order. It is hardly surprising, then, that this aggravates our second concern — namely, that an acquiescence in an ideological view will replace the ideal of an impersonal arbitration over these values with a surrender to their irremediable arbitrariness.

This powerful reservation can at least be partly assuaged by remembering that no arbiter, including "science," oversees the formation of concepts themselves. The perceptions by which we order our observations, whether directed to the heavens or toward earth, spring from our minds and cater to our needs, and make their peace in innumerable ways with our psychic and social domains. There is no escape from this ultimate epistemological frailty — if a recognition of our human estate is a frailty — but that does not undo the possibility of serious, critical work along, or within, the various meanings that can be assigned to science. The task of the scientist commences as he or she works through the implications of a prevailing belief system; considers or tests the consequences that spring from its implications; and examines the conceptual scheme for its compatibility with other construals of reality. In this task, the investigatory process can proceed according to rules aimed at the impartial pursuit of truth, whether or not the "truth" is deemed unchallengeable.

Thus the anxieties aroused by a surrender of the absolutist claims of science can be mitigated by the recognition that scientific work can still be carried on within the accepted modes of social interpretation, be they called "paradigms," "scientific research programs," or simply "ideologies." Different ideologies will bring forth different or differently perceived aspects of the system; but their subsequent measurement, the testing of their interactions, and of greatest interest, the extrapolation of their systemic consequences remain open to the criticism and correction of others.

The recognition of an inextricable ideological content to economics does not therefore envisage a bedlam of conflicting research programs or assertions as to the nature of the economy and its "proper" interpretation. The ascendancy of an ideological conception of economics would be expected to impart a self-consciousness to the discipline, but not a self-destructiveness. In point of fact, I would expect that in the future, as in the past, dominant ideologies are likely to exert their unifying influence, if for no other reason than that we seem to require the stability of a generally accepted world view to carry on systematic investigation. The anxiety aroused by relinquishing such an intellectual base is nowhere more evident than in the extreme difficulties with which Paul Feyerabend, the most eloquent spokesman for methodological anarchy, comes to terms with the counterclaims of his opponent Imre Lakatos: "... at the present stage of philosophical consciousness," Feyerabend writes, "an irrational theory falsely interpreted as a new account of Reason will be a better instrument for freeing the mind than an out-and-out anarchism that is likely to paralyze the brains of everyone" (Feyerabend, 1975, p. 214).[6]

The norm-oriented propensity of the human psyche lends yet one last dimension to the problem of economics as ideology. It involves that responsibility of which I spoke earlier — the responsibility that the self-aware economist feels for the social reality he or she constructs, prior to analyzing it as a "given." Among the constitutive elements of this pre-analytic cognitive act, as Schumpeter called it, we must include deep preconceptions about human "nature," primary among them beliefs about the need for equality versus that for hierarchy, and about the malleability versus the fixity of behavior. These preconceptions, stemming from nurtural and adult experience, are easily "validated" by reference to private or collective life and protected by the very inaccessability of their origins. They seem to me the unrecognized basis for the visions — emancipatory, optimistic, "radical"; bounded, pessimistic, and "conservative" — that underlie the otherwise inexplicable empirical exaggerations or logical lapses that characterize "ideology" in the smaller sense with which we began our analysis of the term.

The role of personal life histories in shaping our construal of social reality adds yet another element of indeterminacy to the problem of what economics is, once we give up the belief that it is the analysis of an unproblematical "research object." Economics must then be understood as a belief system that is not only inherently ideological — that is, enmeshed in the political and social values of its own order — but imbued as well with beliefs as to "human nature" for which there is usually no basis for explanation.[7]

I see no escape from this politically embedded and personally impenetrable starting point for social inquiry, nor do I see any reason to wish for one. Social understanding is a human, not a divine need. Its purpose is to reconcile us to our collective predicament by interpreting it in one coherent way or another — there is no inherent bias toward a radical or conservative view of things, just as there is no touchstone for an unassailable one. Economics conceived as ideology is therefore not a surrender to unworthy motives or remediable weaknesses, and certainly not an invitation to wishful thinking or indifferent analysis. On the contrary, it is a summons to avoid these pitfalls to whatever extent self-reflection and critical thought make possible, not in the vain hope of making economics a "science" but in the ambitious attempt to make it a humanistic discipline.

Notes

[1] The literature is too large to review, but a few benchmarks should be indicated. They include Marx 1947, Part I and 1973, Introduction; Karl Mannheim, 1936, Chapter 2; Peter Berger and Thomas Luckmann, 1966, passim; and Joseph Schumpeter, 1954, Chapter 4.

[2] Adam Smith anticipates some part of this interpretational approach in "The History of Astronomy." There he describes the task of science as "[allaying] the tumult of the imagination" (Smith, 1980, p. 46), a position much in accord with his Humean agnosticism that makes the criterion for closure in scientific debate the attainment of a temporary resting point for the anxieties of the inquirer, not the arrival at some final destination of Truth. This is not a subjective construction of reality, but a subjective construction of the objective of scientific inquiry.

[3] This portion of my argument closely parallels the treatment in my 1988, Ch. 8.

[4] See, for instance, the description of the Walrasian "hard core" in Roy Weintraub, 1985, p. 109.

⁵ In point of fact, the natural world also betrays its connection with the social structures. As Mirowski has written (drawing on the work of Durkheim, Mauss, and Douglas): "Theories of the physical world are shaped by the social relations within the culture that generates them, and these are used in turn to express in reified form the essence of the culture's ideal of order" (Mirowski, 1987, p. 1004). See also the social interpretation of evolution discussed in Richard Levins and Richard Lewontin, 1985, Ch. 1, and passim.

⁶ See the discussion by Rosenberg, 1986, p. 137.

⁷ An unusual opportunity for conjecture as to the personal roots of such preconceptions exists in the case of Schumpeter: see my 1988 Ch. 7, esp. pp. 182–183.

References

Berger, Peter and Luckmann, Thomas. 1966. *The Social Construction of Reality: A Treatise in the Sociology of Knowledge.* Garden City, New York: Doubleday & Co.

Feyerabend, Paul. 1975. *Against Method.* London: Verso.

Friedman, Milton and Friedman, Rose. 1980. *Free to Choose: A Personal Statement.* New York: Harcourt Brace Jovanovich.

Heilbroner, Robert L. 1988. *Behind the Veil of Economics: Essays in the Worldly Philosophy.* New York: W.W. Norton.

——. 1973. "Economics as a 'Value Free' Science." *Social Research* 40(1).

——. 1985. *The Nature and Logic of Capitalism.* New York: W.W. Norton.

Klamer, Arjo. 1983. *Conversations with Economists.* Totowa, NJ: Rowman & Allanheld.

Levins, Richard and Lewontin, Richard. 1985. *The Dialectical Biologist.* Cambridge, Mass.: Harvard University Press.

Lowe, Adolph. 1965. *On Economic Knowledge: Toward a Science of Political Economics.* New York: Harper & Row.

McCloskey, Donald N. 1985. *The Rhetoric of Economics.* Madison, Wis.: University of Wisconsin Press.

Mannheim, Karl. 1936. *Ideology and Utopia: An Introduction to the Sociology of Knowledge.* New York: Harcourt, Brace and Co.

Marshall, Alfred. 1948. *Principles of Economics.* 8th ed. New York: Macmillan.

Marx, Karl. 1973. *Grundrisse.* Harmondsworth, Middlesex, England: Penguin.

Marx, Karl and Engels, Friedrich. 1947. *The German Ideology.* New York: International Publishers.

Mirowski, Philip. September 1987. "The Philosophical Bases of Institutional Economics." *Journal of Economic Issues* 21(3).

Rosenberg, Alexander. 1986. "Lakatosian Consolations for Economics," *Economics and Philosophy* 2.

Schumpeter, Joseph A. 1954. *History of Economic Analysis.* New York: Oxford University Press.

——. 1949. "Science and Ideology." *American Economic Review* 39 (March).

Smith, Adam. 1980. "The History of Astronomy." In: W.P.D. Wightman and
    J.C. Bryce, eds. *Adam Smith: Essays on Philosophical Subjects*. Oxford:
    Clarendon Press.
——. 1983. *Lectures on Rhetoric and Belles Lettres*, ed. J.C. Bryce, Oxford:
    Clarendon Press.
Weintraub, E. Roy. 1985. *General Equilibrium Analysis*. New York: Cambridge
    University Press.

COMMENT BY E. ROY WEINTRAUB[1]

> *While leading you to watch his act of destruction at one point, the "unmasker" is always furtively building at another point, and by his prestidigitation, he can forestall observation of his own moves.*

— Kenneth Burke[2]

Heilbroner's Argument Recapitulated

Section I of Heilbroner's chapter sets out the idea that the language of ideology can provide the interpretational or hermeneutic elements that economic argumentation has lacked. Section II suggests that the tenacity of certain economic analyses in neoclassical theory cannot be explained by their being good science, since theories that assume a symmetry among factors of production are based on "oversights or indifference to logical slips within the argument — slips that are reasonably apparent to a sceptical intelligence." Section III applies the definition of ideology as the construction of social reality to show how economic arguments of the neoclassical variety can be made to reveal a social reality at odds with the "true" reality, justifying for Heilbroner his concern with ideology. Section IV presents the view that attention to the ideology of (neo-classical) economics will uncover the intrinsically political beliefs of the society in which that economics is considered "explanatory." Section V further contends that economics, as an ideology, ignores or masks the political core function of the market system, a system that serves "to mobilize and allocate labor power for ends that are not those of the laborers themselves." Section VI concludes by noting that an ideology-free economics is not, however, possible; what may be possible, and desirable, is rather self-consciousness about the discourse of economics.

Heilbroner's chapter constructs two distinct and incompatible arguments: sections I–V are at odds, as I will show, with the remarkably judicious and sensitive final Section VI.

Heilbroner's False Start

If an oyster makes pearls out of irritation, Robert Heilbroner's grain of sand is his belief that:

> ... such concepts as monadic individuals and isomorphic factors of production continue to be embraced even after their internal difficulties have been

117

revealed. There is no sign in the regnant economic view of an abandonment of these ideas although their self-contradictory or misspecified natures have long been known. It is this intellectual rigidity that suggests the need to impute to the belief systems of economics a sociological basis capable of explaining their resistance to, or insulation from, conceptual challenge. That is the intent of the vocabulary of *ideology*. . . .

Heilbroner invites his reader to share some common ground, particularly the belief that labor and capital are not sensibly treated as factors of production, and the further belief that the social grounding of individual choice theory vitiates any idea of an individualistic theory. These claims are not self-evident, and it must be obvious to all readers of this book that the former claim, at any rate, is associated with one of several positions variously termed Marxist, neoMarxist, neoRicardian, Post-Keynesian, etc. The notion that "real" labor is somehow different from the labor of the new labor economics of human capital theory, and different from the labor of the new home economics, is a claim loaded with doctrinal and discourse history. For clarity, I shall ignore this particular claim for the present.

But his example about choice theory is singularly ill-chosen; to suggest that choice requires an allocation of income, and income assumes other individuals, and thus a sociopolitical system, is simply wrong. Robinson Crusoe, allocating his collected mussels between food-mussels and wave-skipping mussels, needs no Friday. My choice of spending time writing about Heilbroner's chapter or writing a short story does not need anyone to have "given" me time.

The first part of the chapter justifies Heilbroner's concern with attention to ideology. This part contains, as noted, some of his public reasons for believing that ideology must be at the heart of discourse in economics: why, he wonders, do economists not change their methods of analyses and their concern with specific problems and theoretical insights rooted in what to him are the self-contradictory or fallacious doctrines of neoclassical economics?

We should note, because Heilbroner does not, that this is an old and well-travelled path of questioning. It is associated with the idea of revolutionary change in science and has shaped the past twenty years of discussion in the philosophy of science. Why, it is there asked, does a theory supplant another; why does one set of ideas give way to another set of ideas? This is, of course, the obverse of Heilbroner's query of why does one set of ideas *not* give way to another, in particular why has neoclassical (or what I have elsewhere (Weintraub, 1985) termed neoWalrasian) analysis not collapsed. The philosophers would answer Heilbroner's question by suggesting either that: (1) neoclassical economics has not been falsified or (2) neoclassical analysis is a progressive research program or (3) neoclassical analysis solves problems put to it or (4) it is useful for prediction, etc.

Heilbroner asks his reader to put such defenses of neoclassical theory aside because he, Heilbroner, has knowledge that the neoclassical theory is either false or self-contradictory. On the first claim, I note that he offers no basis for assessing truth or falsity; indeed, Heilbroners' apparent approval of McCloskey's antifoundationalist position suggests that he cannot have any epistemological basis for his claim, but only a moral one: he is using "false" in the sense of moral disapprobrium, as in "do not believe in neoclassical economics for it is a doctrine fraught with what you, my reader, must surely agree are undesirable consequences for the way people treat one another."

Or perhaps Heilbroner believes that neoclassical analysis is not a progressive program in Lakatos's (1970) sense; but this belief requires him to have some notion of another program that is then relatively progressive itself, for the notion of abandoning a program or a research agenda requires that there be an alternative to replace that which is lost: we never abandon a program except for a rival program. For Heilbroner to defend his views from this perspective, this must mean that the Post-Keynesian program, or neoMarxian program, or Program X is "better" in some well-defined sense of solving some problems better than does the neoclassical program.

If it is not the case that Heilbroner convinces us that neoclassical theory is false, does he at least convince us of the truth of his claim that its root concepts are self-contradictory? No: in fact he nowhere attempts to do this, except for his failed deconstruction of "monadic individual" in his choice theory example. And, frankly, the case he makes for automatically rejecting self-contradictory theories is naive: consider the two sentences, "Mathematics is the science of significant forms of order and relationship" and "Mathematics is the science of infinity." Note that "Each of these definitions taken by itself is a deep truth in the sense of Neils Bohr: its negation is also a deep truth" (Browder, 1988, p. 286).[3] What must be rejected, which "theory" must be cast out, if I assert the simultaneous truths that "Man is rational" and "Man is irrational?" Might I not be simultaneously a neoclassical economist and a Jungian?

Heilbroner reminds me of the philosopher who is assigned to teach a freshman introductory course. He calls, on the first day, for a show of hands of all those who do not believe in God. Fifteen hands go in the air. He then presents Aquinas's ontological proof of God's existence. Then he asks the fifteen whether they could detect any flaws in the proof, and none so indicate. He then asks how many *now* believe in God, and none of the fifteen raise their hands. Must we invoke ideology to explain the steadfastness of disbelief in God or the unshaken trust in neoclassical economics?

I think not. It is not outrageous to argue that, in Kuhn's (1970) terms, the neoclassical paradigm is robust because it is successfully performing the tasks of normal science, and there are no anomalies so severe that an alternative paradigm offers greater explanatory play. It is not foolish to claim that, in Lakatosian terms, the neoWalrasian research program is, at least with respect to all rivals, relatively progressive in the sense that its successive theories have excess empirical content and some of that content is corroborated. Nor is it idiotic to maintain, as I have done most recently (Weintraub 1989) and as McCloskey (1988) continues to do, that neoclassical economics is the discourse of an interpretive community that has judged the central concerns of the group to be worthwhile and productive and usefully engaging.

Consequently the first two sections of Heilbroner's chapter, justifying his concern with ideology, are not necessary to the argument contained in sections III through VI, which show how ideology can help "unpack" certain economic analyses.

This illustrates the difficulty of any beginning; for there is no necessity to deny Heilbroner's conclusion just because of a weakness of his premise. We can take seriously his claim that there is something worth discussing in the idea that Economics can be construed as Ideology without having to accept the basis on which Heilbroner himself justifies concern with such a framing of the idea. I can, as an afficionado of neoWalrasian general equilibrium analysis and historian of modern economic thought, find much to interest me in his claim and much to engage my scholarly attention, at the same time that I enthusiastically reject the perspective that Heilbroner invites me to share. Thus one does not have to be a Post-Keynesian to take part in a discussion of ideology and its role in economic discourse. Heilbroner begins his chapter badly if his aim is to persuade larger rather than smaller groups of readers. His appeal to his readers as economists hostile to neoclassical theory is both audience-limiting and unnecessary. A reader's fondness for Heilbroner's conclusions does not entail a love of his assumptions: from "if P then Q" and "Q," "P" does not follow logically. What follows instead is my attempt to reconstruct what is meritorious in Heilbroner's argument.

Belief Systems

Heilbroner uses ideology to refer to the construction of "social reality — that is, the frameworks by which societies perceive and interpret the arrangements that order their lives." He is thus using ideology in a very coherent way, as the organizing framework by which social groups or communities order their worlds, which is of necessity a social ordering of a social reality. This perspective is not new, except to economists perhaps, though literate economists have been aware of the themes suggested by Heilbroner's formulation at least since McCloskey, if not more directly before. It is well-handled in more literary discourses.

Stanley Fish (1980), in his development of the idea of interpretive communities, articulates for me what is central in the kinds of issues Heilbroner is attempting to address:

> Interpretive communities are made up of those who share interpretive strategies not for reading but for writing texts, for constituting their properties. In other words these strategies exist prior to the act of reading and therefore determine the shape of what is read rather than, as is usually assumed, the other way around.... [But] an interpretive community is not objective because as a bundle of interests, of particular purposes and goals, its perspective is interested rather than neutral; but by the same reasoning the meanings and texts produced by an interpretive community are not subjective because they do not proceed from an isolated individual but from a public and conventional point of view... [M]embers of the same community will necessarily agree because they they will see (and by seeing, make) everything in relation to that community's assumed purposes and goals; and conversely, members of different communities will disagree because from their respective positions the other "simply" cannot see what is obviously and inescapably there.... The business of criticism, in other words, was not to decide between interpretations by subjecting them to the test of disinterested evidence but to establish by political and persuasive means (they are the same thing) the set of interpretive assumptions from the vantage of which the evidence (and the facts and the intentions and everything else) will hereafter be specifiable... [T]he entities that were once seen as competing for the right to constrain interpretation (text, reader, author) are now all seen to be the *products* of interpretation. (Fish, 1980, pp. 14–16)

To translate, in Heilbroner's terms, a particular ideology is that which is shared, and is taken to define, a specific interpretive community of economists: Keynesian macroeconomists, neoRicardians, Lewis-Becker Chicago labor economists, New Classical economists, etc. In Lakatosian terms, an ideology is that which adherents to a particular (scientific) research program take as given, and use to construct evidence and theories, and is the background for the instantiation of the hard core of the program. In Kuhnian terms, it is the linguistic context of the paradigm. Gloss Fish's "community" as "subculture of economists adhering to a particular theoretical perspective" and their "texts" as their "articles, books, in which are presented their models, theories, and arguments" and you have Heilbroner's discussion of ideology and its role in economics encapsulated. Translate "criticism" as "methodological discourse" and you have a role for discussions *about* economic arguments not based on a metatheoretic perspective (cf. Weintraub, 1989).

That Heilbroner is arguing some postmodernist points that have been well-argued and developed elsewhere is no criticism. There is something rather scandalous in the incessant and *ongoing* borrowings by economists from modernist thought in literature, philosophy, sociology, history, and science, as if the last several decades of postmodernist intellectual life outside of economics did not ever exist. For example, the number of citation studies in history of thought articles, establishing priority of discovery and transmission of new theories, is thoroughly Mertonian sociology of science, and was presented to economists initially by Stigler. But for the past fifteen or more years most of the intellectual action, as it were, is rather in what is now termed the sociology of scientific knowledge, originally associated with the so-called strong program: but how many economists know the work of Collins, Bloor, Geertz, Woolgar, Mulkay, Barnes, Latour, and Knorr-Cetina? Where is the recognition that economists, as is true and now well-understood about biologists, physicists, chemists, astronomers, anthropologists, do not find their facts but rather establish "facticity" through their own efforts (Woolgar, 1988; Collins, 1985; Knorr-Cetina, 1981; etc.)? Science makes worlds, not discoveries.

All of which is to say that Heilbroner is not only not alone in thinking, and arguing, that ideology (or something similar) is a profoundly important conceptual organizer for thinking about economic discourse. He is quite in the intellectual mainstream; it is methodological discourse in economics that is in the scholarly backwater.

Constituting Heilbroner's Own Argument

It is now time to engage Heilbroner's own argumentation directly for, as I shall argue the matter, he succumbs to the unpeculiar temptation to claim, from his own antifoundationalist position, to be providing a set of foundations from which to launch criticisms of practice, of particular work in economic analysis. He does not seem to realize that his own arguments are not exempt from his own criticisms.

> Theory can be seen as an effort to guide practice in two senses: 1) it is an attempt to *guide* practice from a position above or outside it..., and 2) it is an attempt to *reform* practice by neutralizing interest, by substituting for the parochial perspective of some local or partisan point of view the perspective of a general rationality to which the individual subordinates his contextually conditioned opinions and beliefs.... The argument *against* theory is simply that this substitution of the general for the local has never been and will never be achieved. Theory is an impossible project which will never succeed. It will never succeed simply because the primary data and formal laws necessary to its success will always be spied or picked out from within the contextual circumstances of which they are supposedly independent. The objective facts and rules of calculation that are to ground interpretation and render it principled are themselves interpretative products: they are, therefore, always and already contaminated by the interested judgments they claim to transcend. (Fish, 1985, p. 110)

Consider Heilbroner's claim that the economic structure consists of "the activities of provisioning and of the means of coordinating these activities that can be discovered in all societies." He goes on to discuss the implication of this view, and ends the discussion with a perspective on the boundaries of the economy within a society constituted politically and socially too. He is thus able to argue that only with the rise of capitalism is the economy separate from, clearly discernable from, "the community below and the state above." He continues:

> The specifically "ideological" aspect of economics consists in its normal depiction of these activities [provisioning, etc.] and means in terms that ignore and conceal the sociopolitical structure whence they spring and which they serve. "Economic categories" writes Marx, "are only the theoretical expression, the abstraction, of the social relations of production."

What we have here is Heilbroner having his cake and eating it too. He has presented us his readers with a strong case for a situated subject constrained by a belief system called an ideology. He has thus forced us to acknowledge ourselves, as we are engaged as economists or as we are engaged in methodological discourse about economics, as situated and constrained. He then goes on to say that this requires us to think of economic categories as having arisen in a manner associated with Marxian tradition, as having a grounding in a particular theoretical perspective. This cake of course does not need to be consumed.

These two aspects of Heilbroner's argument are intertwined throughout the paper: the "good" or antifoundationalist Heilbroner continually, and without apparent cognitive dissonance, segues into the "bad" Post-Keynesian foundationalist Heilbroner.

The argument of the good and bad Heilbroners carries one along on language both persuasive and exhortatory:

> [The] deepest aspect of ideology enters in another guise, namely the denial of any trace of political power in the orchestration mechanism of society — its price system . . . [The] economic celebration of market choice as freedom masks any recognition of its function as a medium for social power . . . [with] the priority accorded to the rights of property in the division of the product to which labor and capital have each freely contributed. . . . In a word, as an ideology, economics ignores or does not perceive the political core function of the market system — i.e., its capacity to mobilize and allocate labor power for ends that are not those of laborers themselves.

Notice what we have here. Heilbroner tries to persuade us that he has uncovered the ideological component of economic analysis and takes it as given that economics is neoclassical economics in its most unsophisticated form, that presented by the only economist quoted in the previous section, Alfred Marshall. Why would Heilbroner not use, say, the Kenneth Arrow of *The Limits of Organization* or, on the more technical vision of the capital and equilibrium issues, the Christopher Bliss of *Capital Theory and the Distribution of Income*? Why is economic analysis understood to be so monolithic, and coherent?

Leaving those issues, Heilbroner uncovers ideological meat apparently independent of Marxian categories, but they turn out Marxian anyway. The solution to the question of why this is so is that Heilbroner too is a situated subject, and his beliefs are not independent of the perspective he thinks he is using. He believes that he can establish a perspective apart from the theories he himself holds; he believes that in his critical work he is metatheorizing from a perspective apart from, separated from, and distinctly independent of the theories he believes are true.

This is, of course, not possible.

Heilbroner believes in Theory in the sense of Methodology, theory in the sense of a perspective apart from economic analysis that structures and governs the way economic analysis can be appraised.

> Theory cannot guide practice because its rules and procedures are no more than generalizations from practice's history (and from only a small piece of that history), and theory cannot reform practice because, rather than neutralizing interest, it begins and ends in interest and raises the imperatives of interest

— of some local, particular, partisan project — to the status of universals. (Fish, 1985, pp. 111–112)

Put another way, Heilbroner apparently believes that attention to ideology, an attention coerced by the recognition of the situated subject, the situated creator or author of the bit of economics analysis, will lead to a better economics, one in which the political nature of the claims, the political nature of the argument itself, will be brought to the fore and thereupon can be used to deconstruct the theoretical conclusions. But Heilbroner's claim itself is deconstructed by the situated nature of his own theoretical beliefs, beliefs that claim his adherence even prior to his attempts to ground those beliefs in a perspective apart from those beliefs. Since he cannot ever ground those beliefs, for they are simply the context for his seeking a grounding in the first place, he cannot stand apart from the theory he seeks to replace standard economics with. There is no perspective that will permit adjudication between the Marxist, neoclassical, or neoAustrian theories, say. There is no neutral place, no ideology-free Platonic cave, where the various theories can meet to allow pure thought to effect comparisons and relative appraisals among them.

Heilbroner Resplendent

Heilbroner's belief, apparently arrived at from his extra-belief or Foundationalist Metatheory, or Theory, or Methodology, is that attention to ideology will compel a different economics, but he is too wise, too sensible, to be comfortable with the apparent conclusion that "our economic perceptions are perforce ideological suggests that we must apply a kind of political corrective to restore 20–20 vision to our social inquiry."

One of the pleasures of being a member of the economics profession for me is that I can claim association with someone who can write: "The perceptions by which we order our observations, whether directed to the heavens or toward earth, spring from our minds and cater to our needs, and make their peace in innumerable ways with our psychic and social domains. There is no escape from this ultimate epistemological frailty...."

Heilbroner goes on to argue that this bind is less a failure than a fact of life, and we do our analyses recognizing the social and political character of our work. Ideology is not a corrective to the work, but a context for that work. And, to be truthful, psychology matters too, for our construction of social reality is not independent of our construction of personal reality: "The role of personal life histories in shaping our construal of social reality adds yet another element of indeterminacy to the problem of what economics is, once we give up the belief that it is the analysis of the unproblematical research object" (p. 21).

And Heilbroner the preacher ends with the lesson:

> Social understanding is a human, not a divine need. Its purpose is to reconcile us to our collective predicament by interpreting it in one coherent way or another — there is no inherent bias toward a radical or conservative view of things, just as there is no touchstone for an unassailable one.

The wisdom, and force, of these observations should not blind us to their nature, however. For while the reader can hardly take issue with the notion that, to discuss the enterprise, or the program, or the activity of doing neoclassical economics, we need to understand the context of that work, and that context requires attention to the matrix of beliefs that sustain the activity, there is nonetheless no imperative that likewise constrains the neoclassical economics itself. That is, no attention to ideology will lead one to provide a better explanation of black-white earnings differentials, or transitions out of unemployment for white teenagers, or the rate of introduction of new chemical compounds by pharmaceutical firms.[4] That is not to say that neoclassical economics is "above ideology" or that neoclassical economics is different in *this* respect from Post-Keynesian economics, or Marxist economics, or Austrian economics, etc. The point is simpler, and stronger: *doing economics is a different activity from talking about doing economics.* And the communities, and discussions within those communities, change as the activity changes. That neoclassical analysis of black-white earnings differentials is done is not in question, nor can it be doubted that such work will continue to be done well or ill independent of the attention paid to ideology. But Heilbroner's residual point must be granted, namely that in discussing the black-white earnings issue, and placing that work in context, the context is richer than a mere citation of previous articles on the subject would suggest, for the context is associated with a construction of a reality in which blacks and whites are separate categories to be taken seriously, and in which there is a presumption that there is a problem to be addressed.

Conclusion

Heilbroner makes a convincing case for the value of the language of ideology in discussing the situated subject called the neoclassical economist, but he has presented no case at all for a criticism of neoclassical economics. Nor could he have done so from the antifoundationalist position he invites us to share.

Notes

[1] Professor of Economics, Duke University, Durham, NC, 27706. This comment was improved by comments and discussion with Neil de Marchi, Marina Bianchi, and Craufurd Goodwin and was completed during the author's tenure as a Fellow at The National Humanities Center, in Research Triangle Park, North Carolina. Support from the NHS is gratefully acknowledged.

[2] Cited without specific reference in Eugene Goodheart, "A Limit to Ideology," *National Humanities Center Newsletter*, 9, 3–4, 1988, p. 3.

[3] I must note here that the eminent sociologist of science, of the strong program group, Harry Collins, even rejects self-contradiction as a reasonable preliminary cut at what constitutes good science. That is, Collins argues that the assertion of belief in a logical norm like "p or not-p" will never confer an explanatory advantage on the believer vis-a-vis the unbeliever: "What things cannot happen in a society because of the law of contradiction which might have happened if the law of contradiction did not hold? When logically aware anthropologists visit new unfamiliar cultures, what work can they avoid while their less aware colleagues press on in ignorance.... In social psychology, the theory of cognitive dissonance, which is about the way people cope with internalised contradictions, has foundered on the difficulty of determining what people experience as contradictory" (Collins, 1988).

[4] I have argued this point in considerable detail in my paper "Methodology Doesn't Matter But The History Of Thought Might," which will appear in Spring 1989 in the *Scandinavian Journal of Economics*. The major point is that no position outside discourse is possible; there is no privileged position, from which one may criticize "analysis," for all positions are themselves constituted out of the analysis. A Marxist critique of a neoclassical analysis of black-white earnings differentials will be more or less successful depending on the discussion of black-white earnings differentials, not alternate conceptions of history. Indeed, the "relevant" Marxist history lesson is precisely the Marxist analysis of those differentials; there is no such category as "context-free Marxist theory" which may be applied to a particular problem "apart" from the Marxist theory.

References

Browder, Felix E. 1988. "Mathematics and the Sciences." In: William Asprey and Philip Kitcher, eds. *History and Philosophy of Modern Mathematics: Minnesota Studies in the Philosophy of Science, Vol. XI*. Minneapolis: University of Minnesota Press.

Collins, Harry. 1985. *Changing Order: Replication and Induction in Scientific Practice*. London: Sage Publications.

Collins, Harry. 1988. "The Meaning of Experiment: Replication and Reasonableness." In: L.A. Pignansi and H. Lawson, eds. *Dismantling Truth: Science in Post-Modern Times*. London: Weidenfield.

Fish, Stanley. 1980. *Is There a Text in This Class?* Cambridge: Harvard University Press.

Fish, Stanley. 1985. "Consequences." In: W.J.T. Mitchell, ed. *Against Theory*. Chicago: University of Chicago Press.

Goodheart, Eugene. 1988. "A Limit to Ideology." *National Humanities Center Newsletter* 9:3–4.

Knorr-Cetina, Karin D. 1981. *The Manufacture of Knowledge: An Essay on the Constructivist and Contextual Nature of Science*. Oxford: Pergamon.

Kuhn, Thomas. 1970. *The Structure of Scientific Revolutions*. 2nd edition. Chicago: University of Chicago Press.

Lakatos, Imre. 1970. "Falsification and the Methodology of Scientific Research Programmes." In: Imre Lakatos and Alan Musgrave, eds. *Criticism and the Growth of Knowledge*. Cambridge: Cambridge University Press.

McCloskey, Don. 1985. *The Rhetoric of Economics*. Madison: University of Wisconsin Press.

McCloskey, Don. 1988. "Thick and Thin Methodologies in the History of Economic Thought." In: Neil de Marchi, ed. *The Popperian Legacy in Economics*. New York: Cambridge University Press.

Weintraub, E. Roy. 1985. *General Equilibrium Analysis: Studies in Appraisal*. New York: Cambridge University Press.

Weintraub, E. Roy. 1989. "Methodology Doesn't Matter, But the History of Thought Might." *Scandinavian Journal of Economics*, forthcoming.

Woolgar, Steve. 1988. *Science: The Very Idea*. London: Tavistock Publications.

5 THE TEXTBOOK PRESENTATION OF ECONOMIC DISCOURSE

Arjo Klamer

Economic discourse is elusive and frustrating to anyone who tries to enter its maze of questions, terms, diagrams, and models. Most freshmen glare incomprehensibly when the scarcity of resources is urged upon them. When they hear "production possibility curves," "rational choice," and "upward sloping supply curves," they may believe themselves to be in some foreign language class. The mapping of their world in geometric patterns and algebraic formulas does not make much sense. Even though they are constantly bombarded with abstractions in their cultural environment, the thinking in abstract terms that economists do is not natural to most students. The incongruity with common talk makes economics hard.

Yet, the hardness does not seem to dissuade students. Even if we set aside those who perceive in economics courses close substitutes to busi-

I began this study with Michel Grimaud (French/cognitive sciences, Wellesley College), who has responsibility for its methodological part. I am grateful to participants at the H.E.S. conference of 1986, the Middlebury conference on The Spread of Economic Ideas, the Wellesley faculty, and Warren Samuels for comments, and to Chrystal Sharpe for research assistance, and the N.E.H. for its financial support.

ness courses, the large number of economics majors suggests that economists make a convincing case for their discipline. The question is how do they do it?

The obvious place to start is the introductory textbook. What follows is a reading of the introductory chapters in the twelve editions of Paul Samuelson's introductory textbook.

This reading is informed by the rhetorical perspective. Even though the rhetorical perspective goes back a couple of thousand years, it has entered the world of economists only recently.[1] It guides the student of economics to look beyond the propositions that economists produce and consider their discursive practice in its entirety. Thus the rhetorical perspective makes one alert to the various rhetorical devices that economists use to make their case. In other studies I have highlighted the variety of arguments in economic discourse.[2] The lessons learned there inform the reading here.

The intent is to find out the arguments that Samuelson uses to sway innocent readers to the economists' way of reasoning.

Preliminaries

There are many economics textbooks that can be the target of a rhetorical reading, but Samuelson's textbook is the obvious choice. Its influence is beyond questioning; it sets the standard for the post-WW II textbooks and has been the first encounter with economics for millions of students throughout the world, myself included. (I learned from its eighth edition and taught its eleventh and twelfth editions.) Furthermore Samuelson's twelve editions add a historical dimension that turn out to benefit their interpretation.

My reading is inevitably constrained. The purpose is to learn about the way in which economics gets presented to first-time students of economics. Yet, textbooks are only half the story of what happens to those who venture into the field of economics. It is the more formal half. Much else happens in the classroom, in the messages that the teacher conveys.

The concentration on the introductory chapter limits the scope of the study even further. Students do not have an incentive to read the chapter. So who cares about it, one may ask? I do because I presume that the author and the teachers do. The introductory chapter sets the tone for the presentation that follows and reveals to those who select texts what kind of textbook this one is. I grant, however, that the link between the introductory chapter and the subsequent chapters deserves further exploration.

The Textbook As Genre

The rhetorical inquiry begins with the question, What type of text are we looking at? In terms of literary criticism, the textbook would be called a genre, to be distinguished from the genre of research papers, monographs, or surveys.[3] Thomas Kuhn, in the *Scientific Revolutions*, includes textbooks in the genre of popularizing texts and gives the following characterization:

> They address themselves to an already articulated body of problems, data, and theory, most often to the particular set of paradigms to which the scientific community is committed at the time they are written ... (They) aim to communicate the vocabulary and syntax of a contemporary scientific language. (1970, p. 136)

No need to be very surprised here. Clearly, the main objective of textbooks is pedagogical. But what is the "already articulated body of problems, data, and theory" to which Kuhn is referring? The rhetorician is on guard when reading such a phrase. The body of knowledge in physics and other natural sciences is possibly well-defined. At least that is what Kuhn gives as reason why those disciplines have a well-developed textbook genre.[4] The situation in other disciplines is, according to Kuhn, different.

> In music, the graphic arts, and literature ... textbooks ... have only a secondary role. In history, philosophy, and the social sciences, textbook literature has a greater significance. But even in these fields the elementary college course employs parallel readings in original sources, some of them the "classics" of the field, others the contemporary research reports that practitioners write for each other. As a result, the student in any one of these disciplines is constantly made aware of the immense variety of problems that the members of the future group have, in the course of time, attempted to solve. Even more important, he has constantly before him a number of competing and incommensurable solutions to these problems, solutions that he must ultimately evaluate for himself. (Kuhn, 1970, p. 165)

Kuhn should have made an exception for economics. There the genre of textbooks is well-established with numerous, very similar, books competing for adoption. This suggests that economics has a well-articulated body of knowledge. Indeed, economics texts convey the impression of consensus among economists, of a discipline that meets the standards of a hard science. They do not teach "a number of competing and incommensurable solutions, that (the student) must ultimately evaluate for himself." But I am now running ahead.

From Marshall to Samuelson

Marshall's *Principles of Economics* (first edition 1890, eighth edition 1920) was the major textbook for economics students throughout the first two decades of this century. Yet, it reads more like a treatise. Although Marshall intended it to be "a general introduction to the study of economic science," its genre is clearly different from a prototypical textbook, such as *Economics Principles and Modern Practice* (1942, 1947) by Henry R. Mussey and Elizabeth Donnan. For example, Marshall never identifies first-year students as his target audience; Mussey and Donnan do. Marshall's book has short summaries in the margin, as was common practice at the time, but no questions for study as the Mussey-Donnan book. Marshall wrote the book as an economist who sought — and received — professional recognition for his efforts; the book does not only represent the state of the art but advances it as well. The organization of the Mussey-Donnan book bears remarkable resemblance to Marshall's organization, but, as befits an introductory text, it *translates* the work of practicing economists, Marshall included, in a form that is comprehensible to students with no economics background. The book did not have academic pretense and, accordingly, did not pay off in terms of professional recognition.

Samuelson's approach is like Mussey and Donnan's. He addresses beginning students, noting that he wrote the book for those who do not necessarily want to pursue economics beyond the introductory level; he adds questions for discussion to facilitate the study (a list of key concepts appears for the first time in 1957, in the fourth edition.)

The book did not strike its reviewers from the *AER* and the *Economic Journal* as extraordinary. Albert Hart noted in the *AER* (1948, pp. 910–915) the contrast between the mathematical and micro-oriented Samuelson of the *Foundations of Economic Analysis* and the nonmathematical and macro-oriented Samuelson of *Economics: An Introductory Analysis*. He was bothered by the organization of the book, in particular by the placing of the macro chapters before the micro sections and the minimal treatment of international economics. In the *Economic Journal* Honor Croome described Samuelson's book as belonging to the encyclopedic and inductive kind written in the American tradition. The book differs, according to him, from those with an "austerely stripped and essential statement of first principles, to be supplemented by readings and oral teaching," i.e., those books that are preferred in the English tradition.

Even though Samuelson's book was not the first in its kind, it soon dominated the textbook market and became the example to imitate.

Food To Be savored

In the seventh edition, Samuelson tells that he aspired to emulate other textbooks, such as *The Principles of Psychology* by Williams James and *Differential and Integral Calculus* by Richard Courant. Both of these books are comprehensive surveys of their respective disciplines. Both are carefully outlined and present the material in a nonargumentative, this-is-what-you-need-to-know tone. James places his introduction "close to the point of view of natural science"; he clearly defines the subject, begins with the beginning — namely the functioning of the brain — and takes the student through the material in a systematic manner under the motto, articulated by Samuelson,

> Nothing unnecessarily hard, but nothing essential omitted as being beyond the grasp of the serious student; and above all, nothing that later must be unlearned as wrong. (seventh ed. p. v)

Throughout the twelve editions, Samuelson claims to represent the state of the art in economics. In the twelfth edition, Samuelson (with Nordhaus) characterizes his text as *authoritative, comprehensive,* and *clear*. The this-is-what-you-need-to-know tone of the text affirms its authority. Samuelson presents economics as ready-made food that is to be savored and enjoyed. Ever since the ninth edition he has wished his reader "Bon appetit!"

The food metaphor plays to the tune of economics as a body of received knowledge. There is no need to peek into the kitchen and watch the preparation of the food. All students need to do is eat the apples of wisdom. Just like in physics.

The Methodological Argument: Economics as a Science

The next and major stage in the rhetorical inquiry is a scrutiny of the arguments in the text. Let us first consider the methodological arguments.

As I have tried to show in my *Conversations with Economists* (1984), disagreements among economists are mainly fought on methodological grounds. These are fights on how to do economics; they produce most vicious insults, such as that the others do not do science, use "ad hoc" assumptions, or are ideologically biased.

Methodological arguments concern the proper strategies of gaining knowledge as well as the rules for assessment of gained knowledge. They are meta-arguments: they are *about* the discipline. Often they are implicit, expressed in the strategy chosen. Samuelson's text, however, contains several explicit methodological arguments.

When Samuelson began to write his textbook, methodological musings were not standard. The Mussey-Donnan text (1947), for example, is virtually without methodological argument. It refers to economics as a study and merely mentions its "methods of analysis" and that is that. In contrast, Samuelson's first edition is remarkably self-conscious.

Samuelson pauses, for instance, to comment on the proper strategies for gaining knowledge:

> The first task of modern economic *science* [emphasis added] is to describe, to analyse, to explain, to correlate . . . it is necessary to *simplify*, to *abstract*, . . . to *idealize* . . . (first edition, pp. 4, 8)

It must be clear to the student: economics is a science. If still in doubt, she should be aware that economists respect the scientific requirement that theories be subjected to empirical tests:

> The test of a theory's goodness is its usefulness in illuminating observational reality. Its logical elegance and fine-spun beauty are irrelevant. (first edition, p. 8)

Less explicit are the methodological arguments that come through in the numerous references to the natural sciences. While Samuelson confesses that economists cannot hope to attain the precision of such sciences and perform the likes of their controlled experiments, he insists on physics and chemistry as models for the pursuit of scientific knowledge in economics. Thus Samuelson deviates from Marshall's penchant to celebrate biology as the model science. The change is symptomatic of the then occurring shift from an organic root metaphor to the mechanic root metaphor in economic discourse, a shift for which Samuelson's scientific writings bear part of the responsibility.[5]

In line with the this-is-what-you-need-to-know tone, Samuelson does not betray the argumentative character of his views. It is to be expected: the very notion of arguments is incongruent with the concept of science that he tries to impress on innocent minds. Yet, his methodological position, which he developed in subsequent editions, is unmistakably an argument, provoking counterarguments.

Several critics, for example, found Samuelson's presentation too "soft" on the scientific character of economics. E.C. Harwood (1962) wrote a scathing review of the fifth edition in which he reproached Samuelson for downplaying the scientific standards of economics. Lipsey went a step further and presented the same argument in the form of an alternative textbook, *Positive Economics* (1963). Influenced by the views of Popper,[6] Lipsey (who is joined in later editions by Peter Steiner and Douglas Purvis) stresses the importance of "the systematic confrontation of theory with observations." This Samuelson does not deny, but Lipsey, in accordance with Popperian dogma, makes clear that only scientific topics are to be included in an economics text. Because welfare economics is nontestable and thus nonscientific, he excluded it from his text. In line with this scientific bias, the Lipsey text stresses the scientific methods in economics more than Samuelson's first six editions do. It even has separate chapters on "Economics as a Social Science" and "The Role of Statistical Analysis."

As the editions advance, the pro-science arguments in Samuelson's text become more pronounced. The seventh edition (1967) marks a significant turn with new sections on the methodology of science and statistics, the latter complete with diagrams of the consumption curve and normal distribution curve. In the summary of its introductory chapter we read that "economics uses the deductive methods of logic and geometry, and inductive methods of statistical and empirical inference." The eighth edition (1970) adds the image of economics as the "Queen of the social sciences," with the just established Nobel prize as supporting evidence. Finally, the twelfth edition (1985) mentions this most characteristic feature of "scientific" economics, the model "as a simple, often mathematical, representation of a more complex reality" (p. 12).

Interestingly, Samuelson only uses the terms "positive" and "normative" economics when Nordhaus joins the team. The distinction is after all the established way to teach students about the difference between economics as a science (to describe, explain, predict) and economics as an art (to determine what is best for a group or society as a whole). Samuelson did allude to the distinction, identifying in the first edition ethical questions as being outside the domain of economics and in later editions mentioning "value judgments." This was not good enough for Lipsey, and he called his book *Positive Economics*, to allow no mistake of its scientific (or positive) focus.

The argumentative character of the distinction between positive and normative economics is exposed in radical introductory texts. Samuel Bowles and Richard Edwards, for instance, write in their text (published in 1985) that the separation is artificial and untenable:

> Debate about economics involves not only *what is* but *what should be . . .* Economics inevitably involves values. This is as it should be. (pp. 20–21)

The continuous references to the natural sciences, the talk about scientific methods, and the later introduced positive-normative distinction portray the economic discipline as a science. The reader is encouraged to think of physics and chemistry while reading the text, not history, arts, and literature.

Yet Samuelson's text is ambiguous since it does not cut off the connections with the humanities altogether. Paradoxically, the humanistic strokes in his portrait of economics become more explicit just when the scientific features get more pronounced.

It is as if Samuelson tries to get it two ways. He intimidates the reader with the "hard" language of science and then softens the impact by playing to their humanistic sensibilities. In all editions he acknowledges the limitations of economics as a science, mentioning the impossibility of controlled experiments as a major drawback. In the seventh edition, the very same edition with the first section on scientific methodology, he calls attention to

> the irreducible subjective element of our perception of facts depending upon the theoretic system *through* which we look at those facts. (seventh edition, p. vi)

Through the now famous drawing of birds — are they rabbits, or maybe antelopes? — students are made to realize that facts are what you make them out to be. Thoughtful students may be puzzled since these admissions undo the earlier claims that economics is an empirical science. After all, if facts are subjective there is no empirical basis from which to assess economic theories. Samuelson opens the door to this relativizing perspective even further when he, referring to Kuhn's *The Structure of Scientific Revolutions*, concludes:

> When you adopt a new systematic model of economic principles, you comprehend reality in a new and different way. (seventh edition, p. 10)

Suddenly, economics seems less hard, less scientific.

The moment has arrived for a trivia question. The reader is invited to identify the author of the following passage:

> C.P. Snow, scientist and novelist, once called for an end to the separation of "the two cultures," humanities and science. Economics is part of both these

cultures, a subject that combines the rigors of science with the poetry of humanities.

You guess Donald McCloskey? It is a good guess, but the right answer is Paul Samuelson. The passage appears in the seventh and later editions in a section with the humanistic heading "Light and Fruit." In the early editions Samuelson had argued that "logical elegance and fine-spun beauty are irrelevant" but it seems he has changed his mind. He notes:

> economic principles display some of the logical beauty of Euclid's geo-metry.... Of course, mere beauty is not enough. One studies economics for the light it sheds; any pleasure along the way is an incidental bonus. (seventh edition p. 6)

The humanistic features of Samuelson's portrait are further accentu-ated by the plays with words. Even though he has warned in all editions except the last one against the "tyranny of words," Samuelson himself demonstrates a love for words and poetic phrases. Hemmingway's *For Whom the Bell Tolls* lures the reader into the introductory chapter. And what about the phrase "Light and Fruit?" Brief quotations adorn the beginning of each chapter. In contrast, the writing of Lipsey, Steiner and Purvis is terse and prosaic, devoid of any poetic or literary allusions. No funny quotations in their text!

The humanistic features probably appeal to the numerous students who are deterred by "hard-sounding" terms such as "science," "rational-ity," "numbers," "empirical tests," and all that. But further reading exposes the fruit as mere decoration, that is, as misleading rhetoric. The humanistic strokes are without support in his substantive presentation of the discipline. This becomes especially manifest in the treatment of differ-ences among economists and the history of the discipline.

Differences among Economists

According to Kuhn, a student in the social sciences

> has constantly before him a number of competing and incommensurable solu-tions to ... problems, solutions that he must ultimately evaluate for himself. (Kuhn, 1970, p. 165)

The sociological textbooks that I have seen more or less concur with this observation: they systematically represent alternative approaches (such as the functionalist perspective, Weberian conflict theory, Marxian theory, and interpretive perspectives). No synthesis is constructed and the reader is left with the task of making up his or her own mind.[7]

With his humanistic strokes Samuelson makes the reader believe that his presentation of economics will be open-minded and respectful of alternative approaches. The text that accompanies the bird-or-is-it-an-antelope picture in the seventh edition says:

> If you look at wage problems through the spectacles of Marxian economics, you may think you see exploitation of workers by capitalists. If you look at problems of depression unemployment through pre-Keynesian glasses, you may think little of it due to forces that government tax and expenditures policies can change. (seventh edition, p. 10)

Admittedly, both sentences disappeared with the arrival of the twelfth edition, but in that edition Samuelson and Nordhaus emphasize the following statement:

> *When you adopt a new systematic model of economic principles, you comprehend reality in a new and different way.* (twelfth edition, p. 9)

With these remarks and the discussion of "subjective facts" the text seems to prepare the reader for a divided world in which alternative approaches compete for attention. But Samuelson is unwilling to go that far.

The unwillingness shows in the treatment of disagreements among economists. Table 5-1 indicates a subtle but nevertheless interesting change in how much of the confusion among the cooks is exposed to the readers. "Careful students" become "most — not all! — economists," and an "increasingly greater agreement" becomes "fairly close agreement." Insofar as disagreements occur, so the first eleven editions reassure economic novices, they pertain to political and ethical, that is, noneconomic issues.

The twelfth edition seems to break with the image of scientific harmony. The opening paragraph in the preface mentions the existence of competing schools of economics (Post-Keynesian eclecticism, monetarism, rational expectations, Chicago libertarianism, Marxism, and radical economics). The introduction includes a new section "Why economists disagree," and for the first time acknowledges disagreements on economic issues, in particular macroeconomic issues. Later in the book, after a discussion of the monetarist debate, Samuelson and Nordhaus note:

> An elementary physics text cannot settle the frontier disputes about black holes and the expanding universe. An economics text, similarly, should not attempt to render a final verdict between respectable warring scientific paradigms [sic]. (twelfth edition p. 330)

Table 5–1.   Samuelson on Disagreements in Economics

Edition	Text
1 (1948)	"It appears that careful students are coming into increasingly greater agreement on the broad analytical outline of the forces determining national income and full employment.... This does not mean that economists agree in the *policy* field." (p. 5)
2, 3, and 4 (1951–1958)	"On basic economic principles concerning prices and employment most economists are in pretty close agreement. This does not mean that economists agree in the *policy* field. [...] Basic questions concerning right and wrong goals to be pursued cannot be settled by economists as such." (p. 5)
5, 6, and 7 (1961–1967)	"On the basic principles concerning prices and unemployment, most economists are in *fairly* close agreement." [Continued as above, emphasis added]
9, 10, and 11 (1970–1980)	"On many basic principles concerning prices and unemployment, most — not all! — economists are in fairly close agreement." [the remarks in the second edition]
12 (1985)	Sentence removed. Added a section on "Why economists disagree." The thrust: disagreements are on normative rather than positive questions. Conclusion (p. 7): "Economists are quite divided on central issues of macroeconomics, particularly the role of money. A substantial amount of accord is seen in the microeconomic theory of prices and markets. But on the broad political and ethical issues economists are as divided as their parents or cousins."

The break with the previous monistic interpretation of economics looks complete.

However, these remarks are quoted out of context and give the wrong impression. Even though the preface cites the different schools in macro-economics, it also announces that a *new synthesis of modern macro-economics* follows. The section on disagreements includes a reference to a survey that downplays the disagreements among economists.[8] The "reasonable" voice dominates, reassuring, for example, after a discussion of the monetarist debate that "the truth lies in between the shrill extremes" (twelfth edition, p. 331).

The emphasis on synthesis and compromise isolates the discussion of the irreducible subjectivity of facts and the possibility that economists comprehend reality in different ways. The discussion is not followed through as in the sociology textbooks and the radical text by Bowles and Edwards, and thus loses its meaning.

The History of Economics According to Samuelson

The humanistic side of Samuelson's portrait stirs expectations of historical sketches that bring depth to the present. One would expect the human touch in depictions of human souls who wrested the truth from a reluctant and chaotic reality. And history is important to any discipline, according to Kuhn. Reflections on the past will reveal the discontinuities and revolutions with which scientific discourse moves through time. Introductory textbooks, he notes ruefully, tend to repress such consciousness, thus distorting the picture of what science is like.

> They inevitably disguise not only the role but the very existence of the revolutions that produce them.... Textbooks thus begin by truncating the scientist's sense of his discipline's history and then proceed to supply a substitute for what they have eliminated. [They] make science seem cumulative, as if it progresses in a straight line. (Kuhn, pp. 137–138)

Samuelson's book would not escape Kuhn's verdict, its humanistic allusions notwithstanding. Like nearly any other economics textbook, the book paints the last layer of economic discourse as the only layer to know. The paint is so thick that the underlying texture is almost entirely smeared over.

Admittedly, unlike Lipsey et al., Samuelson's *Economics* lets some of the history of the discipline shine through but that history has no consequences for his representation of the present. The argument is in the positioning of the history. A brief discussion of Heilbroner's *Wordly Philosophers* appears in the introduction of the third edition (1955). And that is that. In the fourth edition (1958) the last chapter gets an appendix, "Thumbnail Sketch of History of Economic Doctrines." The appendix survives in the fifth edition (1961), but the discussion of *Wordly Philosophers* does not. In the sixth edition (1964), the appendix disappears too; all the history of thought left is in a chapter on growth and development.

The place of history becomes more prominent in the ninth edition (1973), which contains an entire chapter dedicated to the history of economic "doctrines." The twelfth edition (1985) combines that chapter with a discussion of Marxism and alternative systems ranking the history of thought once again among the to-be-left-out-when-time-runs-out topics.

The ninth edition contains a brief comment on the place of history of thought in the introduction of economics. The master-ironist is here at work. At first the reader is made to believe that history of thought is serious business:

> The brand new chapter "Winds of Change: Evolution of Economic Doctrines" brings into the elementary course — at long last — a view of where political economy fits into the history of ideas and the intellectual history of our times...

But this is a trap; the unsuspecting humanist stands corrected with what follows:

> Political economy is about the economic system, not about economists.... At the end of a long book, though, we may *indulge* ourselves with a brief excursion into the history and present status of economics as a scholarly discipline and as a chapter in the intellectual history of mankind. (ninth edition, pp. ix, 839, emphasis added)

The history of the discipline is here presented as a sweet dessert, without real nutritional value. Such presentation is consistent with Samuelson's insistence that economics is an evolutionary science (the latter phrase is repeated five times in the preface and introduction of the twelfth edition). Nothing about the past is allegedly critical for living the present; all insignificant theories have been weeded out and all that is important is incorporated in the current body of knowledge. It surely is a comforting message to the students.

One argument for including history of thought is that only in comparison with other modes of discourse, such as past modes, can we understand the currently prevailing one. Another argument is simply that the practitioner can learn from the way things went in the past. It may be useful to know, for instance, that changes in economic discourse can be quite dramatic. As a matter of fact, the successive editions of Samuelson's text teach that very lesson. Table 5–2 shows that the changes from one edition to another were quite major indeed. Even Samuelson himself feels compelled to call attention to this historical fact. In the tenth edition he notices that

> although to a superficial observer one edition may look much like its predecessor, a careful comparison will reveal that there is as great a difference between this edition and the original edition as there was between that edition and the earlier nineteenth-century texts of Marshall and Mill! One must be acute to see

Table 5–2. The History of Thought in Samuelson's Text*

Edition	Text
1 (1948)	Central theme is National Income; special attention for the issues of unemployment and depression.
2 (1951)	A shift in emphasis away from unemployment to inflation. Discussion on the conditions for growth and security.
3 (1954)	New chapter on growth and development. An emphasis on efficient growth and productivity. "Repeatedly throughout the book I have set forth what I call a 'grand neoclassical synthesis.' "
4 (1957)	Greater emphasis on microeconomics (goods and factor pricing, the market mechanism. New macro topic: monetary policy and inflation. New micro topics: economics of energy and automation.
5 (1960)	More emphasis on price theory, distribution theory, capital theory. (Introduction of the micro definition of economics.) New topics: cost-push inflation, economic growth in advanced economies, international position of the United States.
6 (1964)	Reorganization of microeconomics section. Development of theory of competitive pricing. New macrotopics: structural unemployment, balanced growth, social overhead, capital and the gold drain against the dollar. (New chapter on the theory of growth.)
7 (1967)	Major thrust is again microeconomics. Introduction of different categories of costs and of oligopoly theory (kinked demand curve). More attention to the methodology of economics. New macro topics: structural unemployment, poverty programs, incomes policies, fiscal drag, full employment surplus, sliding peg. Mentions victory of "new economics." Introduction of Phillips curve in appendix.
8 (1970)	New emphasis on welfare aspects of competitive and other pricing; stress on externalities, public goods and interpersonal equity considerations. New chapters on "Poverty, Affluence and the Quality of Life" and "The Economic Problems of Race, Cities and Polluted Environment." Brief treatment of Von Neumann game theory added. More attention to dissent with "new economics" (ideas of Galbraith, Friedman, and radicals get a "dispassionate" hearing). Phillips curve moved from appendix to main text.

Table 5–2.   (*cont.*)

Edition	Text
9 (1973)	Particular emphasis on "involved problems of modern economics" (p. ix): cost-push inflation, GNP versus N.E.W. (quality of life versus economic growth). Addition of chapter on History of Thought. More attention for Marxist and libertarian criticism.
10 (1976)	Full discussion of the monetarist debate. New macrotopics: stagflation and international finance (flexible exchange rates). New micro topics: energy economics, new microeconomics (economics of time, marriage and parentage, human capital, crime and punishment).
11 (1980)	New evidence on stagflation and on monetarist debate. First discussion of rational expectations and efficient markets. New micro topics: economics of law, altruism, sociobiology, entropy economics. (Section on game theory removed.)
12 (1985)	Introduction of AD/AS diagram. Extensive treatment of rational expectations, monetarism, and supplyside economics (to a lesser extent). Acknowledgment of a critical role for money. Micro: new analysis of efficiency; game theory reintroduced; antitrust theory and policy discussed.

* As discussed in the preface of each edition.

the small hand of the clock move; but, over time, it does mark off profound epochs. (tenth edition, p. ix)

Remarkable changes are, for instance, the revival of microeconomics as the place where all analysis begins, the acknowledgment of the role of money, the introduction of the Phillips curve, and, most recently, the re-introduction of the AD/AS framework. Kuhn could have had Samuelson's book in mind when he observes that

> [Textbooks] being pedagogic vehicles for the perpetuation of normal science, have to be rewritten in whole or in part whenever the language, problem-structure, or standards of normal science change. (Kuhn, 1970, p. 137)

Economics as a Research Activity?

Samuelson presents economics as food to be enjoyed and digested. It may contain some "fruit" (some poetic stuff) but most of it is solid food that promises: Eat me and thou gaineth wisdom.

Table 5–3. Description of Scientific Methods

Edition	Text
1 (1948)	No explicit discussion. Reference to ceteris paribus assumption (p. 7); (it is necessary) to *simplicy*, to *abstract* from the infinite mass of detail (. .) to *idealize* "(p. 8); the test of a theory's goodness is its usefulness in illuminating observational reality" (p. 8).
3 (1955)	As above plus a mentioning of "the tools of economic analysis." (p. v)
5 (1961)	As in the third edition plus reference to methods of probability statistics.
7 (1967)	As in the sixth edition plus new section on methodology. "It introduces the modern approach, borrowed from the 'more exact' natural sciences, that insists on the irreducibly subjective element of our perception of facts depending upon the theoretic system *through* which we look at those facts" (p. vi). "observation and quantitative measurement, mathematical model-building, patient attendance to empirical facts and systematic reasoning." (p. 7)
12 (1985)	As in the seventh edition plus remarks on the scientific method in practice: "the process of observation, hypothesis formation, testing, interpretation, synthesis. It is at once logical and messy, rigorous and intuitive and profoundly un-predictable. But is just this process, occurring hundreds of time, that leads to the mutation and evolution of economic science." (p. 12) Brief discussion of model-building. "Facts are central to an empirical science like economics, but facts never tell their own story. Facts must be organized and arrayed by means of the development and testing of economic theories." (p. 6)

The metaphor is appealing, but it is also misleading. To exploit the metaphor further, eating the food is one thing, preparing it quite another. Admittedly, doing economics involves digesting the products of other economists, but who can *know* economics without knowing how it gets prepared? Yet Samuelson keeps the kitchen door closed.

Admittedly, the introductions to the twelve editions give an increasing number of hints at what happens behind that closed door (see table 5–3). They allude to the methods through which economists prepare economic knowledge. In this respect the book outscores the radical introduction by Bowles and Edwards — which gives practically no hints at all — but falls short of Lipsey's book, which dedicates an entire chapter to the role of statistical analysis.

Only in rare cases do the hints receive concrete illustrations in the remainder of the book. The method of abstraction may get conveyed, but even though Samuelson et al., and to a greater extent Lipsey et al. stress the importance of testing, references to empirical tests are minimal throughout either text. In their discussion of the demand for money, for example, Samuelson and Nordhaus merely mention empirical studies that show its interest-sensitivity; they also report different estimates of the multiplier, but nowhere in their text will the reader get even as much as a peek at the empirical procedures that economists use. Of course, they also do not learn numbers that compare with, say, Planck's constant. We all know that those do not exist in economics, but that cat Samuelson does not let that out of the bag. Furthermore, the students will not learn how economists construct their models. The most important argumentative strategies in economics are kept out of sight.

In contrast, textbooks in psychology and sociology invariably include chapters or sections on methods and techniques. Note the plural: the message is that various methods are used, among which are survey methods, experiments, participant observation, fieldwork, statistical techniques, content analysis, and simulation. As a consequence, the portraits in these textbooks acquire some resemblance to a research activity or process of inquiry. In other words, they draw the attention to what happens in the kitchen.

At one point, Samuelson and Nordhaus refer to the process as "at once logical and messy, rigorous and intuitive and profoundly unpredictable" (twelfth edition, p. 12). Such an observation intrigues but nowhere in the text do they follow it up. The sentence, therefore, is a throwaway: it reads well but has no consequences.

The image of economics as food to be enjoyed and digested is affirmed through the presentation of the material. Whenever questions are raised or problems stated, the discussion leads to a synthesizing or compromising conclusion that *is printed in red*. The student is persuaded to study the conclusions rather than the problems and the process of reasoning. The concomitant message is that there are clear answers in economics.

Samuelson's Text as Argument

The Economic Argument

The repression of economics as a research activity strongly weakens the case that economics is a science. After all, what is a science without research? And what is an empirical science if there are no empirical results? The scientistic rhetoric of the Samuelson text is further undermined when its presentation of economics is considered next to the presentation of other texts. This rhetoric tells students that logic and fact drive the pursuit of economic knowledge, but the text itself shows that economics is much more than that. Most importantly, Samuelson's text advances economic arguments that compete with alternative arguments. There is, thus, no "body of knowledge to which the scientific community is committed."

The first edition of Samuelson's text is a compelling argument for the Keynesian macro position. That becomes clear in a comparison between its outline and the outlines of two other contemporary texts (see table 5–4).

The books by Mussey-Donnan (M-D) and Garver-Hansen (G-H) basically follow the organization of Marshall's *Principles*. The emphasis is on production, business organization and demand and supply. Additions are the parts on money and banking (in both books), international relations (in G-H), and government (M-D). Samuelson, through the outline of his book, takes issue with this perspective. The arguments are serial and spatial: macro (part II) precedes micro (part III)[9] and gets 196 pages versus 156 pages for micro.

A major argument concerns the importance of the Keynesian perspective. G-Hs book dates from 1937 and hence the fact that it includes only a brief discussion of Keynes's *General Theory* (in a chapter on business cycles) is not saying much. M-D revised their book around 1946 but clearly did not consider the *General Theory* relevant for first-year students. Keynes's theory is introduced as an alternative explanation of the business cycle in a chapter on "Unemployment and Business Fluctuations." The placing of this chapter in part III ("Distribution and Consumption of Income") is odd, at least to those who got used to Samuelson's ordering. In his text, the entire part II is basically an introduction to Keynesian macroeconomics.

(Samuelson was by the way not the first textbook writer to present the pro-Keynes argument to students. Lorie Tarshis made the same argument in *The Elements of Economics*, which was published in 1947. The book contains a part entitled "National Income and Employment," which is unmistakenly Keynesian. An interesting difference is that the micro part precedes this macro part.)

The economic arguments are further borne out in confrontations with those textbooks that have been written as alternatives to conventional texts such as Samuelson's. For instance, Joan Robinson and John Eatwell

Table 5–4. The Argument According to the Table of Content

Mussey-Donnan (1947)	Graver-Hansen (1937)	Samuelson (1948)
I. The economic system/production	I. Production	I. Basic economic concepts and national Inc (includes: economic system, income, business organization, government, labor union
II. Business organization	II. Value (idem)	
III. Value and price (demand and supply)	III. Money and prices (including business cycles)	
IV. Money and banking (including international relations)	IV. Distribution of income (functional and institutional)	II. Determination of income and its fluctuations (including banking and international finance)
V. Distribution and cons. (including business cycles)		III. Composition and pricing of national output (demand and supply, international trade, economic welfare)
VI. State and enterprise (regulation/ public finance)		

wrote a textbook to take issue with their uncritical reliance on neoclassical economics and distortion of Keynes's economics (Robinson and Eatwell, 1973). *Understanding Capitalism, Competition, Command, and Change in the U.S. Economy* by Samuel Bowles and Richard Edwards (1985) presents a radical alternative. It introduces a historical approach and argues that an understanding of capitalism does not only require an understanding of the market process (as Samuelson's text suggests) but also of the process in the work place.

The Ideological Argument

Part of the argument is ideological. Samuelson employs the voice of reason and communicates values of intellectual tolerance and open-mindedness, but ideology marks also his text, as it does any text. The ideological components are not made explicit; they have to be teased out in dialogue, in confrontation. The ideological argument becomes apparent where a line gets drawn, when the conversation is stopped. It often shows in the negative, in the exclusion of particular possibilities.

One such ideological confrontation is Marc Linder's two volume *Anti-Samuelson* (1977). The effect of his critique on Samuelson's text appears to be nil: it is like water on a duck's back. Yet the silence brings out the ideological argument.

One of the allegedly ideological concepts that Linder points out in Samuelson's text is the concept of the marketplace. The rhetorician would say that Samuelson makes his reader believe that explanations for economic phenomena must be sought in market situations. In rhetorical terms, the market is a *topos*,[10] or the place where neoclassical economists look for explanations. Scarcity and individual choice have a "natural" place in such a situation. Economics, according to Samuelson,

> is the study of how people and society choose to employ scarce resources that could have alternative uses in order to produce various commodities and distribute them for consumption, now and in the future, among various persons and groups in society. (twelfth edition, p. 4)

As Linder makes painstakingly clear, this definition allows Samuelson to take his reader right away, without historical preparation, into the choice situation as it is posed by the *topos* of the market.

The *topos* that Linder develops as an alternative is that of the work place. In such a *topos* scarcity and individual choice do not enforce themselves as primary concepts; the attention turns instead to the relationships of production, to (class) conflict, exploitation, and alienation. Bowles and Edwards (1985) show in their radical text how a commitment to this *topos* of the work place produces a text that is radically different from Samuelson's. They offer, for example, the alternative characterization of economics as

> the study of how people interact with one another and with their natural surroundings to produce their livelihoods. (p. 19)

The deletion of the concepts of "scarcity" and "choice" is deliberate. They argue, namely, that our choices and perceptions of scarcity are socially constituted and cannot be presumed given as in Samuelson's text.

Another ideological component of Samuelson's text might be its neglect of the historical and social conditions in which current economic arrangements have come about. Linder makes a major persuasive effort urging the reader to think of capitalism as an historical stage, and thus to be sensitive to the possibility of (revolutionary) change. In his introduction, Samuelson recognizes the role of history for economics. That role, however, is one of the provider of case studies from which lessons can be learned (like the case of the German hyperinflation). Bowles and Edwards practice what Linder preaches: their first chapter presents, under the title "Capitalism Shakes the World," a brief historical analysis of the genesis of capitalism. Thus historical change is impressed on the reader's mind as a concept integral to economic discourse.

Samuelson displays his tolerance in the treatment of Marxist economics, but betrays his true colors by the dramatic shifts in emphasis in subsequent editions.

Unlike Lipsey, Steiner and Purvis (1984) who refer to Marx only four times in their textbook, Samuelson and Nordhaus seriously discuss the ideas of Marx and his followers in their chapter 35, "Winds of Change: Economic Alternatives." This treatment of Marx — carefully tugged away under the covers of history — is modest compared with earlier treatment.

In the early editions Samuelson was least well-disposed to Marx's theories. He had things to say about the boils of Karl Marx (see table 5–5), but in the ninth edition he scoffed at his own denigrating remarks. The neglect of Karl Marx was then a "scandal," and he deserved treatment as a serious secular scholar. Samuelson approvingly quoted Marx's famous maxim — "Up till now philosophers have interpreted the world in various ways. The point, though, is to *change* it!" We read 1973, a year that rounds off a period of political turmoil on American campuses. That Samuelson was playing to his audience shows in his subsequent retraction of the generous apologies. Marx's incitement to change the world gets dropped in the twelfth edition.

Table 5–5. Samuelson on Marx and Marxian Doctrines

Edition	Text
1 (1948)	Final chapter includes a discussion on Marxian Communism among other social/political systems.
3 (1955)	Reference to Heilbroner's *Wordly Philosophers* in introduction. Marx described as, "The black sheep in the family history of economics who was beyond the pale of the true classical tradition. Karl Marx, an exile from Germany, worked away at the British museum vowing that the bourgeoisie would pay for the suffering his boils caused him as he sat working out his theories of the inevitable fall of capitalism." Discussion in final chapter remains.
4 (1958)	Addition of the suggestion that "[Marx's] own biography reads more like a Balzac novel, not like a sociological science." Extended discussion of Marx's ideas in a new chapter on the history of economic thought.
5 (1961)	Remarks in introduction are dropped. Discussion in final chapter remains.
7 (1967)	Short historical summary in introduction. Re. Marx: "Thus almost at the halfway point, there appeared the massive critique of capitalism by Karl Marx. . . . A billion people, one-third of the world's population, blindly regard *Das Kapital* as economic gospel. And yet, without the disciplined study of economic science, how can anyone form a reasoned opinion about the merits or lack of merits in the classical, traditional economics?" Further discussion in final chapter on alternative systems.
9 (1973)	New reference in introduction: "It is a scandal that, until recently, economic majors in economics were taught nothing of Karl Marx except that he was an unsound fellow. This was not out of intimidation by the plutocratic interests, but rather reflection of the fact that such independent and impassioned teachers of the last generation as John Maynard Keynes thought Karl Marx sterile and dull. In this edition I have tried to treat Karl Marx as neither God nor Devil — but as a secular scholar whom half the world's population deem important. The rudiments of mature Marxism, as well as the insights of the resurrected young Marx, are newly discussed in this revision (p. x)." Discussion of Marx and Marxism in new chapter: "Winds of Change: Evolution of Economic Doctrines."
10 (1976)	Paragraph in introduction is dropped.
12 (1985)	"Winds of Change" chapter combined with chapter on alternative systems. Marxian section included, just as in pre-ninth edition.

Conclusion

The rhetorical perspective provides a mode of inquiry. It may eventually affect the way economists view the world — I have argued it should[11] — but for now it guides explorations of what it is economists do.

The study reported here is an exercise in rhetorical reading of an economics text. It takes its cue from the rhetorical insight that economists argue. They argue to persuade — and that brings the audience into the picture.

The conventional picture of science deletes the role of the audience altogether. It highlights the products of scientific research and makes it seem as if they are inscribed in stone expressed in a universal language (logic). The premise of the rhetorical inquiry is that such a universal language does not exist and that the knowledge products are generated within, and derive their meanings from, local discursive practices. A practice is local in the sense that it only works with a specific audience.

Alertness to the audience is a crucial element in any rhetorical reading. In the case of Samuelson's textbook, the audience seems obvious, namely the students. But let us not forget the economics instructors at colleges and universities. The latter, after all, choose the text for their courses and review it for the publisher. If my rhetoric has depicted Samuelson as the perpetrator of misleading scientistic rhetoric, I should mitigate the verdict at this point. Textbook writers are severely constrained by the perceptions and expectations on the demandside for their market. The dehistorization of the subject may have been as much a product of those constraints as Samuelson's own conscious preference.

The dual audience is a major problem for any textbook writer. It may partially account for the schizophrenic character of Samuelson's rhetoric, which the preceding reading has brought out. The "science" that Samuelson's rhetoric writes all over the face of economics is needed to please the instructors as well as those students who expect to learn something solid. On the other side, the literary phrases and relativizing remarks comfort those students who are humanistically inclined and fear "science." (This side undoubtedly also satisfies Samuelson's own penchant for literary flourish.)

The humanistic touches have an ironic effect as they seem to undo the scientistic rhetoric. But the latter ends up dominating the presentation anyway. The humanistic side of the portrait proves to be merely decorative, misleading students into believing that economics is "kind and gentle" anyway. This the rhetorician calls bad rhetoric.

Other successful economics textbooks tend to avoid Samuelson's literary flourishes. Teachers apparently want the positive-normative distinction, remarks on model building, and references to empirical testing. Yet, the scientistic rhetoric is misleading as Samuelson's text shows. (Other texts do not appear to do any better on this count.) Nowhere do the readers get a taste of what the research economists do. They do not learn about research strategies, including empirical testing. The text invites them to stuff themselves with the food offered and discourages curiosity about the preparation of the food, its ingredients, and its nutritional content.

The scientistic rhetoric of Samuelson's textbook mimics a similar rhetoric in academic writing (cf. McCloskey, 1986). It serves to suppress the arguments that the text unequivocally contains. Thus students are deluded and tricked into believing that what they get is hard. Economic discourse is not like that. It is rhetorical as Samuelson's text demonstrates. It argues a point of view, an ideology, too.

The scientistic rhetoric, it could be objected, appears to work. Yet, the creation of false expectations is risky. The expectation that economics produces "scientific" answers is bound to be frustrated. And frustrated people tend to be suspicious, if not outright hostile. Currently, economics programs ride the tide of mass anxiety that propels the young in pursuit of marketable skills. Students ignore the hardness and strangeness in their classes because credit in economics still looks good. But when frustrations accumulate, more people may dare to point out that the emperor does not wear any clothes. The consequences will be especially severe when those people are officials of foundations or university administrators. Economists might do better if they were to be more honest about their practice. They could begin with their textbooks.[12]

A more truthful presentation of economic discourse is conceivable. It would highlight economics as a research discipline and emphasize its rhetorical character. Students would learn that economics involves the art of argument and that disagreement is the spice of economic discourse. History will be a lively part of the exposition. Given where economics discourse is at, the expectation that such a text would work may be unreasonable. But the rhetorical perspective is having an impact, as this book shows, and disillusionment with the old scientific vision appears to be growing strong. The time may soon be ripe for an alternative.

Notes

[1] See McCloskey (1986) on rhetoric in general and economic rhetoric in particular; Klamer (1983) on argumentation; Klamer (1984) on economics as discourse; Miroski (1984, forthcoming) on physical analogies in economics; Heilbroner (1988) on ideology in economics; and Klamer et al. (1988) for various articles on the subject.

[2] See Klamer (1983, 1984, and 1987).

[3] See for a discussion of the concept of "genre" Wayne Booth, *The Rhetoric of Fiction* (1961).

[4] Even in physics, textbooks differ. The textbooks that were written in the aftermath of the Sputnik debacle resembled handbooks for technicians to meet the perceived need of applied knowledge. Current college textbooks deemphasize technical applications and concentrate on a "survey of physics as it is seen by contemporary physics" (cf Philip Stehle, *Physics, The Behavior of Particles*).

[5] See for an exposition of these root metaphors Stephen C. Pepper, *World Hypotheses* (1942).

[6] For an excellent account of Lipsey's relationship to the Popperian dogma, see Neil deMarchi (1988).

[7] A good example of such an approach is Percell (1984). Levin and Spates (1985) does not systematically treat alternative viewpoints but ends with a chapter on sociological controversies.

[8] A survey that David Colander and I did among graduate students contradicts that conclusion (Klamer and Colander, 1989).

[9] In a later edition, Samuelson justifies this ordering with the reason that macro is more interesting for students than micro.

[10] Or commonplace. It indicates the place or domain where people within a particular discursive practice look for arguments.

[11] In two forthcoming articles.

[12] Donald McCloskey and I are trying to write a textbook that conveys the image of economics as discourse or conversation.

References

Booth, Wayne. 1961. *The Rhetoric of Fiction*. Chicago: University of Chicago Press.

Bowles, Samuel and Edwards, Richard. 1985. *Understanding Capitalism, Competition, Command, and Change in the U.S. Economy*. New York: Harper & Row.

de Marchi, Neil. 1988. "Popper and the LSE Economists." In Neil de Marchi, ed. *The Popperian Legacy in Economics*. New York: Cambridge University Press.

Darver, Fred B. and Hansen, Alvin H. 1928, second edition, 1937. *Principles of Economics*. New York: Ginn & Company.

Harwood, E.C. 1962. "Betrayal of Intelligence: A Review of Samuelson's *Economics, An Introductory Analysis*." In *Reconstruction of Economics*, Third Edition. American Institute for Economic Research.

Heilbroner, Robert L. and Thurow, C.L. 1984. *Understanding Macroeconomics*. Eighth Edition. New York: Prentice Hall.

——. 1988. *Behind the Veil of Economics*. New York: Basic Books.

Hodges Percell, Caroline. 1984. *Understanding Society, An Introduction to Sociology*. New York: Harper & Row.

Klamer, A. 1984. *Conversations with Economists: New Classical Economists and*

Their Opponents Speak Out on Current Controversies in Macroeconomics.
Totowa, NJ: Rowman and Allenheld.
——. 1984. "Levels of Discourse in New Classical Economics." *History of Political Economy* Summer:263–290.
——. 1987. "A Rhetorical Interpretation of the Panel Discussion on Keynes." In Warren Samuels, ed. *Research in the History of Economic Thought and Methodology*, JAI Press.
——. 1988. "Economics as Discourse." In Neil de Marchi, ed. *The Popperian Legacy in Economics*. New York: Cambridge University Press.
Klamer, Arjo and Colander, David. 1989. *The Making of an Economist*. Boulder, Co.: Westview Press.
Klamer, Arjo, McCloskey, Donald, and Solow, Robert M., eds. 1988. *The Consequences of Economic Rhetoric*. New York: Cambridge University Press.
Kuhn, Thomas. 1970. *The Structure of Scientific Revolutions*. Second enlarged edition. Chicago: University of Chicago Press.
Lavoie, Don. "Getting Economics Back to the Real World: Hermeneutics and the Interpretive Study of Business." In *Economics and Hermeneutics*. Forthcoming.
Levin, Jack and Spates, James L. 1985. *Starting Sociology*. Third edition. New York: Harper & Row.
Linder, Marc. 1977. *Anti-Samuelson*. Volume one and two. New York: Urizen Press.
Lipsey, Richard G., Steiner, Peter O., and Purvis, Douglas D. 1984, first edition 1963. *Economics*. New York: Harper & Row.
Marshall, Alfred. 1890, 1920. *Principles of Economics*. Eight editions. London: MacMillan.
McCloskey, Donald. 1986. *The Rhetoric of Economics*. Madison: University of Wisconsin Press.
——. Forthcoming. "Storytelling in Economics," in Lavoie (ed).
Mirowski, Phil. 1984. "Physics and the Marginalist Revolution." *Cambridge Journal of Economics* 8:361–379.
——. Forthcoming. *Heat and Light*. New York: Cambridge University Press.
Mussey, Henry R. and Donnan, Elizabeth. 1947 (1942). *Economic Principles and Modern Practice*. Second edition. New York: Ginn and Company.
Pepper, Stephen C. 1942. *World Hypotheses*. Berkeley: University of California Press.
Robinson, Joan and Eatwell, John. 1973. *An Introduction to Economics*. Maidenhead: McGraw-Hill.
Samuelson, Paul A. 1948, 1951, 1955, 1958, 1961, 1964, 1967, 1970, 1973, 1976, 1980, 1986. *Economics*. New York: McGraw Hill.
Toulmin, Stephen, Rieke, Richard, and Janik, Allen. 1979. *An Introduction to Reasoning*. New York, MacMillan.

COMMENT BY JANET A. SEIZ

Introduction — The Rhetoric Approach

Keynes offered his *General Theory* to the public before its arguments had all been made formally tidy, and presented the work in a manner calculated to produce controversy: he caricatured the ideas of his "classical" adversaries and made very strong claims about the degree to which his ideas departed from and invalidated theirs. He explained to friends that his contentiousness was quite deliberate: he wanted to "raise a dust," because he believed it was only in the ensuing fracas that it would be made clear what he was really saying. Above all else, he feared having his arguments absorbed into the dominant theory as minor modifications of it; thus he refused to express his ideas in the dominant theory's language or to provide a translation from that language to his own. "I am frightfully afraid," he wrote, "of the tendency . . . to appear to accept my constructive part and to find some accommodation between this and deeply cherished views which would in fact only be possible if my constructive part has been partially misunderstood" (Keynes, 1973, p. 548).

Perhaps a similar rhetorical strategy is being pursued by Arjo Klamer and Donald McCloskey as they develop their "rhetoric approach" to economic discourse. Certainly their work has provoked considerable controversy since its first appearance six years ago (McCloskey 1983, Klamer 1984a,b); they suspect their ideas are often misunderstood, and express frustration at readers' attempts to incorporate their arguments into the standard "conversation" on economic methodology.[1] Like Keynes, they assert that their portrayals are more useful for understanding the real world than are the idealized representations of reality offered by their opponents: the rhetoric approach, they believe, offers most importantly a more *realistic* account of how economics is practiced, and of what can be hoped for from the discipline, than is provided by the dominant "modernist" or "scientistic" rhetoric about economic inquiry. Finally, like Keynes, they not infrequently find themselves branded "irresponsible" by their critics, who accuse them of abdicating the methodologist's responsibility to help economists choose criteria by which to appraise arguments and analytical techniques.

Literary theorists have taught us that each individual brings a particular set of concerns and presuppositions to the reading of a text; and there are ambiguities in McCloskey's and Klamer's writings, as in any texts. Thus very different readings of their work are possible. My own reading, as will become clear, is a very sympathetic one. I would summarize their central arguments as follows:

155

1. *Epistemology*. Klamer and McCloskey are antifoundationalists: they believe "there is no certitude to be had, with any methodology" (McCloskey, 1985, p. 61). Economic theories can be at best persuasive, useful, or appealing. No number of confrontations with empirical evidence can prove a theory to be either true or false.

2. *Methodology*. Economists should not accept guidance from philosophers of science, whose preoccupation with epistemology and demarcation leads them to promulgate "rule-bound methodologies" that stifle inquiry. Economic practice should not be straitjacketed by falsificationism, predictionist instrumentalism, or any other "modernist" methodological precept. Instead, economists should conduct their discourse in accordance with a set of *ethical* (not demarcational) rules which McCloskey calls *Sprachethik*. Examples include, "Don't lie; pay attention; don't sneer; cooperate; don't shout; let other people talk; be open-minded; explain yourself when asked; don't resort to violence or conspiracy in aid of your ideas" (1985, p. 24; see also McCloskey, 1988b).

3. *Analysis of economic discourse*. Historians of thought should not try to force economic discourse into any of the molds offered by philosophers and historians of science (Popperian, Lakatosian, Kuhnian, etc.). Instead, they should investigate how economists "actually" do their work, paying particular attention to the "rhetoric" of economic writings, the devices economists employ to persuade their audiences. Argumentation in economics is much richer than the "scientistic" view admits: the reception of economists' theoretical and empirical propositions is influenced by a variety of factors, including the language in which propositions are articulated, the feelings and associations evoked by economic metaphors, the use of appeals to authority, etc.

Klamer and McCloskey call for a new sort of critical examination of economic texts, which they believe will lead to a better understanding of the history of economics and (ultimately) the improvement of economists' argumentative practice. "The task of an economic criticism would be to dissect samples of economic argument, noting in the manner of a literary or philosophical exegesis exactly how the arguments sought to convince the reader" (McCloskey, 1985, p. 69). "The point is to figure out why some arguments work in economics and others don't" (Klamer and McCloskey, 1988, p. 11). Klamer's essay here is a case study in rhetorical criticism.

Though McCloskey and Klamer would both, I think, agree to the above statements, there are important ways in which they differ. McCloskey (1985) emphasizes the extent to which economists agree, while

Klamer (1984a,b, 1988b) focuses on disagreement (see also Klamer and McCloskey, 1988). McCloskey (1985) finds neoclassical economics persuasive and successful, while Klamer (1987) is much more critical. And while McCloskey concentrates on analyzing economic texts, Klamer (1984a, 1987, 1988a,b) calls for a much wider inquiry encompassing the "sociology" (or anthropology) of economics, the broad "conditions of production" of economic discourse.[2] Klamer's essay reflects both what he shares with McCloskey and his own distinct views and priorities.

Critics of the rhetoric approach (Caldwell and Coats, 1984; Coats, 1988; Maki, 1988; Rappaport, 1988; Rosenberg, 1988; and Solow, 1988) have usually agreed with Klamer and McCloskey that knowledge is never certain, and have acknowledged that economists' efforts to persuade involve the use of many devices that would not be sanctioned by the official rhetoric on economics-as-science. But they have been frustrated with statements such as McCloskey's that if economists find a theory "persuasive, interesting, useful, reasonable, appealing, acceptable, we do not also need to know that it is True.... The serious issues are rhetorical — how we become persuaded, in the actual case at hand — not epistemological." (1985, p. 47) It is one thing to investigate which arguments economists *have* found persuasive at particular times, and why — to study, as does the Strong Program in the sociology of science, "how scientists choose what to believe," without judging those choices. It is another matter altogether to offer *assessments* of how far scientists' beliefs are "really warranted." Klamer and McCloskey, critics complain, are not being clear about whether they are pursuing only the first task, or also the second (which is the standard concern of methodologists): if they do mean to make judgments about the worthiness of economic arguments (as it would appear from the critical case studies in McCloskey, 1985), they should specify the criteria they wish to see used for such assessments.

Another important criticism is the accusation that McCloskey (1985) "underestimates the importance of power and politics in determining the course of the economic conversation," and thus "is far too optimistic about the ease with which heretics, Marxists for example, can be admitted" (Stewart, 1987, p. 84; see also Heilbroner, 1988).[3] On one hand, the rhetoric approach is clearly well-suited for investigating the political elements in economic discourse: it encourages us to identify the ideological content or political implications of an economic argument, and to ask how far those features determine how the argument is received by the profession. On the other hand, an exclusive focus on texts will produce an incomplete picture of how economic discourse is shaped, since it will miss the extent to which the "silences" in the discourse are produced by mechanisms of censorship. The rhetoric approach, as broadly conceived by Klamer, overcomes this limitation: it invites us to also ask how far "politics" determines whether an argument gets any hearing at all — whether the arguer is granted the credentials that give her a professional voice, whether her research is funded, and her writing published.

Klamer's essay provides (implicit) responses to both these criticisms. It clarifies the grounds on which the rhetoric approach enables us to evaluate economic writing, and it has something to say about the operation of power in the economics profession. In both areas, much remains to be said, and some of my remarks here will be devoted to building upon the illuminating suggestions that Klamer provides.

Klamer on Samuelson

Klamer's essay examines the first chapters of the twelve editions of Samuelson's economics textbook. An introductory textbook, he observes, provides a portrait of a discipline; a very successful text, one might say, has been accepted as a discipline's "self-portrait."[4] A textbook offers authoritative characterizations of both the *practice* of a discipline and the *subject* of its inquiry: here, it says, is how economists "discover" things about the economic world and an overview of "what they've found." To one who is unaware of the extent to which knowledge is a contested terrain, the textbook may seem simply to convey important information and teach useful skills; but, as Klamer notes, textbooks also serve other ends. Tomorrow's practitioners of the discipline will emerge from today's classrooms, and the ways in which economics and the economy are portrayed there will have considerable impact upon the selection process. Many students will not pursue economics beyond the introductory course; for them, the textbook helps shape their attitudes toward economic institutions and policies and helps establish the authority of economists, whose pronouncements they will continue to encounter long after they have left school. The textbook, in claiming to provide an authoritative characterization of the state of knowledge in the discipline, is both weapon and prize in the battles among economists: it legitimizes some arguments and approaches, and delegitimizes others.

Because of its considerable "political" importance, the introductory economics text has also been studied by Marxist and feminist economists. Marc Linder, whose work (1977) Klamer discusses briefly, performed an exhaustive examination of the "ideological" content of Samuelson's text, confronting its arguments point by point with arguments developed from a Marxist perspective. Susan Feiner and Barbara Morgan (1985, 1987) examined a number of introductory texts to see how often and how well they dealt with issues of race and gender; they concluded that most texts gave far too little attention to race and gender issues, reinforced sexual and racial stereotypes, underemphasized the extent of discrimination, and undermined arguments for social change by insisting that achieving greater "equity" necessarily involved sacrificing "efficiency."

Those studies look at how introductory texts portray *economic reality*. Klamer's work complements them, focusing upon how Samuelson's text portrays *economics*. He finds the following:

1. Samuelson portrays economics as a "science" comparable to the natural sciences, one which utilizes both deductive and inductive reasoning and continually subjects its theories to empirical tests.

2. Samuelson downplays disagreements among economists. He sometimes acknowledges that there are important theoretical disputes (e.g., between Keynesians and monetarists), but asserts that most disagreements among economists concern ethical/political value judgments. When he does present conflicting theories, he immediately offers a "synthesis," giving the impression that disputes in economics are resolved or easily resolvable. He gives only the slightest lip service to methodological disagreements, and the reader is told very little about non-neoclassical approaches.

3. In accordance with the picture of economics as a "science," the basic ideas and facts of which are well-established, Samuelson presents his book as a "comprehensive" and "authoritative" overview of "what you need to know" (as in Kuhn's "well-developed textbook genre").

4. Samuelson presents arguments (e.g., Keynesian macroeconomics) that are far from agreed upon by the profession, without acknowledging the disputedness of his claims.

5. Samuelson writes as though it is not very important to study the history of economics, as though "all that is important is incorporated in the current body of knowledge." The image is one of continuity in economic discourse, a linear progression toward "the truth."

6. Samuelson mentions the concrete labors of economists (e.g., "observation and quantitative measurement, mathematical model-building, patient attention to empirical facts"), but he does not show how things are done, how a model is constructed or an empirical test performed. He provides students only with the conclusions of analysis, not with a taste of the process of inquiry.

7. Samuelson's work embodies an ideology: capitalism is to be under-

stood by studying market exchange relations (the realm, Marx observed, of freedom and equality), not by looking at the production sphere's relations between agents with very unequal power. His political biases are further revealed in his oscillating but generally dismissive treatment of Marx.

These findings are fascinating: Samuelson's rhetoric in his first chapters, Klamer shows us, is skillfully crafted to establish his authority and to convince students of the *definiteness* of economic knowledge. The presentation is more intimidating than empowering: the student is not enabled to pursue economic investigation on her own, nor is she presented with (in Kuhn's words) "a number of competing ... solutions to [economic] problems" that she must evaluate for herself. This surely helps to explain why so many of our students, having endured the introductory course, refuse to pursue the study of economics further; those of us who teach should ask ourselves whether this is the sort of pedagogy we really wish to be practicing.

Klamer does not merely reveal to us the nature of Samuelson's rhetoric: he also criticizes it. He does so on two principal grounds. Sometimes he argues that Samuelson offers a *misleading characterization* of economics: his evaluative standard here must be reference to economics as "actually practiced." At other times he says that Samuelson's rhetoric is "bad," or *ineffective*: and here he must refer to some (only implicitly specified) guidelines on how to present a persuasive case.

The first sort of criticism follows from the critique of "scientism" or "modernism" throughout Klamer's and McCloskey's writings. Samuelson's "scientism," his downplaying of disagreements, and his neglect of history misrepresent the way economic discourse actually proceeds and exaggerate the conclusiveness of economic knowledge — thus Samuelson is a "perpetrator of misleading scientistic rhetoric," rhetoric that is dangerous because it creates "false expectations."

Klamer's second sort of criticism focuses on Samuelson's effectiveness as a writer. He says that Samuelson's "humanistic touches" — such as the allusions to poems and novels and the reference to C.P. Snow — are "mere decoration," because they are "without support in his substantive presentation of the discipline," which emphasizes hard science. A passage on different schools of economics in which Samuelson appears "open-minded and respectful of alternative approaches" is dismissed because it "is not followed through ... and thus loses its meaning." And a sentence referring to the concrete methods of economic inquiry is said to be "a throwaway," because it "has no consequences." Klamer says Samuelson is trying unsuccessfully to "get it two ways" and suggests that these "schizophrenic" moments result from Samuelson's need to make his text appeal to a "dual audience" of students and instructors; since the rhetoric is "bad," neither group, presumably, *should* be deceived by it.

My own reading is slightly different: I see Samuelson as trying "to be all things to all people," to establish his authority (and by extension, the economist's) as strongly as possible by the way he constructs his authorial persona. He appears the dispassionate, white-lab-coat-clad, "objective" man of science, but he is also the tweedy, well-read, humane man of letters. He is the embodiment of scientific knowledge that confers power, but he is also the intellectual sophisticate familiar with the work of philosophers of science who challenge his epistemic authority. He is the expert practitioner of the most prestigious sort of economic analysis (neoclassical) — indeed, so expert that he is able to stand above his peers and produce "syntheses" of their conflicting views — but he is also knowledgable and open-minded about approaches that differ from his own. It is true that some of Samuelson's statements are "bad rhetoric" in the sense that they are not supported or "followed through"; but their overall effectiveness for establishing the character-based authority of the author may still be quite considerable.

So far as exploring the relationships among statements in the text is concerned, I would suggest that Klamer's work in this essay might best be viewed as *deconstructive*: that is, he is not merely uncovering and assessing Samuelson's persuasive devices one by one, but rather identifying *tensions* in the text, apparent contradictions in it, or points at which Samuelson undermines his own central arguments. As Klamer observes, Samuelson devotes much effort to characterizing economics as an "empirical science" but also acknowledges the theory-dependent nature of "facts." Samuelson says a textbook should not "attempt to render a final verdict between respectable warring scientific paradigms," but he presents only one "paradigm," and he continually renders "final verdicts" in theoretical disputes by offering a "synthesis" of conflicting views. In cases such as these, the problem is not merely that statements are not "followed through" and thus carry little persuasive weight; rather, it is that Samuelson is offering statements that appear incompatible, building a structure whose elements do not cohere. Here he can't "have it both ways," because logic forbids it.

What accounts for all these tensions in Samuelson's texts? Perhaps it is partly the dual audience being addressed, and partly Samuelson's desire to construct a quite "large" authorial persona. But consider the possibility that the tensions reflect the "schizophrenia" of the discipline itself. If Samuelson's work is a portrait of neoclassical economics, it is perhaps a more revealing one than Samuelson himself realized. It depicts the neoclassical majority of the profession as trying to cling to a coveted "scientific" status despite a growing awareness that "positivism is dead"; acting as if neoclassical work *is* "economics," despite the increasing availability of sophisticated articulations and applications of alternative methodological views; and denying the extent and persistence of disagreement among economists about both how the economic world works and what sorts of inquiry best enable us to understand that world. To accept this portrait as an accurate one is not necessarily to accuse neoclassical economists of intellectual bad faith or abuse of power: it is simply to note that methodological (or philosophical) thought in economics is in a very unsettled state. Economists are having considerable difficulty coming to terms with philosophers' declarations of the "death of positivism," and we have made rather little progress in addressing the longstanding question of the relationship between moral/political worldviews and methodological stances.[5] Many economists are aware of these problems, but we are far from agreed about what they mean for our day to day practice of our discipline. And it is this uncertainty that makes many of us receptive to the work of McCloskey and Klamer.

Conclusion

Klamer clearly hopes that revealing the inaccuracy and incoherence of Samuelson's portrayal of economic discourse will awaken in his readers a desire to see economics presented differently. His critique of Samuelson's (and similar) books will only be complete, he might say, with the appearance of his own alternative portrayal in the introductory textbook he is writing with McCloskey. We may infer from Klamer's essay that that text will present economic discourse more "honestly," introducing students to conflicting methodological and theoretical views, providing more information about how economists actually construct models and perform empirical tests, offering much more discussion of history, and generally emphasizing the *unsettledness* — rather than the definiteness — of economic knowledge. Many readers, myself included, will find the idea of such a text very exciting.

But as Klamer and McCloskey are no doubt well aware, there are strong forces operating to discourage economists from adopting textbooks so different from those to which we are accustomed. First there are "political" problems: many economists choose to believe that neoclassical economics as a body of analytical techniques is "value-free" and that alternative approaches (particularly Marxian economics, but also institutionalist, Post-Keynesian, and Austrian work) are "value-laden" and thus less legitimate. Many instructors who would like to offer students an inclusive, pluralistic introduction to economics will fear (not without reason) that to do so would jeopardize their standings in their departments.

Klamer and McCloskey will also have to deal with the "practical" or "pedagogical" objection: if so much additional material is to be "put in" the introductory course, what is it that is going to be "taken out?" What institutional facts, what concepts, what basic models will be eliminated, put off to higher-level courses? These questions are of course also partly political: the same issues appear in the debates among our colleagues in literature concerning "the canon." "If we put Toni Morrison and Richard Wright into our course on the Modern American Novel," the question goes, "whose work do we take out? Hemingway's? Fitzgerald's? Faulkner's? It's impossible!" All too often, conversation — and curricular reform — stop here. We may hope that this will not be the case in our own discipline; certainly the work of Klamer and McCloskey has created a "discursive space" in which economists may openly discuss these quite fundamental issues. We must recognize that those of us who seek to transform economics teaching and to promote pluralism in the profession as a whole have a long and difficult job ahead.

Notes

[1] See McCloskey's responses to critics (1984 and 1988c).

[2] Some of these differences appear less sharp in McCloskey's recent work. For example, McCloskey (1988b) calls for inquiry into the sociology of economics and notes that much of the work being done by sociologists and historians of the sciences overlaps considerably with rhetorical criticism.

[3] McCloskey responds to this criticism in his 1987 and 1988a.

[4] An earlier version of Klamer's essay, presented at the History of Economics Society meetings in 1986, was titled "Self-Portrait of a Discipline: Economics Through Its Textbooks."

[5] The question is whether a particular methodology — a set of analytical techniques and a language for articulating propositions — "embodies" a particular moral-political worldview, restricting what questions the knowledge-seeker can ask and what explanations she can suggest. Marxists have long argued that the very form of neoclassical analysis — its focus on individual rational choice — serves to obscure the operation of power in economic relationships. I have asked (Seiz, forthcoming) whether neoclassical economics embodies an "androcentric" (gender-biased) view of economic reality.

References

Caldwell, Bruce J. and Coats, A.W. June, 1984. "The Rhetoric of Economists: A Comment on McCloskey." *Journal of Economic Literature* 22 (June):575–578.
Coats, A.W. 1988. "Economic Rhetoric: The Social and Historical Context." In Arjo Klamer, Donald N. McCloskey, and Robert M. Solow, eds. *The Consequences of Economic Rhetoric*. New York: Cambridge University Press.
Feiner, Susan F. and Morgan, Barbara A. 1985. "Discrimination: The Case of Economics Textbooks." *Challenge* Nov.–Dec.:52–54.
——. Fall, 1987. "Women and Minorities in Introductory Economics Textbooks: 1974 to 1984." *Journal of Economic Education* 18(4):376–392.
Heilbroner, Robert L. 1988. "Rhetoric and Ideology." In Arjo Klamer, Donald N. McCloskey, and Robert M. Solow, eds. *The Consequences of Economic Rhetoric*. New York: Cambridge University Press.
Keynes, John Maynard. 1973. *The Collected Writings of John Maynard Keynes*. Vol. XIII. *The General Theory and After, Part I: Preparation*. Edited by Donald Moggridge. New York: Macmillan and Cambridge University Press.
Klamer, Arjo. 1984a. *Conversations with Economists: New Classical Economists and Their Opponents Speak Out on the Current Controversy in Macroeconomics*. Totowa, NJ: Rowman and Allenheld.
——. 1984b. "Levels of Discourse in New Classical Economics." *History of Political Economy* 16:263–290.
——. 1987. "As If Economists and Their Subjects Were Rational." In John Nelson, Allen Megill, and Donald McCloskey, eds. *The Rhetoric of the Human Sciences*. Madison: University of Wisconsin Press.
——. 1988a. "Negotiating a New Conversation About Economics." In Arjo Klamer, Donald N. McCloskey, and Robert M. Solow, eds. *The Consequences of Economic Rhetoric*. New York: Cambridge University Press.
——. 1988b. "Economics as Discourse." In Neil de Marchi, ed. *The Popperian Legacy in Economics*. New York: Cambridge University Press.
Klamer, Arjo and McCloskey, Donald N. 1988. "Economics in the Human Conversation." In Arjo Klamer, Donald N. McCloskey, and Robert M. Solow, eds. *The Consequences of Economic Rhetoric*. New York: Cambridge University Press.
Linder, Marc. 1977. *Anti-Samuelson*. Two volumes. New York: Urizen Press.
Maki, Uskali. 1988. "How to Combine Rhetoric and Realism in the Methodology of Economics." *Economics and Philosophy* 4:89–109.
McCloskey, Donald N. 1983. "The Rhetoric of Economics." *Journal of Economic Literature* 21 (June):481–517.
——. 1984. "Reply to Caldwell and Coats." *Journal of Economic Literature* 22 (June):579–580.
——. 1985. *The Rhetoric of Economics*. Madison: University of Wisconsin Press.
——. Fall, 1987. "Reply." *Review of Radical Political Economics* 19(3):87–91.
——. 1988a. "The Consequences of Rhetoric." In Arjo Klamer, Donald N.

McCloskey, and Robert M. Solow, eds. *The Consequences of Economic Rhetoric*. New York: Cambridge University Press.

——. 1988b. "Thick and Thin Methodologies in the History of Economic Thought." In Neil de Marchi, ed. *The Popperian Legacy in Economics*. New York: Cambridge University Press.

——. 1988c. "Two Replies and a Dialogue on the Rhetoric of Economics." *Economics and Philosophy* 4:150–166.

Rappaport, Steven. 1988. "Economic Methodology: Rhetoric or Epistemology?" *Economics and Philosophy* 4:110–128.

Rosenberg, Alexander. 1988. "Economics is Too Important to Be Left to the Rhetoricians." *Economics and Philosophy* 4:129–149.

Seiz, Janet A. Forthcoming. "Gender and Economic Research." In Neil de Marchi, ed. *The Methodology of Economics*. Boston: Kluwer Academic Publishers.

Solow, Robert M. 1988. "Comments from Within Economics." In Arjo Klamer, Donald N. McCloskey, and Robert M. Solow, eds. *The Consequences of Economic Rhetoric*. New York: Cambridge University Press.

Stewart, Hamish. Fall, 1987. "Review of The Rhetoric of Economics." *Review of Radical Political Economics* 19(3):83–85.

6 HERMENEUTICS, SUBJECTIVITY, AND THE LESTER/ MACHLUP DEBATE: TOWARD A MORE ANTHROPOLOGICAL APPROACH TO EMPIRICAL ECONOMICS

Don Lavoie

What is the status of modern economics from a hermeneutical standpoint?[1] Since hermeneutics is essentially a philosophy of understanding, a philosophy that shows us what understanding is, how it happens, and what it depends on, this question can be rephrased: How well do economists understand understanding? What difference would it make to our scholarly practices if economics were to become more hermeneutically sophisticated in this respect?

My own impression is that were economists to understand what hermeneutics has to say they would have to dramatically change the way they do both theoretical and empirical research. I am convinced that it would foment a major revolution in the discipline, as far reaching as, for example, the marginalist revolution of the 1870s. Which is to say that this chapter cannot be expected to anticipate all the ramifications of so profound a transformation.[2] Instead, the chapter is limited to three related tasks:

1. I want to identify one of the many changes I believe economists would have to make if they were to take hermeneutics more seriously, that is, that it would need to "become more anthropological." It needs to

168

pay more serious and more "close-up" scholarly attention in its empirical research to the life-world, the world of everyday meanings.

2. I want to get a rough gauge on how sophisticated, hermeneutically speaking, the contemporary economist's view of understanding is.

3. I want to show how these first two points are connected to each other. The reason economics is "insufficiently anthropological" can be traced to shortcomings in its view of understanding. These shortcomings are evident in the way a particular debate from the 1940s, the Lester/Machlup debate, has been interpreted by most economists.

The late Fritz Machlup is a key figure whose methodological work can help to develop and connect these themes. On the one hand, his famous answer to Richard Lester is widely interpreted as a reason economists do not *need* to "become anthropological." I will argue, on the other hand, that he was one of the most hermeneutical economists in the profession, who can be interpreted as saying that economists in fact do need to be anthropological.

Toward a More Anthropological Economics

Economics *begins*, both historically as a systematic discipline and individually in the education of everyone who learns it, with the everyday world of business. The dominant philosophical attitudes of our time — attitudes that I think hermeneutics could help us to overcome — have gradually led to the circumstance that economics *only* begins there, and that the more it "develops," the more remote from the real world it gets. Every new generation of graduate students seems less equipped to understand the world they occupy; every volume of the "top" journals seems less oriented toward addressing the real problems from which the economy continues to suffer. The systematic undervaluation of what I would call the interpretive dimension of economics has led to a gradual loss of relevance of what we consider our most "advanced" and "sophisticated" research and has caused a loss of crucial skills our profession had once developed.

Were we to better understand what economic understanding is, we would, I think, turn much more of our attention back to the everyday world our discipline began by trying to understand. The understanding of economists needs to come into closer relation with that of the economic "agents" we are supposed to be talking about. There is already a discourse taking place in the economy before the economists arrive to invent "scientific" discourses about it. Our understanding of words like "price" is shaped by the fact that we who try to understand already live in the world we are trying to understand and that world has prices in it. Thus we need to do things like study the history of particular corporations, conduct interviews with leading and ordinary actors in the economy, or use questionnaires to find out how everyday actors think. We should get into closer touch with the language of business, acquaint ourselves with current developments in management techniques, marketing theories, accounting methods, financial institutions, and organizational theories, in terms of which the "agents," who we are supposed to be trying to understand, think.

Economists should become more like anthropologists, in the sense that they should do more of their empirical work "up close" through participant observation rather than only from the distance required for statistical work. The fact that virtually all the empirical work economists undertake is preoccupied with the application of statistical techniques brings about a corresponding need for large sample sizes. It is widely assumed that the only way a test can be made convincing is to achieve a sufficiently large sample to permit statistically significant and thus generalizable conclusions.[3] A more interpretive approach to empirical economics would challenge this whole attitude, both about what it means to do empirical research and about what it takes to see general lessons in such research. Indeed, I would argue, the best empirical work in economics has not sought large sample sizes at all but instead has tried to see a few cases "up close." The case study, which pays attention to how individual choices were made under specific circumstances, is able to explicate empirical facts that simply cannot be seen from the distance required for most statistical studies.

Modern economics strives to be some sort of Newtonian physics of human affairs[4] from which the qualitative interpretation of the meaning of human purposes has been thankfully extracted. Many economists take pride in the claim that they have liberated their science from what they see as the ambiguities surrounding the interpretation of meaningful human expressions, ambiguities that are thought to keep other human sciences, such as psychology, sociology, and especially anthropology, from attaining the high standards of objectivity to which economics adheres. Economists are clearly of the view that anthropological sorts of empirical methods are frought with difficulties, and best avoided if possible.

Economists are not so clear about why they think this. On the one hand, it sometimes seems as if they consider understanding the discourse of the life-world to be "too easy" to be the topic of serious scientific research. When hermeneutics seems to say that science is nothing more than conversation, this makes many would-be "hard scientists" in economics nervous. Without a privileged status for the scientist's rigorous conversation, they fear that "reducing" science to "mere" discourse destroys any possibility of building reliable explanations of the world around us.[5]

On the other hand, much of the resistance economists have to taking up this everyday level seems to come from a fear that understanding is "too difficult." It embroils us in tangled philosophical or psychological complications and thus would distract economists from their more straightforward investigation of the real world. Finding regularities in quantitative data is hard enough; discerning what is "inside the heads" of the agents whose actions are reflected in that data sounds like a supremely difficult task, unachievable by mere mortals.

Whether understanding the meanings operative in everyday life is taken to be below them (and best left to undergraduates) or above them (and best left to angels), economists seem to agree that their scientific discourse of economics should dissociate itself from the everyday discourse of the economy. I would like to turn the tables on such economists by arguing that, precisely because they are dissociated from the life-world, they are already dangerously out of touch with the real world they think they are investigating. Theories of discourse such as hermeneutics might be seen not as a threat to the economist's realism but as a way to bring economists into closer contact with reality, of bringing theory and empirical work into a closer relationship with one another.

My claim here is not the usual complaint that economic theorizing, for example in the Walrasian general equilibrium tradition, is increasingly remote from reality.[6] Rather, my charge is that in the very part of their research economists consider strictly empirical they typically fail to get close enough to the world they think they are examining.

The closest the empirical economist usually gets is access to a dataset on which he can exercise his econometric techniques. The data was in most cases put together by a government bureau ostensibly to describe some feature of the real world, but where the numbers originally came from, how they were put together, or what meaning they might have had to those who first reported them are not taken to be the economist's concern. Economists generally do not consider empirical research to involve something like, say, actually *talking* to a flesh-and-blood businessperson once in a while. The conversations of economists about a particular industry rarely intersect with the conversations taking place among business-people and workers in that industry.

The mainstream economist has a ready response to this kind of argument. We do not need to know how those in business think in order to explain their actions, and in any case we cannot find out because that would require "getting inside their heads." Questionnaires are notoriously misleading, and talking to businesspeople is futile. People lie. Rather than wallow in subjective opinions like the other social sciences, economists prefer to work with "hard" data, quantitative evidence on what businesspeople do, regardless of what they *say* about what they do.

This is what they take to have been conclusively shown in Fritz Machlup's famous critique of Lester. Lester, the usual interpretation goes, somewhat naively thought he had found evidence that "marginalism" was wrong on the basis of responses to a mailed questionnaire sent to business executives. The businesspeople reported that profit was not the most important consideration, that they did not know or care what their elasticity of demand was, and that average costs were more often the crucial consideration than marginal costs. Ahah!, Lester concluded, marginalism is refuted. Machlup leveled a devastating critique of Lester's meager argument, a critique that almost could be said to have been too successful, in the sense that it effectively silenced this whole line of criticism of neoclassical economics. The lesson most modern economists think was learned from Machlup's critique is that economics need not concern itself — in an anthropological manner — with what everyday actors in the economy think. In effect, it is widely thought, Lester was being "too subjectivist" and thus threatened the scientific status of economics.

The simple answer to this line of argument is of course that it proves too much. If people can lie when you talk to them, they can certainly lie when they fill out the government forms that go into the production of the "hard" datasets. In fact it is easier to find out if lies or other kinds of misleading statements are contaminating ones empirical research if one gets closer to the sources. In an interview, after all, cross examination of the witnesses is possible.

A more extensive response is required here. Many economists who are fully aware of the problems with bad data are nevertheless leery about the kind of anthropological-type research I am recommending. Some light can be shed on this bias against close-up research by examining Machlup's "subjectivist" methodological position, and then his application of this view in his critique of Lester.

Subjectivity in Theory and Practice

How well do economists understand understanding? I would like to use
the economists' idea of "subjectivity," especially as it is interpreted by
Fritz Machlup, as a gauge on this question.[7] For economists "subjectivity" refers to the importance in a choice-theoretic explanation of correctly
identifying the relevant means and ends conditions as they are perceived
by the choosing subject, and not as they are perceived by the observing
scientist. The hermeneutical elements that are hidden within its notion of
"subjectivity" make economics less backward in its view of understanding
than it may appear to the outside observer. Yet, I argue, limitations in its
notion of subjectivity prevent economists from being hermeneutical
enough. Thus from the way economic theorists talk about "subjectivity,"
we can assess the hermeneutical strengths and weaknesses of their view
of understanding.

The chief strength is that subjectivity, particularly in Machlup's interpretation of it, is essentially an assertion that the "life-world," the level of
everyday understanding that hermeneutics insists underlies all understanding, constitutes the relevant reality about which economic theory is
concerned. Applied to empirical research this would suggest that economists should be more like anthropologists. The weakness is that the theoretical principle is often rendered in a way that effectively prevents it from
actually *being* applied to empirical research.

This chapter concludes that Machlup's methodological views in his
debate with Lester have been severely misunderstood. One reason for
this misunderstanding, I think, is that Machlup's view of "subjectivity" is
misunderstood. The reason for this, in turn, may lie in another famous
methodological debate with which Machlup's name is associated, the
Friedman/Samuelson debate, in which Machlup came to Milton Friedman's defense. This has led many to identify Machlup's methodological
position with Friedman's, and it is notorious that in Friedman's there is
an insulation of theoretical assumptions from realism. This position would
seem to deprive anthropologically oriented empirical work of anything
but a marginal role. Machlup is partly to blame for this and in my view
was much too kind to Friedman's article. But the one point on which
Machlup disagreed with Friedman, what he calls "the only serious flaw in
the otherwise excellent essay," is significant for the theme of this chapter.
Machlup agreed with Friedman that "the fundamental assumptions of
economic theory are not subject to a requirement of independent empirical verification." But he insisted, against Friedman, that assumptions are
subject instead "to a requirement of understandability in the sense in

which man can understand the actions of fellowmen" (1955, p. 17).

This requirement of understandability is what Machlup means by subjectivity. He quotes a passage from the phenomenological sociologist Alfred Schütz (1953, p. 34) to illustrate this point:

> In order to explain human actions the scientist has to ask what model of an individual mind can be constructed and what typical contents must be attributed to it in order to explain the observed facts as the result of the activity of such a mind in an understandable relation. The compliance with this postulate warrants the possibility of referring all kinds of human action or their result to the subjective meaning such action or result of an action had for the actor.
>
> Each term in a scientific model of human action must be constructed in such a way that a human act performed within the life world by an individual actor in the way indicated by the typical construct would be understandable for the actor himself as well as for his fellowmen in terms of common-sense interpretation of everyday life. Compliance with this postulate warrants the consistency of the constructs of the social scientist with the constructs of common-sense experience of the social reality.

Although few contemporary economists have as sophisticated a view of subjectivity as Machlup, most would not quarrel with Machlup's statement of it. Many would consider the principle among the most important and fundamental in all of economics, and almost every modern economist gives at least lip service to the idea in principles courses. Introductory textbooks in economics agree that the subject matter of this discipline is not so much an objective world of things, but rather the perception of the world by human subjects. What makes a price go up is not some purely physical cause but subjective thoughts in the minds of human "agents." Indeed, what is called "neoclassical" economics today owes its orientation to the marginalist revolution in value theory that took place in the last years of the nineteenth century and that is sometimes called the "subjectivist" revolution. In rebellion against classical value theory, which came to be considered too "objectivistic," neoclassicism stressed that value phenomena are determined by subjective preferences. It is not some intrinsic characteristic of a commodity that gives it value but its *meaning* to the human subjects who might buy or sell it. When economists praise a theory for being "choice-theoretic" or for being connected to its "microfoundations" they are really calling on their understanding of subjectivity.

There is definitely something of the spirit of hermeneutics in this principle of subjectivity and especially in Machlup's Schützian interpretation of it. And Machlup considered this hermeneutical notion to be specifically relevant to his dispute with Lester. Machlup opens his argument against Lester with an exposition of the principle of subjectivity and comes back to the point repeatedly throughout the paper (1946, pp. 521–524, pp. 533–536, pp. 548–549). He seemed to think all he was doing here was elaborating a point that was almost universally accepted in neoclassical economics. The numbers with which empirical economists deal, he insists, are not "objective" measures of some sort that could be "calculated by disinterested men." The background context of the numbers is what renders them intelligible. "It should hardly be necessary to mention that all the relevant magnitudes involved — cost, revenue, profit — are subjective — that is, perceived or fancied by the men whose decisions or actions are to be explained (the business men)" (1946, p. 521). In other words, these numbers are only meaningful in terms of the interplay among the various plans of the agents themselves. Machlup emphasizes the tacit nature of the judgments businessmen make, which he characterizes as "an ability to size up a situation" (1946, p. 523), and compares such judgments to the parking and driving of a car without resorting to measurement (1946, p. 523, pp. 534–536). He specifically points out that businessmen often act on the basis of routines, citing George Katona's psychological studies, but points out that routine "is based on principles which were once considered and decided upon" (1946, p. 524).

Moreover, Machlup points out, these contexts differ radically from agent to agent so that there is a profound divergence of perspectives. Machlup goes to great lengths to stress that the apparently objective written accounting records of the past cannot fully capture the meaning of the decisions businesspeople make. Such records "may form a firm point of departure for evaluating prospective and hypothetical cost and revenue figures" but "anticipations alone are the relevant variables in the marginal calculus of the firm" (1946, p. 523). These anticipations depend on the time horizon of the agent, which can vary in a number of different dimensions:

> What is the time-range of the significant anticipations? How far into the future do they reach, and what period, if any, is given special emphasis? Is tomorrow more important than next year or several years hence? Is it the "short run" or the "long run" which controls current action? (1946, p. 523)

If empirical research posed questions like these more often it would become more anthropological, and it would also be more consistent with its own theoretical pronouncements about the principle of subjectivity.

Since the principle is so widely accepted "in theory" and thrusts so strongly in an anthropological direction, why does empirical research remain so biased against anthropological research? Economists' specific wording of the point about subjectivity, the way they express the principle, is indicative of what would nowadays be considered a distinctively un-hermeneutical presumption. If their statements of this principle are among the most hermeneutical-sounding statements economists make, the hermeneutics it sounds like is an older and outmoded version.[8]

The way subjectivity is described by most economists is remarkably similar to the way that Gadamer, in what he called Romantic hermeneutics, described understanding. Wilhelm Dilthey is often criticized by contemporary hermeneutical philosophers for his notion of "empathy."[9] To understand is to somehow "get inside the head" of the person one is trying to understand. This certainly does sound mysterious or metaphysical. Even when this empathic act is admitted to be strictly impossible, Romantic hermeneutics sets it up as the ideal of correct understanding. One should strive, as far as humanly possible, to erase one's own prejudices and to adopt the point of view of the person under study. To properly understand, for example, the cost of a particular person's choice would be to see the choice the way the person saw it at the moment the choice was made and not allow one's view to be tainted by what we the observers think of the choice, from our later and different perspective.

This is exactly what economists say about the principle of subjectivity. To analyze a person's choice is to somehow get into the private domain of one's thinking at the moment of choice. Those who are thought of as "purists" about the idea of the subjectivity of cost (for example writers in the L.S.E. cost tradition, or followers of George Shackle, or the Austrian economists), often insist on the inaccessibility of opportunity cost to third parties. Costs are made up of "private, subjective appraisals" that are not "publicly visible."[10] There is, I think, a valid point to be made here. One cannot analyze an actor's decision adequately without taking great care to see what the actor thought he or she was doing. But this way of putting subjectivism in terms of "inaccessibility" would seem to make empirical work on cost completely impossible. Subjectivity taken to its logical extreme appears to lead into an anti-empirical trap.

Thus, many contemporary economists accept this principle of "subjectivity" for economic theory and draw from it the conclusion that it is hopeless in practice to "get inside people's heads" so that empirical economics needs to work with more "objective" forms of evidence. The point is admitted "in theory" that the relevant real world with which economics is ultimately concerned is a world of subjective meaning and not of objective things, but then, because of the way they understand what subjective meaning is, they abandon any hope of actually *getting at*

this real world in concrete empirical research. Since to be a purist about
subjectivity is to make empirical research altogether impossible, subjectivity must remain a strictly theoretical principle. What is needed is a
"marrying" of subjectivist and objectivist theory, a relaxation of the
purism about subjectivity, in order to retain "positive and predictive
content" in the discipline.[11]

Gadamer's critique of Romantic hermeneutics suggests that the problem with the notion of empathic understanding is not that it is "too
subjectivistic" in the economist's sense but that it is not subjectivistic
enough. The way to avoid the anti-empirical trap of considering cost
inaccessibly private is not to cheat on the principle of subjectivity but to
take it more seriously. Yes, what matters is the way the decision looked
to the human subject making it, but what matters about "the way the
decision looked to the subject" is the way *this* looks to another subject:
the social scientist. There is what Anthony Giddens calls a "double
hermeneutic" in the human sciences, where what is involved is not only a
subjective interpretation of the world by the agent, but also a subjective
interpretation of this interpretation by the observing scientist.

The subjectivist economist is not being subjectivist enough. He acts as
if there is such a thing as an objective account of subjective choices. The
language of "ends" and "means" is misleading here, for the economist
seems to think that it is possible to objectively identify the list of all the
subjective ends being pursued by actors, and all the means the actors
subjectively think are at their disposal. This list of subjective ends and
means is then thought of as itself strictly objective. Economics is thus an
objective science of subjective acts of choice.

But is it really possible to identify "all" the ends and means of any
actual human action? To be sure, in theory building we can always simply
specify the entire choice framework of the "agents" we invent for our
models. In practice, however, when we are talking about real human
action, aren't we necessarily involved in asking certain questions of such
action, examining certain selected aspects of the ends and means which
we, the observing scientists, consider significant? That is, aren't we
involved in a hermeneutical circle, where we are faced with two subjective perspectives that we are trying to bring into a fusion of horizons with
one another?

Let's say, for example, an entrepreneur is weighing alternative technologies to employ in business, oil or coal powered turbines, and we, the
observing scientists, happen to know that at this time a third technology,
solar power, is under consideration by competitors and will later prove
to be more profitable. Now the "pure subjectivist" wants to make the

point that since solar power is not in our entrepreneur's choice set, our analysis of his action must not treat solar power as the opportunity cost of choosing oil. We can only say his cost was the next best opportunity *he* chose to set aside, which was coal. Again, I think there is a valid theoretical point here, that we need to be true to what the entrepreneur was choosing between and not transpose our own assessment of his situation into our account of his actions. But as soon as we act as empirical economists, our task is precisely to ask such questions as why the entrepreneur did not consider solar power, and whether he lost to his rivals because he neglected this opportunity. That is, when we act empirically we need to take into account another subjective view of the world — our own — in order to assess the significance of this action. To us, there was another option the actor ignored. It wasn't, strictly speaking, his opportunity cost, as he perceived his choice, but it was, from our subjective perspective, the cost of his choice. Were we to try to really view the situation as the entrepreneur saw it, we would only nullify our own view of the situation. We would only make understanding impossible. The empirical researcher isn't trying to eliminate what he knows, and "get inside the head" of the entrepreneur, he is trying to mediate between his own and the entrepreneur's perspective.

As Gadamer sees it, the problem with empathic understanding is its latent objectivism, its presumption that the social scientist has to — or can — utterly erase his own perspective and adopt that of the agent. Understanding is a mediation of the perspective of the observer and the observed. It is not a matter of getting an exact copy of the other person's private mental picture, a complete account of his ends/means framework, but of interpreting one perspective from the standpoint of another one. We understand differently when we understand at all, is Gadamer's famous aphorism.

Moreover, understanding in Gadamer's view does not entail some kind of mysterious access to the private contents of minds but takes place through the public medium of language. It is because meaning is essentially social and public, shared through participation in the life world, that understanding has nothing to do with "getting into heads."

Machlup's Critique of Lester Reconsidered

Machlup's anwer to Lester is cited as the locus classicus for the "getting inside people's heads" problem. It is supposed to show why economists do not need to try to get into any heads, and thus it shows why subjectivity needs to be confined to a purely theoretical principle. Certainly Machlup realized that the agent need not understand the intricacies of marginalist analysis in order for that analysis to be acceptable. But Machlup never intended his critique to be used by economists as an excuse to avoid coming to grips with the level of everyday understanding that Lester wanted to bring to economists' attention. What economists think they have learned from the debate is that it is not necessary for them to make any interpretive contact with the real agents of the economy in order for them to know that their theory is correct. This is the wrong lesson.

What makes Machlup's critique so persuasive is not his disconnection of economic theory with everyday understanding but his ability to connect them. It is this very ability that is suffering alarming deterioration today. Indeed neoclassicism was lucky to have had a Machlup around at the time to interpret it in so reasonable a fashion and defend it from so unreasonable a critic. The one point that can be made in Lester's favor is that he noticed early the tendency toward formalism that has by now become a serious obstacle to progress.[12] In the mid-1940s most economists still maintained a firm enough grasp on the "real world" of business to be able to successfully deflect a critic of this kind. By the 1940s a process of atrophy had just begun that has led to our producing fewer and fewer economists with the kinds of interpretive skills Machlup exemplifies. In other words the "neoclassicism" that Machlup defended from Lester is not the same thing as the one that dominates the profession today. Indeed we could learn a great deal from Machlup about how we might recover the interpretive dimension of our empirical research.

Machlup's understanding of "marginalism" is that it is an interpretive tool useful for understanding the everyday world of business. The point is not only that Machlup happened to have had direct experience in business and knew many business people personally, though these factors certainly helped. The point is rather that he considered it the responsibility of the profession to strive for a close-up understanding of the business world.

The lesson we should draw from his critique of Lester is neither that finding out how business people think is "below" us, and that we need not bother, nor that it is virtually impossible, as many contemporary economists seem to think. The lesson is that it is more difficult than someone like Lester imagines, but that it definitely can and should be done. The standard view of the debate is essentially that Lester was taking his subjectivism too far in his use of questionnaires, and that

Machlup was insisting on more "objective" scientific methods. I contend that, as with Gadamer's critique of Romantic hermeneutics, the problem is on the contrary that subjectivism is not being taken far enough. Machlup was not saying that economists need not get *as close* to the understandings of economic agents as Lester wanted to, he was saying we need to get *closer still*. Lester is criticized not for trying to find out what business people think, but essentially for treating this as a matter of copying instead of understanding. Lester's questionnaires naively asked business people about their decisions in the vernacular of marginalist discourse, and as is to be expected, his results indicate a failure of communication. In contrast, Machlup insists that to do what Lester wanted to do requires much more intimate contact with his subjects. It requires what hermeneutical philosophers call the development of a common language in a dialogue, the fusion of horizons, the translation of utterances from one perspective to another.

It is important to recall that Machlup's position is not Friedman's. He is not claiming that there need be no relationship between the everyday level and the analysis of the academic economist. He is not endorsing the kind of "as-if-ism" that economists so often invoke to escape responsibility for finding out what is going on in the everyday world. He points out, to be sure, that "A mental process in everyday life may often be most conveniently described for scientific purposes in a language which is quite foreign to the process itself" (1946, p. 537). But this linguistic gulf is precisely what he is saying the empirical researcher needs to bridge. If the economist is to make up questions for this purpose he needs to make sure that "the questions are readily formulated and adapted to the peculiarities of the particular man and his business" (1946, p. 537).

Machlup does suggest that there are serious difficulties in doing this kind of research by the use of standard questionnaires but not for the reason most contemporary economists would. The problem is not that subjectivity entails an attempt to "get inside heads" and is therefore suspicious, or simply that people lie. One of the main shortcomings of Lester's study was that the relevant data he needed to do what he wanted was of a psychological nature that cannot be ascertained or evaluated "for the large number of firms contained in a representative sample" (1946, p. 548). For neoclassical economists today sociology and, even more so, anthropology are suspect for being too subjectivistic, too oriented to finding our what people think. For Machlup's version of neoclassicism, the study of business requires more of an anthropological method of participant observation, rather than the sociologist Lester's use of standardized and general questions.

To ask a business man about the "elasticity of demand" for his product is just as helpful as inquiring into the customs of an indigenous Fiji Islander by interviewing him in the King's English. But with a little ingenuity it is possible to translate ideas from the business man's language into that of the economist, and vice versa. (1946, p. 537)

This translation does not only mean that the "mere" everyday language of business people has to be brought "up" to the more precise language of economists. Like any real translation this has to be a bidirectional communicative process in which economists may have as much to learn as business people if they are to come to an understanding together. "Often it will be necessary to know a good deal of the technology, customs and jargon of the trade, and even of the personal idiosyncrasies of the men, before one can ask the right questions" (1946, p. 537). Instead of trying to rely on a mailed questionnaire with a "set formulation of questions," Machlup recommends "the more subtle technique of analyzing a series of single business decisions through close personal contact with those responsible for the decisions".[13]

Neoclassical economists tend to hold paradoxical beliefs about the possibility of grappling directly with the discourse of the business world. They seem to believe that this is at once too easy and too hard. It is too easy in the sense that since it is what everyday people do all the time it appears unworthy of the scientist. It is too hard in the sense that to do it "rigorously" it is practically impossible to do at all.

Hermeneutics provides a response to both sides of these beliefs. Understanding the discourses going on in the everyday world is harder than some economists think, in that it is not a matter of copying what the agent thinks into our heads but of interpreting his views in light of our own theoretical and historical situation. This is not "too easy" and cannot be left to undergraduates or journalists. It is, however, easier than some economists think because it really does not involve getting inside anybody's head in the first place. That is a remnant of an outmoded, Cartesian view of the mind as an isolated entity with a-linguistic thoughts buried deep inside of skulls. Hermeneutics, along with the other philosophies of discourse, would move the relevant unit of analysis from the individual brain to the whole language-speaking process. To live in human societies is already to partake in an understandable web of meaning. We do not need to pry into skulls to discern meaning, our whole everyday lives are full of spoken and written "texts" that are readily accessible for interpretation.

Acknowledgment

Special thanks are due to Arjo Klamer for showing me how powerful anthropological methods can be within economics, in his book *Conversations with Economists*; and for turning this perspective to the study of the agents within the economy, in his unpublished paper, "Towards the Native's Point of View, or, the Difficulty of Changing the Conversation."

Notes

[1] A good collection of some of the classic works of the hermeneutics tradition is Mueller-Vollmer (1985). Excellent summaries of Gadamer's approach are provided by Warnke (1987), Linge (1976), and Bernstein (1983). Sympathetic attempts to relate hermeneutics to economics include Ebeling (1986), Lachmann (1986), Lavoie (1986), and Madison (1986, 1988). My own attempt to summarize the main points of hermeneutics in relation to the natural and human sciences is contained in Lavoie (1987).

[2] When two discursive communities are as distant from one another as hermeneutics and economics are, it is difficult to explore the implications they might have for one another. So far there has only been the most tentative efforts by economists to consider the nature of hermeneutics, and contemporary hermeneutical philosophers have said remarkably little about economics. For example, discussion of economics was conspicuous by its absence in an otherwise excellent collection of essays on interpretive social science edited by Rabinow and Sullivan (1979). Some of the earliest attempts at communication have been filled with accusations of methodological sins of all kinds, and little has yet been done in constructive fashion to see what these discourses may have to say to one other.

Of all the human sciences economics has probably been the least affected by the recent resurgence of hermeneutics. Much of the attention economists have paid to hermeneutics has been to react to it in horror. In a recent article in *KYKLOS*, a highly respected journal of economics, the Popperian philosopher, Hans Albert (1988), dismissed hermeneutics as, at best, having nothing whatever to say about the methodology of economics, and at worst, representing a dangerous threat of historicism and relativism. This article shows an amazing inability to listen to what hermeneutics is trying to say. Albert thinks he is launching an attack on contemporary hermeneutics when he accuses the nineteenth century historian, Johann Gustav Droysen, of the vice of historicism. For a critique by a contemporary hermeneutical philosopher of Droysen's historicism, see Gadamer's *Truth and Method*, 1984, pp. 187–192. Other attacks by economists on hermeneutics have been as bad or worse. See, for example, Hands (1987) and Rothbard (1988).

[3] McCloskey (1985, ch. 9) has elaborated on the way economists delude themselves about what their significance tests really mean. Edward E. Leamer (1983) has elaborated on the serious robustness problems of much of the empirical work economists publish.

[4] On the way early marginalist economists borrowed metaphors and modeling strategies from physics and the way this has distorted the economists' discourse, see Philip Mirowski (1984, 1986a, 1986b).

[5] This view that understanding the everyday level is "below" the scientist is reflected in the way everyday problems get treated at introductory levels but are not deemed relevant to

advanced research. The most valuable things economists have to say that help us get a handle on the real world are only said to our students in lectures or to lay people in journalism, not to each other in the scholarly journals.

[6] It is true, I think, that the theorists are often worse in the sense that at least the empirical economist *wants* to be in touch with reality. But since the theoretical investigation of any sort of unrealistic world might prove to be productive to the economist's imagination, unrealism of theory is not necessarily a problem. Although I will not take up this issue here, modern economic theory can certainly be criticized from a hermeneutical point of view for having become an end in itself, rather than a device for understanding the real world.

[7] It is important to keep in mind that the basic meaning and connotations of the word "subjectivism" for economics differ considerably from its meaning in philosophy. It does not necessarily claim, for example, "that there are a priori structures of transcendental subjectivity that ground both our scientific objective knowledge and the pregiven *Lebenswelt* of everyday experience" as one philosopher describes Edmund Husserl's "subjectivism" (Bernstein, p. 11).

[8] Although Machlup's version of the principle is among the best, it is noteworthy that he and his teacher, Ludwig Mises, got the idea from Schütz and Max Weber, who got it from Wilhelm Dilthey. Schütz's stress on intersubjectivity and the life-world under the influence of Edmund Husserl is the beginning of an important advance from the Romantic hermeneutics of the early Dilthey. But like Husserl's, Schütz's position is still trapped in the objectivistic presuppositions that contemporary hermeneutics criticizes.

[9] It is significant that Dilthey himself moved away from this empathic view of understanding, and his later work points in a direction much closer to Gadamer's. See Ermarth (1978).

[10] These words are taken from the Austrian-school economist, Israel Kirzner (1986, p. 149), who, like Machlup, was a student of Ludwig Mises. See Buchanan (1969) and Buchanan and Thirlby (1973) for the classic statements of the L.S.E. subjective cost theory where the ephemeral and inaccessible character of cost is stressed.

[11]See Buchanan's introduction to Buchanan and Thirlby (1973, p. 16). Yeager similarly warns against the "ultrasubjectivists" who are "overstating the subjectivist position" (1987, pp. 21–29).

[12] In the opening paragraph of his article Lester (1946, p. 63) pointed out that "the trend over the past decade has been to devote more and more space in elementary textbooks to complicated graphs illustrating marginal relationships and to detailed discussions of marginal analysis under a variety of assumed circumstances." He was already wondering why textbooks needed to "spend so much of the students' time on the mathematics of profit maximization" and the "minutiae of marginalism."

[13] Machlup (1946, pp. 537–538) is here quoting an earlier article in which he went into great lengths about how this kind of close-up empirical research ought to be done (1939).

References

Albert, Hans. 1988. "Hermeneutics and Economics: A Criticism of Hermeneutical Thinking in the Social Sciences." *KYKLOS* 41:573–602.

Bernstein, Richard J. 1983. *Beyond Objectivism and Relativism: Science, Hermeneutics, and Praxis*. Philadelphia: University of Pennsylvania Press.

Buchanan, James M. 1969. *Cost and Choice*. Chicago: University of Chicago Press.

Buchanan, James M. and Thirlby, G.F. 1973. *L.S.E Essays on Cost*. New York: New York University Press.

Ebeling, Richard M. 1986. "Toward a Hermeneutical Economics: Expectations, Prices, and the Role of Interpretation in a Theory of the Market Process." In Kirzner, 1986b, pp. 39–55.

Ermarth, Michael. 1978. *Wilhelm Dilthey: The Critique of Historical Reason*. Chicago: University of Chicago Press.

Gadamer, Hans-George. 1976. *Philosophical Hermeneutics*. Berkeley: University of California Press.

——. 1984. *Truth and Method*. New York: Crossroad.

Hands, D. Wade. 1987. "Charles Taylor's *Human Agency and Language: Philosophical Papers I and Philosophy and the Human Sciences: Philosophical Papers II*." *Economics and Philosophy* 3:172–175.

Kirzner, Israel M. 1986a. "Another Look at the Subjectivism of Costs" In Kirzner, 1986b, pp. 140–156.

—— ed. 1986b. *Subjectivism, Intelligibility, and Economic Understanding: Essays in Honor of Ludwig M. Lachmann on his Eightieth Birthday*. New York: New York University Press.

Lachmann, Ludwig M. 1986. "Economics as a Hermeneutical Discipline." Paper presented at the conference on *Interpretation, Human Agency, and Economics*, March 28, 1986, George Mason University, Fairfax, Virginia.

Lavoie, Don. 1986. "Euclideanism vs. Hermeneutics: A Reinterpretation of Misesian Apriorism." In Kirzner, 1986b, pp. 192–210.

——. 1987. "The Accounting of Interpretations and the Interpretation of Accounts: The Communicative Function of 'The Language of Business'." *Accounting, Organizations and Society* 12:579–604.

Leamer, Edward E. 1983. "Let's Take the Con Out of Econometrics." *American Economic Review* 73 (March):460–472.

Lester, Richard A. 1946. "Shortcomings of Marginal Analysis for Wage-Employment Problems." *American Economic Review* 36(March):63–82.

——. 1947. "Marginalism, Minimum Wages, and Labor Markets." *American Economic Review* 37(March):135–148.

Linge, David E. 1976. "Editor's Introduction." In Hans-Georg Gadamer *Philosophical Hermeneutics*. Berkeley:University of California Press.

Machlup, Fritz. 1939. "Evaluation of the Practical Significance of the Theory of Monopolistic Competition." *American Economic Review* 29.

——. 1946. "Marginal Analysis and Empirical Research." *American Economic Review* 36(Sept.):519–554.

——. 1947. "Rejoinder to an Anti-marginalist." *American Economic Review* 37(March):148–154.

——. 1955. "The Problem of Verification in Economics." *The Southern Economic Journal* 22:1–21.

Madison, G.B. 1986. "Hans-Georg Gadamer's Contribution to Philosophy and Its Significance for Economics." Paper presented at the conference on *Inter-*

pretation, Human Agency, and Economics, March 28, 1986, George Mason University, Fairfax, Virginia.

——. 1988. "How Individualistic is Methodological Individualism?" Working paper #8806 of the Groupe de Recherche en Epistemologie Comparee, University of Quebec at Montreal.

McCloskey, Donald N. 1985. *The Rhetoric of Economics*. Madison: University of Wisconsin Press.

Mirowski, Philip. 1984. "Physics and the Marginalist Revolution." *Cambridge Journal of Economics* 8:361–379.

——. 1986a. "Shall I compare These to a Minkowski-Ricardo-Leontief-Metzler Matrix of the Mosak-Hicks Type? Or, Rhetoric, Mathematics, and the Nature of Neoclassical Economic Theory." Paper presented at the conference on *The Rhetoric of Economics* April 17–19, 1986. Wellesley College, Wellesley, Mass.

——. 1986b. "Mathematical Formalism and Economic Explanation." In Philip Mirowski, ed. *The Reconstruction of Economic Theory*. Boston: Kluwer-Nijhoff.

Mueller-Vollmer, Kurt. 1985. *The Hermeneutics Reader*. New York: Continuum.

Rabinow, Paul and Sullivan, W.M. 1979. *Interpretive Social Science: A Reader*. Berkeley: University of California Press.

Rothbard, Murray N. 1988. "The Hermeneutical Invasion of Philosophy and Economics." *The Review of Austrian Economics* 3:45–59.

Schütz, Alfred. 1953. "Common-Sense and Scientific Interpretation of Human Action." *Philosophy and Phenomenological Research* 14:1–38.

Shackle, G.L.S 1972. *Epistemics and Economics: A Critique of Economic Doctrines*. Cambridge: Cambridge University Press.

Warnke, Georgia. 1987. *Gadamer: Hermeneutics, Tradition and Reason*. Cambridge: Polity Press.

Yeager, Leland. 1987. "Why Subjectivism?" *Review of Austrian Economics* 1:5–31.

A COMMENT BY SHEILA C. DOW

Lavoie makes an important case for a return to old-fashioned empirical methods, to an understanding of the business world rather than the amassing of data series. Not only should economists understand economic agents as engaging in hermeneutics in their own understanding of their economic environment, but we should ourselves engage in hermeneutics to promote our own understanding. We must translate individual agents' understanding into economic terms before theorizing about it.

This argument is supported, surprisingly at first glance, by Machlup's exchange with Lester. Rather than arguing against "realistic" representations of individual behavior, Machlup was arguing that realism required a translation from case-study understanding to formal models. Series of data referring to economic variables had limited value because they could not account for the subjectivism inherent in the series: cross-industry cost data for example could not reflect the different understanding of what is meant by costs on the part of individual suppliers of data. Formal models should be realistic by "making sense" in terms of our understanding of individual behavior, not in the sense of being confirmed by empirical tests using data series.

The argument is a good one and is persuasive, expressed as it is in a subjectivist, microeconomic context. Where it needs further development, on the one hand, is in its relevance to macroeconomics (and indeed to the macrofoundations of microeconomics) and, on the other, to extend it beyond the subjective context employed by Lavoie.

The need for development in terms of macroeconomics is parallelled by a serious lack in rational expectations theory. Machlup's argument is popularly interpreted as justifying "as if" assumptions: company managers act "as if" they know their marginal costs and marginal revenues. This argument in turn is used to justify the assumption of rational expectations theory that economic agents act "as if" they know a complete macroeconomic model and, in the case of the strong hypothesis, the correct macroeconomic model. But, in hermeneutic terms a business manager's understanding of company costs is of a quite different order from any economic agent's understanding of macroeconomic variables like the money supply, far less a complete macroeconomic model.

Even for macroeconomics seen as an aggregation of microeconomics, then, economists have a difficult task in formalizing agents' understanding of macroeconomic variables. This ground has been well covered by Hayek. The task becomes even more difficult for macroeconomics seen as having a life of its own, as it were, that impinges in an objective sense

185

on the subjective perceptions of individual agents: relevant macroeconomic variables in this context include "state of confidence" as well as "the rate of inflation." If realism requires an understanding of process (as advocated by Lawson, 1989), then macroeconomists must understand macroeconomic processes. There is no macroeconomic equivalent of rhetorical understanding at the micro level: we cannot converse with the macroeconomy.

This is not to undermine Lavoie's argument, but to extend it. Lavoie argues that economists should be anthropological in their understanding of their subject matter; macroeconomists must then look to social anthropology, which studies society's impact on the individual. Indeed, there is a standard classification of social relationships in social anthropology (see Mitchell, 1969) according to their structural, categorical and personal aspects. Lavoie does not develop what he means by anthropology, but it would be helpful to spell it out in relation to economics. (These categories seen to have parallels in the categories macro; industry; firm.)

An example that springs to mind (to engage in hermeneutics at yet another level) of an economist who employed social anthropology is Keynes. He is an important example in that he pioneered modern macroeconomics in the hermeneutic mode advocated in Lavoie's paper. Keynes's great strength was the breadth of his experience in business and government life, as much as in academic life. His personal understanding of speculative behavior, for example, allowed him to understand the processes of speculative activity and its interaction with the rest of the economy. As a result of this combination of understanding of individual behavior with an understanding of macro process, Keynes in fact avoided putting artifical barriers between microeconomics and macroeconomics. Our contemporary thought is constrained by these barriers. But the type of argument presented in this chapter leaves the way open for a coalescing of the two fields, if hermeneutics can be understood to encompass more than the individual level.

Particularly when the discussion departs from the level of individual decision-making, however, the relationship between subjectivism and hermeneutics becomes more tenuous. Lavoie emphasizes the connection between the two, but it was Keynes again who posited a more complex combination of objectivism and subjectivism at the level of individual understanding (see Lawson, 1988). The significance to Lavoie's argument of the possibility of objective evidence is that there may still be a role for aggregative data series. First, the regularities that emerge from such series, in spite of changing economic structure on the one hand and changing subjective perceptions on the other, are the very stuff of macroeconomics: the series underlying the consumption function are a good example. The consumption function is a particularly good example too of the need at the same time for anthropological understanding, which is essential to prediction of when and if the regularity is going to break down. (The money demand function would be another example.) Second, aggregative phenomena, like the state of market confidence, impinge on the subjective understanding of individual economic agents. However subjectively generated, the state of confidence has objective significance.

In conclusion, then, Lavoie's argument is a good counterpoint to logical positivism but runs the risk of overstating the case. The argument would be stronger if it left room for macroeconomics and data series *in combination with* anthropological understanding.

References

Lawson, T. 1988. "Probability and Uncertainty in Economic Analysis." *Journal of Post Keynesian Economics* 11(1):38–65.
Lawson, T. 1989. "Realism and Instrumentalism in the Development of Econometrics." *Oxford Economic Papers* 41(1):236–258.
Mitchell, J.C. 1969. *Social Networks in Urban Situations*. Part I, Manchester: Manchester University Press.

7 WALRAS' "ECONOMICS AND MECHANICS": TRANSLATION, COMMENTARY, CONTEXT

Philip Mirowski and Pamela Cook

Mathematicians are like Frenchmen: whatever you say to them, they translate into their own language, and forthwith it is something entirely different.

— Goethe

The place of Leon Walras in the history of Western economic thought would appear honorable and secure. One of the earliest to proclaim his stature was Joseph Schumpeter (1954, p. 827): "So far as pure theory is concerned, Walras is in my opinion the greatest of all economists. His system of economic equilibrium, uniting as it does, the quality of 'revolutionary' creativeness with the quality of classic synthesis, is the only work

We should like to acknowledge the support of the National Endowment for the Humanities program in Science, Technology and Society in the preparation of this translation and commentary.

by an economist that will stand in comparison with theoretical physics." In the interim, this conviction has become institutionalized to such an extent that the recipient of the 1983 Nobel Prize in economics could assert that, "Walras wrote one of the greatest classics, if not the greatest, in our science" (Debreu, 1984, p. 268).

The central presupposition of this homage is the rhetorical linkage between the work of Walras and the elevation of the study of the economy to the status of a "science." Both Walras and his modern followers persistently asserted that the Walrasian model has put economics on a scientific footing, raising it above the endless disputes of literary classical political economy. The most precarious aspect of such appeals is their lack of philosophical and historical perspective: we doubt any two neo-Walrasian economists can agree upon what precisely characterizes "science"; and worse, in the interim it has been forgotten that the scientific status of the Walrasian model has repeatedly come under attack, even during Walras' lifetime. We cannot hope to convince anyone with respect to the overarching philosophical problems of an appeal to science in this venue,[1] and therefore we have no ambitions to do so. However, we would like to bring some historical evidence to bear on the issue of the scientific status of Walras' endeavors: It was the case that many scientists of repute expressed grave reservations about the Walrasian program, which provoked Walras to pen the text that we have translated in this chapter, his last published work in economics. It is our conviction that bringing this entire episode to the attention of economists and historians of economic thought will begin to reveal the pitfalls and dangers of associating the name Leon Walras with science.

One of the authors of this chapter has suggested elsewhere (Mirowski, 1987) that recent writings on rhetoric in economic discourse such as McCloskey (1985) have not taken the lessons of literary criticism sufficiently to heart, and that this might be attributed to the desire of that author and others to come up with some modern defense of neoclassical economic theory. The present chapter is intended to serve, not as some further abstract "methodological" discussion of economic rhetoric,[2] but instead as demonstration of how older or repudiated forms of writing may indeed alter our perceptions of the actual subject matter. In this particular instance, we have opted for a thoroughly discredited and outdated format, the "translation and scholium." Science itself possesses certain specific rhetorical tropes (Markus, 1987); in our opinion, the best way to analyze them is to find an Archemedean point outside that mode of discourse in order to better display the distance between the intentions of an author, the implicit social structures of the rhetoric, and what a subsequent tradition has made of that author's project.

Mathematical Economics as Social Physics

With the help of Jaffe's incomparable edition of Walras' correspondence, it is now possible to make some definitive statements about the influences surrounding the genesis of neoclassical economic theory. In Mirowski (1984; forthcoming) one of the present authors has argued that the supposed simultaneous discovery of neoclassical value theory — the constrained optimization over a field of utility — was no discovery at all, but rather the appropriation of the mathematical formalisms of potential energy recently innovated in the science of physics. While this mathematical model provided the common denominator of discourse for a disparate collection of far-flung theorists who were at first unaware of each other's endeavors, each individual did not propose an exactly *identical* model: a fact that previous historiography has generally passed over in silence, or at least without explanation. Under a revised understanding of the meaning of scientific discourse, this phenomenon becomes comprehensible, and important for our present narrative.

In the 1870s, a number of individuals possessing varying degrees of mastery of the energy model proposed to import it into the economic context with differing intentions and widely varying facility with the metaphorical implications of their exercise. In the case of Walras, the sequence of events by which the model was transported across the boundaries was of particular significance for its later elaboration and realization. Walras, it must be noted, was a poor mathematician by most any standards, a fact frequently admitted in his correspondence; but that did not stop him from pursuit of his life's goal, which was to recast his father's concept of *rareté* into a scientific framework. In his first effort to mathematize the concept in 1860, he toyed with a Newtonian model of market relations, positing that the "price of things is in inverse ratio to the quantity offered and in direct ratio to the quantity demanded" (Walras, 1965, v. I, pp. 216–217). As Jaffe notes, it was a "sorry performance" (in Black et al., 1973, p. 216); more importantly, it reveals a lack of familiarity with the more novel energy formalisms, as well as the physical metaphor of the "field." Nevertheless, Walras did not give up in his quest to imitate physics. As he wrote to Jules de Mesnil-Marigny in December 1862, he needed financial support to develop "an original creation," a "new science . . . a science of economic forces analagous to the science of astronomical forces. . . . The analogy is complete and striking" (Walras, 1965, v. I. pp. 119–120). Unfortunately, Walras' desire to emulate physics was stronger than either his understanding of physics or his artistic appreciation of metaphor, since his pre-1872 metaphor was neither complete nor striking. It took someone much familiar with mechanics to point out where the metaphor of preference as a field of force might be found.

In the late autumn of 1872, an engineer and professor of mechanics at the Academy of Lausanne, one Antoine Paul Piccard (1844–1920?), wrote a memo to Walras sketching in the mathematics of the optimization of a "quantité de besoin" (Walras, 1965, v. I, pp. 308–311). Jaffe himself calls Walras' paltry acknowledgments of this critical memo "niggardly" because "There was not the slightest inkling of a theory of maximization of utility either in L.W.'s pre-Lausanne papers or in the various outlines and prospectives of his work up to October 19, 1872" (in Walras, 1965, v. I, p. 309). Indeed, Jaffe continued, "It is doubtful whether L.W. who arrived in Lausanne with virtually no mathematics beyond elementary analytical geometry, was able to grasp more than simple algebraic and geometric aspects of Piccard's explanation."

This wobbly inheritance from physics constitutes our point of departure: the basic value theory came directly from the physics via Piccard, whereas the embellishments (and gaffes) were all due to Walras. It was the *metaphor* of mechanics rather than its actual structure of explanation or its specific mathematical structure that fired Walras' theoretical imagination; the rest consisted of the rather more pedestrian and strained attempts to invest his imperfect understanding of the mathematics with economic significance. One observes this time and again in Walras' correspondence, for example when the mathematician Hermann Amstein tried to explain Lagrange multipliers to him (Walras, 1965, v. I, pp. 516–520).

Now, such borrowings across disciplines are not intrinsically flawed or fallacious, as long as the people doing the borrowing treat it as a self-conscious act of metaphorical reasoning: maintaining a certain level of agnosticism, one should proceed to weigh the advantages and drawbacks of the metaphor from various points of view (Mirowski, 1987). However, this could not be said of Walras' exercise. Because he never understood the original mathematical metaphor with any depth or subtlety, he simply was incapable of serious evaluation of its pros and cons. Indeed, it seems clear that he thought the mere act of imitating mechanics and stating propositions in its characteristic mathematical formalisms was sufficient to render economics "scientific." This view was not shared by other *scientists* with whom Walras came into contact.

The Sciences Were Never at War?

It would have been extraordinary that so many economists could so frequently misrepresent the energy model without eventually calling down the wrath of physicists upon their labors. Indeed, one of the skeletons in the neoclassical closet is that around the turn of the century, quite a number of competent physicists turned their attention to this species of proto-energetics and pronounced it wanting: their most perspicacious barbs took the form of accusations that the early "mathematical economists" had misrepresented the energy concept itself and had displayed an incongruous silence concerning conservation principles. While the rhetoric of science declares that the sciences were never at war, the early neoclassicals who bore the brunt of the slings and arrows of cruel or not-so-cruel physicists certainly did not end up feeling that way. It seems clear that they believed imitation of the trappings of science would put an end to all partisan disputes and squabbles. Yet, time and again Walras and others such as Pareto and Fisher met these inquiries with hurt incomprehension, bluster, farrago, protests that the physics was irrelevant, and finally, a feeling of betrayal: how did it come to pass that those in the forefront of trying to render economics a science should be so abused by those whom they were only trying to emulate?

The first instance of such a confrontation was the review by Joseph Bertrand of Cournot's *Recherches* and Walras' *Théorie Mathématique de la Richesse Sociale*, which was a compilation of Walras' previously published journal articles (Bertrand, 1883). Bertrand was well-placed to comprehend the scientific pretensions of the fledgling science: a product of the Ecole Polytechnique, professor at the Collège de France, a specialist in the mathematics of rational mechanics, and the editor of the third edition of Lagrange's *Mécanique Analytique*. Most of his review centered on the thesis that the neglect of mathematical political economy in the French academy had been deserved, because the existing attempts had been devoid of any serious empirical content, not to mention numerous mathematical and conceptual errors. While the preponderance of the review was devoted to Cournot, Bertrand also offered two critiques of Walras' general approach.

In the first, he observed that in general there would exist what is now called in the modern literature "false trading": namely, some exchanges are conducted at nonequilibrium prices in the process of trying to discover the market-clearing price. Bertrand pointed out, quite correctly, that the mere existence of false trading, or indeed any mercantile speculation, would obviate the determinacy of Walras' general equilibrium. It is noteworthy that here Bertrand homed in directly on the one emendation that the neoclassicals had made to the proto-energetics model — the "law" of one price — and demonstrated that it rendered the rest of the model a poor analogy for market activity. Bertrand's second critique centered on the putative path-independence of "rareté." He suggested that if all actors traded only according to the independently given utility functions, that would give one result, but if they calculated gain and loss over time in price terms, that would give entirely another result. Although he did not phrase it precisely in these terms, this clearly was the initial probe of the sore spot of the dearth of explicit conservation principles in a model appropriated from physics.

The story of the hostility of the French academic establishment to neoclassical economics is often told as a moral tale of ignorance and backwardness, but as usual, this was not the way things were perceived at the time. Bertrand's critiques were felt to be devastating in *fin de siècle* France, regularly quoted, and thought in some quarters to justify the rebuff of mathematical economics (Bouvier, 1901a,b; Boninsegni, 1903; Zoretti, 1906). The situation was not helped by the fact that Cournot (having died in 1877) could not retort; and while Walras never directly answered the criticisms, Bertrand's barb did have profound impact upon the fourth edition of the *Elements of Pure Economics* (Walras, 1969; fourth edition, 1954).

Donald Walker has recently shown that, in the case of Walras, the encounter with the physicists plunged the neoclassical general equilibrium model into more confusion (Walker, 1987). He points out that the first three editions of Walras' *Elements of Pure Economics* represent an attempt to construct a model of economic dynamics where purchases of inputs and production of commodities actually occur through time as part of a mechanism of equilibration. However, in the fourth edition of 1900, that is, after Bertrand's blast and Laurent's needling (described below), Walras switched to a different model of "bons" or "pledges," wherein everything is coordinated on papers prior to any and all economic activity: everything is irredeemably static. This later version, of course, is the one that does not violate the proto-energetics model because all trades are virtual, thus ensuring conservation principles are avoided; and this version, of course, is the progenitor of the twentieth-century Arrow Debreu model. The one unfortunate aspect of all this, however, is that Walras himself never reconciled the two models in his text, probably because he never really understood that the problem was one of path-dependence and thus violation of the original energy metaphor; and therefore he merely forced the pledges model into the structure of the *Elements* without eliminating or revising the older theorizing that contradicted it (Walker, 1987). As a consequence, generations of neoclassical theorists have felt free to assert anything they pleased about the "dynamics" of their model, without understanding that their freedom was spurious.

The second instance of a scientist harassing Walras came in 1898. Hermann Laurent, a mathematician at the Ecole Polytechnique and the author of a textbook on rational mechanics (Laurent, 1870) as well as treatises on statistics and actuarial science, wrote to Walras about some things, as he later put it, "ce qui choquera un peu moins les mathématiciens purs" (Walras, 1965, v. III, p. 116). Laurent queried Walras on 29 November 1898 as to his opinion of the appropriate unit of value (Walras, 1965, v. III, letter 1374, pp. 40–41). Walras, after trying to fob him off with compliments, responded with a repetition of the thesis in his *Elements* that it is not proper to speak of a unit of value, only an arbitrary *numéraire* (Walras, 1965, v. III, letter 1377). Laurent, a little perturbed at being patronized, wrote back that he was asking about *dynamics* and the essential role of time but that Walras had only responded with a static argument (Walras, 1965, v. III, letter 1378). Walras, himself getting a little flustered, then accused Laurent of conceptualizing value as an absolute magnitude, in analogy with certain physical magnitudes such as length, weight, and force. He wrote, "A vrai dire, vous tendez à identifier purement et simplement la valeur et la force en prenant pour unité de valeur la valeur de l'unité de force." [To tell the truth, you tend to identify value and force by purely and simply equating the unit of force and the unit of value.] (Walras, 1965, v. III, pp. 47–48). Walras then went on to say that he thought of value as a magnitude *sui generis*, and did not expect that there existed any unit of value which was constant over time and space.

Laurent, at this juncture, was probably beginning to wonder whether Walras was just playing dumb, being obstreperous, or perhaps simply did not understand the physics (Walras, 1965, v. III, letter 1380). By all appearances, Walras' *rareté* was modelled upon a conservative vector field; and the very first implication of such a formalism is that there exists a gradient function, unique up to a scalar multiple, conserved through time. As might be expected, the correspondance concerning value theory then cooled for a while, but upon a friendly letter from Walras a year later, Laurent decided to try one more time. This letter of 13 May 1900 (Walras, 1965, v. III, letter 1452) is a miracle of compression and lucidity. Laurent wrote [our translation]:

Let dq_1, dq_2,... dq_N be quantities of merchandise A_1, A_2,... A_N consumed during time dt. Their total price is

$$p_1 dq_1 + p_2 dq_2 + \ldots + p_N dq_N \qquad [1]$$

where p_i designates the price of a unit of q_i. If one accepts that there is a standard of measure for utility, then one must also accept that expression 1 is integrable after having multiplied by a factor μ, if it is an exact differential. Then one posits:

$$d\Phi = \mu[p_1 dq_1 + p_2 dq_2 + \ldots] \qquad\qquad [2]$$

and

$$\frac{d\Phi}{dq_1} = \mu p_1, \frac{d\Phi}{dq_2} = \mu p_2, \ldots$$

and hence these derivatives are proportional to the prices, such that one would be able to call the *raretés* of A_1, A_2, . . . the partial integrals

$$\int \frac{d\Phi}{dq_1}, \ldots$$

which will be the utilities. But there is one difficulty: the measure of rareté depends on the factor μ. One could respond that it is just a matter of definition, but that does not mean it is any less interesting to interpret the significance of the factors of integration. If the differential equation 1 is null, then the function Φ is constant, and after one hypothesis, will there exist *one* relationship between prices and the quantities consumed?

This threw Walras into a tizzy. In a reply dated 22 May 1900 he compared his own work with that of the early progenitors of the calculus, who knew their techniques worked, although they were unsure of its principles. Then he insisted that there were other economists who were also good mathematicians, such as "Bortkevitch, Pareto, and Barone," who also started from the same point of departure without quibbling about these issues: such consensus is rare. (He seemed to be implying that there was safety in numbers.) He then proceeded by suggesting that the integrating factor is equal to the ratios of marginal utility to price, and to rewrite Laurent's equation 1 as a system of individual demand and supply equations. Finally, he reiterated that he did not see any need for a standard or measure of utility (Walras, 1965, v. III, letter 1454).

Amazingly, Laurent doggedly tried one more time on 24 May 1900, writing that Walras still had not answered his question. Patiently he asked: why is equation 1 an exact differential, and what is the economic interpretation of the factor of integration? (Walras, 1965, v. III, letter 1455). In exhaustion, Walras ignored the question about the exact differential entirely and responded by shifting his premises to instead insist that the integrating factor is the marginal utility of the *numéraire*; he claimed that this was similar to Marshall's discussion of the marginal utility of money (Walras, 1965, v. III, letter 1456). From this point onwards Walras started suggesting to others that Laurent was part of a plot against him (Walras, 1965, v. III, letter 1469). Both sides then retired to nurse their bruised egos, and Walras in particular his "tête assez sérieusement malade" (Walras, 1965, v. III, p. 132), never to correspond again concerning this issue.

Laurent should be considered one of the unsung heroes of neoclassical economic theory, because of his avid devotion to getting the content of the physical metaphor correctly specified. Strange at it may seem, Laurent thought of himself as a supporter of the Lausanne school of economics throughout the entire episode. So just when the Walras correspondence looked to him like it was going nowhere, he decided to try one of the neoclassicals who might possess a little better comprehension of the issues involved. In an effort clearly above and beyond the call of duty, early in 1899 he composed a number of letters to Vilfredo Pareto, essentially posing the same queries.[3]

Perhaps the most incongruous aspect of this particular episode is that Laurent persisted in seeing himself as a partisan of the Lausanne school of mathematical economics. In 1902 he published his *Petit traité d'économie politique mathématique*, which was little more than a pastiche of brief observations on a sequence of mathematical models; nevertheless, it was written with the intention of defending the Walrasian program. Curiously enough, the section on price theory merely recapitulates the contents of his letters cited above, minus the parts questioning why equation 1 is an exact differential. His questions along those lines were never adequately answered by the protagonists, and so it appears he just avoided them in his own treatise. Reading between the lines, however, he does offer two hints about conservation principles. The first shows that equilibrium at a point in time outside of a Robinson Crusoe world requires the further condition that $\Sigma dq_a = 0$, $\Sigma dq_b = 0, \ldots$ and so forth, which we would now recognize as "Walras' Law"; a better way of stating it would be that motion in commodity space is a zero-sum game and hence path-independent (Laurent, 1902, pp. 10–11). Secondly, he observes that enjoyment of goods must be independent of time, which we could restate as the condition that the utility function is itself conserved. Here Laurent was one of the first, along with Antonelli, to anticipate later neoclassical attempts to simulate the energy conservation condition by means of an ensemble of auxilliary hypotheses. Finally, in a very brief section, Laurent noted, "There exist between economic facts and those of rational mechanics some analogies which we merely point to without drawing any conclusions" (Laurent, 1902, p. 19).

Meanwhile, Walras was growing increasingly apprehensive about what must have seemed a spate of skeptical evaluations of his program of a "mathematical economics." This can be judged from a letter Walras wrote to Henri Poincaré (1856–1912) on 10 September 1901, practically begging him to act as umpire in this matter (Walras, 1965, v. III, letter 1492). One aspect of Walras' naiveté is revealed by the suggestions in the letter that he did not realize that he was writing to the premier theorist of rational mechanics in France; rather, he had settled upon Poincaré because some of his philosophical writings had been quoted in Bouvier (1901b). Walras adopted a somewhat despairing tone in this letter, complaining about his treatment by Bertrand and the Institute of Actuaries (a veiled reference to Laurent), and enclosing the fourth edition of the *Elements* for Poincaré to endorse. Poincaré, as would anyone else in the same situation of receiving a whining letter from a complete stranger, promised to read the book in the unspecified future; and assured Walras that, "A priori, je ne suis pas hostile à l'application des mathématiques aux sciences économiques, pourvu qu'on ne sorte pas de certaines limites" (Walras, 1965, v. III, letter 1494).

The comment about "limits" was like a red flag to a bull for Walras; he immediately fired off another letter to Poincaré to preempt what he feared would be yet another blast of skepticism from a prominent scientist. Unlike the vague hints of hostility to mathematics in the first letter, Walras gets right to the crux of Laurent's critique, even mentioning him by name, broaching the complaint that mathematicians have denounced *rareté* because it was not measurable. While admitting that he was "putting aside, for the present, all ideas of numerical evaluation," he took the offensive by claiming that physicists also posited inaccessible mathematical entities in their theories, and no one felt that it had compromised mechanics (Walras, 1965, v. III, letter 1495). This section of the letter is very revealing about Walras' competence in physics, as well as providing the germ for the paper translated below. He wrote:

> ... I open Poinsot's *Statique* (8th ed.) to chapter 3: "Centers of Gravity," 134; I see that if defines the mass of a body as the number of molecules which comprise it or as the amount of matter it contains; and I assert that, by so doing, he regards as measurable a magnitude that is not, given that no one has ever counted the molecules of such a body. Yet because of the mass so considered, mathematicians have been able to demonstrate that "celestial bodies attract one another in direct proportion to the masses and in inverse proportion to the square of the distances", and have had success in explaining astronomical phenomena. Thanks to treating *rareté* in the same way, I have been able to show that "merchandise is exchanged in direct proportion to its *rareté*" and I have explained the principal phenomena of economies and outlined a pure mathematical political economy. It seems to me the first attempt justifies the second." (Walras, 1965, v. III, letter 1495)

First, let us unpack the implications of this letter, and then attend to Poincaré's reply, which has been previously misunderstood due to a lack of appreciation of the context. The most important implication is that, irrespective of the numerous attempts by physicists and engineers to acquaint him with the more modern concepts of energy physics, at this late date Walras still believed he was implementing the original Newtonian metaphor that had served as his inspiration as long ago as 1860. Although in textbooks and nonhistorical texts it may be common to conflate Newtonian mechanics and "classical" energy physics, there are many historiographical reasons to make a sharp distinction between the two (Mirowski, forthcoming, ch. 2).

In this instance it is critical to note that all of the mathematics of Walrasian general equilibrium were derived from energy physics (by way of Piccard, Amstein, and others), which Walras himself never actually studied or, by all evidence, ever understood. Indeed, in this letter to Poincaré Walras quotes from Poinsot's *Elements of Statics* (Poinsot, 1842), the rational mechanics text of his youth (Walras, 1965, v. III, p. 149). That text contains no discussion of energy physics (as it could not, since the "discovery of energy conservation" was just taking place in the 1840s/1850s) and, as should be obvious from the title, no discussion whatsoever of dynamics. The body of the text is unremittingly geometric, which would explain why Walras thought he understood mechanics while remaining relatively innocent of the differential calculus prior to 1872. Two "Mémoires" appended to the text did consider d'Alembert's principle (a stepping-stone to Lagrangian dynamics and the energy principle: Poinsot, 1842, p. 459) and the conditions for a conservative vector field expressed in discrete form as individual equations (Poinsot, 1842, p. 397) but these were clearly not intended to be part of the pedagogy of the standard "cours," and in any event, their importance only came to be appreciated after the rise of energy physics.

The significance of these rather arcane considerations is that *every single question* raised by the skeptical physicists was directly related to these *lacunae* in Walras' education. The issue of "false trading," the distinction between statics and dynamics, the problem of the integrability of utility, questions concerning what was conserved in the act of trade, possible disjunctions between "force" (price) and "energy" (utility) — all of these would have been second nature to the physicist familiar with the structure of energy physics but were little more than Greek to Walras. While "measurability" is one corollary of this entire issue — after all, energy is measurable precisely because it is posited to be conserved in a closed system — measurability was not (and indeed, still is not) the crux of the criticism. It is instead (in more modern terminology): don't go positing the existence of some unique equilibrium configuration unless you can guarantee the existence of a path-independent vector field and a gradient of a time-independent scalar field. Otherwise, every little bit of history matters, taking us out of the realm of metaphors from rational mechanics.

Walras' appeal to "mass" as an example of an inaccessible mathematical entity further reveals that he is out of his depth. It was well understood by the nineteenth century that "mass" stood for two different concepts: the first, "inertial mass," defined by Euler as the ratio of impressed force to resulting acceleration, and the second, "density" or "quantity of matter," related to weight. The equivalence of both concepts was noted but not thoroughly understood by the end of the century — clarification had to await the theory of relativity — but on no account did that mean that mass was empirically inaccessible. It was precisely because of the specification of conservation principles that mass could be gauged with great precision. Hence the comparison of mass and *rareté* did not reflect favorably upon Walras' position: there was no equivalent to mass in Walras' equations: there were no "constants" of motion to be measured.

And now to Poincaré's response (Walras, 1965, v. III, letter 1496). Although he did not realize it, Walras was very lucky to have chosen Poincaré as his umpire, because, among other reasons, Poincaré had evolved into an advocate of a philosophical position now called "conventionalism" (Giedymin, 1982). In 1889 Poincaré had demonstrated that certain general classes of mechanical problems, such as the generalized three-body problem, possessed no Hamiltonian invariants that would guarantee an analytic solution; afterwards, he adopted the unusual position for his time that energy was not a descriptive entity but rather the assertion of the ideal of natural law, i.e., a stable time-invariant world independent of our activity or inquiry. Thus invariance principles such as the conservation of energy were not necessarily *true*: they were only *convenient* (Poincaré, 1952). What this meant is that Poincaré believed that mathematical entities are not discovered so much as they are human creations, to be judged as much by their usefulness as their logical consistency.

It is entirely possible that Poincaré's response was intended more to shrug off a troublesome zealot than it was to encourage a fellow scientist. After all, quoting Poinsot to Poincaré would have been rather like quoting Francis Amansa Walker to Gerard Debreu. There is no evidence that Poincaré actually bothered to read the *Elements*; he restricted himself to the question raised in Walras' letter concerning the problem of measurability of "satisfaction." (Even the change in terminology may be significant.) He never addressed Walras' awkward citation of the inaccessibility of mass. Instead, he gave a little lecture on conventionalism, very similar to that found in his philosophical writings:

> I never meant that you had gone past "legitimate limits." Your definition of *rareté* seems to me to be legitimate. Here's how I would justify it. Can satisfaction be measured? I can say that one satisfaction is greater than another, because I prefer one to the other. But I cannot say that one satisfaction is twice or three times greater than another. That makes no sense *per se* and could acquire none except by arbitrary convention. Satisfaction is therefore a magnitude, but not a measurable one. Now, will a non-measurable magnitude be thus excluded from all mathematical speculation? Surely not. Temperature, for example, (at least until the advent of thermodynamics which gave meaning to the words) absolute temperature, was a non-measurable magnitude. It was measured arbitrarily by the expansion of mercury, rather than the expansion of any other body. Temperature could also have been just as legitimately defined by any function of the just-mentioned magnitude, provided that this function was monotonically increasing. In the same way you can define satisfaction....
>
> "In your premises there are going to be a certain number of arbitrary functions; but once these are posited, you have the right to draw inferences from them; if in these inferences these arbitrary functions still figure, the conclusions will not be false, but they will be devoid of all interest because they will be subordinated to arbitrary conventions made at the outset. You must therefore try to eliminate these arbitrary functions, and that is what you are doing." (our translation; Walras, 1965, v. III, letter 1496)

This resembles Poincaré's approach to energy in his *Science and Hypothesis*. One can posit the existence of energy, as long as the energy terms drop out of the final conclusions. Of course, the reason they do so is that energy reifies the conserved nature and path-independence of ideal mechanical phenomena; if it were otherwise, the results would have been "devoid of all interest," since they would be "subordinate to arbitrary conventions made at the outset." But this was precisely the nature of the objections of Bertrand and Laurent! If Poincaré had actually read the *Elements*, he would have undoubtedly recognized the attempt to draw analogies between potential energy and utility and would then very likely have agreed with the objections of his fellow scientists: but of course, this is merely counterfactual history. Unfortunately, this was all beyond Walras' ken. Instead, he believed that he had finally been granted the dispensation, perhaps even the imprimatur of a respected physical scient-

ist, and proceeded to trumpet that Poincaré was a supporter of his brand
of mathematical economics (Walras, 1965, v. II, letters 1505, 1511, 1514,
1532). The letter from Poincaré was obviously a turning point in Walras'
career: he reprinted it as a testimony to his *bona fides* as an appendix to
the article translated in this chapter (Walras, 1909, pp. 326–327); and
more importantly for our present concerns, it marked the debut in
Walras' published work of the idea that an isomorphism should be displayed between rational mechanics and the new economics as part and
parcel of a program of justification of neoclassical theory. This germ took
root in Walras' consciousness; and after a further sequence of errors,
confusions, and failures of communication finally appeared as his last
published paper, "Economics and Mechanics."

Economics and Mechanics

In a book that first appeared in 1905, the mathematician Charles Emile
Picard noted the analogy between a potential function in rational mechanics and the utility function of the Lausanne school (Picard, 1908,
pp. 45–46). Walras, always on the lookout for scientific allies, wrote
to Picard, hinting that respected mathematicians such as himself should
intervene to defend mathematical political economy (Walras, 1965, v. III,
letter 1636). The importance of this incident is that it coincides with
Walras' decision to elaborate upon the analogy in the paper that finally
became "Economics and Mechanics." For most of his life Walras had
been the unwitting conduit for the energy metaphor from Antoine Piccard, Hermann Amstein, and others to political economy; now various
scientists had recognized energy in its new context; and their exclama-
tions provoked Walras to attempt to explore *for the first time in his life*
the extent (if not actually the validity or rhetorical character) of the
mathematical analogy. The ironic circle thus became complete: Walras,
who never understood the social physics he was purveying as political
economy, now set out not to explore the advantages and drawbacks
of the metaphor of utility as potential energy, but instead rather to convince the world of its legitimacy and thus seek his own vindication by
drawing analogies with his outdated pre-energy understanding of rational
mechanics.

The first mention of the manuscript can be found in a letter of 1
December 1907 to Albert Aupetit, which he claims will diffuse "our

method" among mathematicians by comparing maximum satisfaction to the equilibrium of a "balance romaine" (which we have translated as "steelyard") and general equilibrium to universal gravitation (Walras, 1965, v. III, letter 1666). There followed a number of attempts by Albert Aupetit and Pasquale Boninsegni (who occupied the chair in economics at Lausanne after Pareto) to make sense of Walras' tortured and error-ridden version of rational mechanics (Walras, 1965, v. III, letters 1678, 1679, 1706, 1735, 1754). Hermann Amstein, who had earlier provided Walras with mathematical guidance, refused to make detailed comments on the manuscript (Walras, 1965, v. III, letter 1754). Apparently, Walras also consulted another engineer at Lausanne, one Professor Benjamin Mayor, but the letters and notes concerning this consultation were not included in *Correspondence and Related Papers* (Walras, 1965, v. III, p. 420).

All of this assistance was to no avail, for one very important reason: Walras never attained any analytic comprehension of the energy concept, much less the crucial formalism of a potential field. This fact was of critical importance to the history of economic thought: putting it bluntly, since Walras never understood energy, he never understood utility either. And given that he was making a botch of the single-most important mathematical concept in his entire system and misrepresenting the physics he so admired, how could he be credited in any sense with raising the "scientific" tenor of political economy?

Let us just briefly indicate how the text that follows garbles the physics and thus misrepresents the nature of the analogy between physics and neoclassical economics. In the first section of the paper, Walras wanted to draw an analogy between the equilibrium of a lever and equilibrium in exchange. As late as June 1909, and after all of the previous correspondence with Laurent, Boninsegni still was trying to explain to Walras that energy was an integral of forces times displacements (letter 1754). In order to reveal the analogy, one would have to derive the equilibrium of the lever from a gravitational potential; but Walras did not (and probably could not) do so. Instead he began by inscribing a hodgepodge of the static derivation from his copy of Poinsot and some mysterious integrals copied from Boninsegni's letter (1754). A more correct derivation would go as follows.

Let the following variables refer to a lever. Two masses, m_a and m_b are suspended from the ends of a lever, with m_a situated at distance a from the fulcrum, and m_b situated at distance b. Let the displacements from the horizontal be x_a and x_b, respectively. One begins by specifying the

energy equation for the system, where the kinetic energy is the motion of
the masses and the gravitational attraction is the potential energy:

$$E = (1/2)\, m_a \left(\frac{\partial x_a}{\partial t}\right)^2 + (1/2)\, m_b \left(\frac{\partial x_b}{\partial t}\right)^2 + g m_a x_a + g m_b x_b$$

In the case of the lever, the system is subject to the constraint that the
masses can only move through similar triangles, or that $x_b = -(b/a)x_a$.
Incorporating the constraint into the energy equation, we would then
write:

$$E = \frac{1}{2} \left(\frac{\partial x_a}{\partial t}\right)^2 \left(\frac{m_a a^2 + m_b b^2}{a^2}\right) + g x_a (m_a - m_b[b/a])$$

Having written the stated equation in terms of the conserved terms and
the constraints, we would then legitimately bring into play the extremum
principle, in this case the Lagrangean minimization:

$$\partial E/\partial x_a = (m_a - m_b[b/a])g = 0$$

or

$$m_a/m_b = b/a = -x_b/x_a$$

which expresses the law of the lever.

Compare this derivation with the one in Walras' "Economics and
Mechanics." In Walras' purported derivation there is no explicit postula-
tion of the energy terms, no explicit conservation principle, no independent specification of the constraints, and only a very indirect specification
of the extremum principle. Translate these terms into their economic
analogues, and one can see how much of the neoclassical economic
theory is left out: no understanding of the necessary restrictions upon the
utility function, no conception of the necessity that some combination of
utility and the budget must be conserved, no independent appreciation of
the constraints (among which should be the prohibition of negative
prices), and finally, no clear understanding of the role and significance of
the extremum principle. Upon meditation over these *lacunae*, one comes
to realize that Walras never understood his own metaphor, which sub-
sequently became neoclassical economics, with any dependable degree of
penetration. Hence talking to Walras about the relative plausibility,
measurability, or feasibility of utility was like talking to a brick wall.

Boninsegni, to his credit, tried to get through to Walras, especially in
his letter of 14 September 1908:

> In order to measure *rareté* it is necessary to study dynamic equilibrium, some-
> thing concerning which we now have only a vague idea. If a day comes when

we can find an entity resembling acceleration in mechanics, the problem which occupies you will be solved. You have found the fundamental equation of static equilibrium; we hope that one of your students will be able to find an equation similar to that of d'Alembert. (Walras, 1965, v. III, letter 1706)

But of course that day never came, in part because Walras never could be brought to appreciate the entire content of the supposed analogy, and in part because the neoclassical school has *never* settled upon any phenomenon to play the role of the true invariant in the constrained optimization formalizm. Hence the imitation of the physics was and is fundamentally flawed.

The second example in Walras' memoir, as if it were possible, is even more embarassing. He begins with the simple idea of the transitivity of relative prices in general equilibrium, only to wander off into a complete non sequitur concerning the reciprocal Newtonian attraction of bodies in celestial mechanics. As we have indicated above, Walras attempted a Newtonian attraction metaphor earlier in his career only to drop it due to its lack of sense; here we find him trying to revive some sort of analogy, even though it has nothing to do with the later neoclassical model of utility as a potential field. What is worse, he found that he could not even make the celestial mechanics turn out right, making numerous mistakes along the way (Walras, 1965, v. III, pp. 350–351). What the reader was supposed to learn about science from this sorry performance is anyone's guess.

He Blinded Us with His Science

The purpose of this chapter is to call into question the widespread conviction that somehow Walras took what had previously been a sloppy literary discourse about the economy and turned it into something clear, rigorous and *scientific*. Instead, he was a bit like the sort of religious zealot who loses himself in order to speak in tongues; in Walras' case, he was the voice for numerous engineers and physicists who might not themselves have advocated a literal social physics but were willing to help out with bits and bobs of mathematical metaphors for someone who was so willing. The fact that the result impressed some subsequent readers as a step in the scientific direction had little to do with the actual content of Walras' doctrines, and rather more to do with the mere fact of its impenetrable mathematical expression, or its evocation of the trappings of specific calculation and deterministic order. Why and how such a distorted image of "science" should eventually come to dominate half the practitioners of a discourse called "economics" is not our concern here. However, if "science" could so universally come to be associated with the name of Leon Walras, then something has definitely gone awry in the interim.

Translation of Leon Walras' "Economics and Mechanics" (1909)*

> *It seems to me that our science should be mathematical, for the simple reason that it deals with quantities.*

How apt is this remark made by Jevons in the passage entitled *"Mathematical character of science,"* appearing in chapter one of his *Theory of Political Economy*. As soon as a science is applied to things with a capacity for being *more* or *less*, then their interrelationships and their laws are of a mathematical nature. The commonplace laws of supply and demand deal entirely with quantities of merchandise supplied or demanded and express the way in which these quantities vary with prices. As a direct consequence, these laws *are* mathematical. It would be impossible for economists to change the nature of these laws by denying their name; they might just as well try to change red light by calling it blue. That the mathematical laws of economics are formulated in words or by using the usual symbols x, y, z, p, q, etc. is an accident and a question purely of convention. Were we to disregard to cumbersome verbosity, we could tackle the most complicated mathematical problems in ordinary language and prosecute and articulate their solution.

This paragraph of Jevons' is followed by three others entitled respectively: *"Confusion between the mathematical sciences and the exact sciences"*; *"Possibility of an exact measure"*; *"Measure of sentiments and motives,"* which are also very relevant. However, instead of these, I should like to offer the following brief consideration.

Mathematical facts must be placed in two distinct categories.

There are those which are *exterior* and take place in Nature's theatre, where we play no active role. Consequently they appear to everyone, and to everyone in the same way; in addition, for each one of these facts there is a collective and objective *unity*, that is, a magnitude, which is the same

---

* This translation was prepared with the help of a grant from the National Endowment for the Humanities.

for all and which serves as a measure. We shall call these *physical* facts and they will be the objects of *physico-mathematical* sciences.

The other facts are *interior* and take place within us, where our sensibility is their theatre. As a result they do not appear to others as they appear to us and if each of us is able to compare them one to another in terms of magnitude or of intensity, and consider them greater or more intense than each other, in a word to *appreciate* them, then this appreciation remains subjective and individual. We shall call these *psychic* facts and they will be the objects of the *psycho-mathematical* sciences.

Mechanics and *astronomy* belong to the first category; *economics* belongs to the second; probably the first of its kind and unlikely to be the last.

Having established this, it seems that we may now proceed.

Social wealth is the collection of things which are *useful* and at the same time *limited in quantity* and which are for this reason (1) *adaptable*, (2) *valuable and exchangeable*, (3) *industrially producible*. Of these three activities or conditions, the second is incontestably mathematically scientific. This is so, whether it be the value of exchange or the characteristic contained in those things constituting the social wealth which enables them to be exchanged in certain quantifiably determined proportions. Pure economics, of which this is the object, is a mathematical science. However, aside from indicating its object or nature, the theory of general activity encompasses the research into its cause or origin, the enumeration of its species, the enunciation of its laws, and the indication of its consequences. When economics wishes to accomplish its task by stating the cause of exchange value and claiming to discover it by means of the mathematical method, in the *rareté* or the *intensity of the last need satisfied*, non-mathematical economists protest and even mathematicians refuse to accept "that a satisfaction may be measured."[1]

It would be a waste of time to argue with the former group: we simply do not speak the same language. But with mathematicians it is different: we can explain ourselves and perhaps understand each other.

The need which we have for things, or their *utility* for us, is an internal quantitive fact, appreciation of which remains subjective and individual. so be it! Nonetheless it is a magnitude and it is even estimable. Of two useful things which I need and which I could not obtain freely and unconditionally, I know full well which is more useful to me or which I need more. It is simply the one I prefer.[2] It is not a question of whether or not my preference is morally justified or even in my own interests. *Morality* is a separate science and there could be yet another, that of felicity or *hedonism*, which would teach us how to be happy; but there is no question of that in this case. We are dealing here with the determination of prices in perfect competition and which depend upon our preferences, justified or unjustified. This question alone is the object of *pure economics*. Pure economics will not be a *physico-mathematical* science, but one of a *psycho-mathematical* nature. By means of two conclusive examples it seems to me easy to make mathematicians see that its procedure is rigorously identical to that of two of the most advanced and uncontested physico-mathematical sciences, *rational mechanics* and *celestial mechanics*. When we have agreed upon this point, then let the mathematicians judge.

II

Let (A) and (B) be two commodities on the market.

$$u_a = \Phi_a(q_a)$$
$$u_b = \Phi_b(q_b)$$

are the *utility* functions of a trader for these commodities and do not increase proportionally to the *quantity consumed*.

$$r_a = \frac{d\Phi_a(q_a)}{dq_a} = \Phi'_a(q_a), \, r_b = \frac{d\Phi_b(q_b)}{dq_b} = \Phi'_b(q_b)$$

Let r_a and r_b be the equations of *rareté* (*intensity of last need satisfied*), decreasing with the quantity consumed. We can posit the equation of utility maximisation as

$$\frac{d\Phi_a(q_a)}{dq_a} \cdot dq_a + \frac{d\Phi_b(q_b)}{dq_b} \cdot dq_b = 0,$$

or the equation of demand or supply

$$r_a \cdot dq_a + r_b \cdot dq_b = 0 \tag{1}$$

as the fundamental differential equation of pure economics.

Moreover, the commodities (A) and (B) have supposedly been exchanged according to their respective values v_a and v_b. Thus we have the *exchange* equation

$$v_a \cdot dq_a + v_b \cdot dq_b = 0 \tag{2}$$

and, by an easy elimination of the two differentials, we have

$$(r_b/r_a) = (v_b/v_a).$$

Therefore, *maximum satisfaction occurs where raretés are proportional to values*.

Let us now look at how rational mechanics is structured. Let us first note, as does Cournot,[3] that if one takes for measure of force, not the *vis mortua* of Newton and all the French geometricians of the XVIIIth century, including Lagrange, but the *vis viva* of Leibnitz, that is, force multiplied by its *momentum*, (vitesse), the fundamental differential equation of rational mechanics

$$P \cdot \frac{dp}{dt} + Q \cdot \frac{dp}{dt} = 0$$

will appear, not simply as an assumption but as the natural and necessary expression of equality at a given moment of two momenta acting upon each other in perfect balance. Therefore given a machine such as the steelyard, in which, by virtue of the connections of the system

$$\varepsilon_p = \Phi(p) = \int_0^p \Phi'(p) \, dp, \, \varepsilon_q = \Phi(q) = \int_0^q \Phi'(q) \, dq$$

there may be, at the ends of the two arms of the lever, the equations of *energy*, increasing proportionally with the *distances* p and q

$$P = \frac{d\Phi(p)}{dp} = \Phi'(p), \quad Q = \frac{d\Phi(q)}{dq} = \Phi'(q)$$

which are the equations of *force*, or of *limited energy*, constant with the same distances, rational mechanics can posit the equation of maximum energy

$$\frac{d\Phi(p)}{dp} \cdot dp + \frac{d\Phi(q)}{dq} \cdot dq = 0,$$

or the equation of equilibrium

$$P \cdot dp + Q \cdot dq = 0 \qquad [1]$$

resulting in its fundamental differential equation.

If one supposes the arms of the lever to have the same respective lengths p and q, the following equation is easily obtained

$$p \cdot dq + q \cdot dp = 0 \qquad [2]$$

and upon elimination of the differentials gives

$$(P/Q) = (q/p).$$

That is, that: *the equilibrium of the steelyard is achieved by the inverse proportionality of the forces on the arms of the lever.* The analogy is obvious. In addition we have already pointed out that the *forces* or *raretés* are *vectors* on the one hand, and *energies* and *utilities* are *scalar quantities* on the other.[4]

III

The same analogy exists between economics and celestial mechanics.

In economics we show that: *the general equilibrium of the market is achieved only if the price of any two commodities is equal to any third following the formula*

$$P_{c,b} = \frac{v_c}{v_b} = \frac{P_{c,a}}{P_{b,a}} = \frac{v_c/v_a}{v_b/v_a},$$

This is sometimes explained by saying that each of the commodities (A), (B), (C) ... has only one value. On the other hand, we can demonstrate that the prices of all the commodities (B), (C), (D) ... have been expressed in terms of one, (A), taken as numéraire: *When the market is in a state of general equilibrium, the ratio of the raretés of any two commodities, equal to their relative prices, is the same for all possessors of these two commodities* according to the equations

$$P_b = \frac{r_{b,1}}{r_{a,1}} = \frac{r_{b,2}}{r_{a,2}} = \frac{r_{b,3}}{r_{a,3}} = \ldots$$

$$P_c = \frac{r_{c,1}}{r_{a,1}} = \frac{r_{c,2}}{r_{a,2}} = \frac{r_{c,3}}{r_{a,3}} = \ldots$$

$$P_d = \frac{r_{d,1}}{r_{a,1}} = \frac{r_{d,2}}{r_{a,2}} = \frac{r_{d,3}}{r_{a,3}} = \ldots$$

which can also be indicated in this way

$$
\begin{array}{l}
v_a \;:\; v_b \;:\; v_c \;:\; v_d \;:\; \ldots \\
::\; r_{a,1} : r_{b,1} : r_{c,1} : r_{d,1} : \ldots \\
::\; r_{a,2} : r_{b,2} : r_{c,2} : r_{d,2} : \ldots \\
::\; r_{a,3} : r_{b,3} : r_{c,3} : r_{d,3} : \ldots \\
::\; \cdot \quad \cdot \quad \cdot \quad \cdot \quad \cdot \quad \cdot
\end{array}
$$

which says that: *In the state of general equilibrium values are proportional to raretés.*

Finally, let n, p ... being quantities of (B), (C) ... to be exchanged for a quantity m of (A), we can posit the equations:

$$m v_a = n v_b = p v_c = \ldots$$

or, taking v_a for the unit of value, the equations

$$m = n p_b = p \, p_c = \ldots$$

indicating the virtual state of the market from the point of view of *exchange*.

In astronomy it is claimed that: *three given celestial bodies* (T), (L), (S), *gravitate towards each other with uniform acceleration* analogous to free-fall according to the law of gravity,

$$e = (gt^2/2)$$

knowing that (T) and (L) follow the equations which generate

$$(\gamma_L/\gamma_T) = (e_L/e_T)$$

(T) and (S) follow the equations which generate

$$(\gamma_S/\gamma_T) = (e_S/e_T)$$

(L) and (S) follow the equations giving

$$(\gamma_S/\gamma_L) = (e_S/e_L)$$

with the complementary condition:[5]

$$\frac{\gamma_S}{\gamma_L} = \frac{\gamma_S/\gamma_T}{\gamma_L/\gamma_T}$$

which allows us to bring into play *masses* inversely proportional to the *acceleration* according to the equations:

$$\gamma_T m_T = \gamma_L m_L = \gamma_S m_S = \ldots$$

to say, that each of the celestial bodies (T), (L), (S) ... has only one mass in relation to all the others and, finally, taking m_T for the unit of mass, to posit the equations:

$$\gamma_T = \gamma_L \mu_L = \gamma_S \mu_S = \ldots$$

indicating the virtual state of the world from the point of view of *gravitation*.

I refer to my work in what follows, but I cannot resist commenting upon the treatment of celestial mechanics. Letting k be a constant, and introducing the essential condition of *inverse attraction proportional to the square of the distances*, let us posit for any two bodies, for example, (T) and (L), the formula of mutual attraction.[6]

$$a_T = a_L = k m_T m_L / d_{T,L}{}^2,$$

We shall be able to state that *celestial bodies are attracted to each other in direct proportion to the masses and in inverse ratio to the square of the distances*, which is the Newtonian law of universal attraction.

The numerical determination of the general constant k is particularly decisive from the point of view of the value of the mathematical method in the sciences of action and quantitative relations, and is, and rightly so, well known in the history of science. The numerical determination is formed in the following way. Let us also posit the *acceleration* of a celestial body as equal to the *force of attraction* which acts upon it, divided by the *mass*, respectively for both the earth and the moon:

$$\gamma_T = (a_L/m_T) = (km_L m_T/m_T) = km_L$$
$$\gamma_L = (a_T/m_L) = (km_T m_L/m_L) = km_T$$

a double equation which formulates the law of the *equality of action and reaction* and that of the *absolute proportionality of the acceleration of the body attracted to the mass of the attracting body.*

Having accomplished this, let us take the mass of the earth m_T, for the unit of mass, the radius of the earth r, for the unit of distance; and let us suppose the masses of the earth and the moon to be concentrated at their centers. The observation is that, at the distance of $60'3$, the moon tends to fall towards the earth at a rate of $0'''00136$ per second; in other words, its acceleration is $0'''00272$. At a distance of 1^r, this acceleration would be $60.3^2 = 3626$ times stronger, or $9'''8$.

Thus it may be demonstrated that the general coefficient k is nothing other than the g of the physicists, that the coefficient of free-fall is that of universal gravitation, and modern astronomy is established.

IV

Let us now examine as attentively as possible the four theories outlined above: the theory of the maximum satisfaction of the trader and that of the maximum energy of the steelyard, the theory of the general equilibrium of the market and that of the universal equilibrium of celestial bodies. Between the two mechanical theories on the one hand and the two economic theories on the other, we shall find this one difference: due to the existence of common measures for these *physical* conditions, that is, the character of *objective appearance* of the two mechanical phenomena and the unperceived *internal* character of the two economic phenomena, it is possible to witness the conditions of equilibrium of the steelyard and those of the sky. Lacking common measures for *psychic* conditions, it is impossible to reveal all the conditions of equilibrium of exchange and those of the general equilibrium of the market. There are meters and centimeters to establish the length of the arms of the steelyard, grams and kilograms to ascertain the weight supported by these arms; there are instruments to determine the motion of stars. There are none by which to measure the intensities of needs of traders. But it is of no importance, since each trader takes upon himself this operation, consciously or unconsciously, and decides for himself if these last needs satisfied are proportional to the values of the commodities. *Measure*, that is, the comparison of *quantities* and *quantitative relations*, is not prevented by its exterior or interior quality, according to whether the measurable facts are physical or psychic. Consequently neither is science denied its *mathematical* character.

That is not all; and since I have ventured on to this terrain, I shall allow myself to draw the attention of those mathematicians who are detractors, to the seriousness of the problem of the measure of physico-mathematical quantities such as *force, energy, attraction, mass*, etc. A short time ago learned mathematicians did not hesitate to define the mass of a body as "the number of molecules" or the "quantity of matter" therein contained.[7] Perhaps some time from now we shall be able to teach the theory of universal gravitation to young people; allowing them to represent all molecules, in number m, of a celestial body as being linked to all the molecules, in number m', of another by a force of intensity k in inverse ratio to the square of the distance d, there results for the two bodies a reciprocal attraction kmm'/d^2. However, we are not there yet! After quoting and then criticising the essays on the definition of *mass* by Newton, and of Thomson and Tait, of *force* by Lagrange and Kirchhoff, one of the masters of modern science concluded that: *masses are the coefficients which are conveniently introduced into the calculations.*[8] Fine! This candor encourages one to enquire as to whether all these concepts, those of *mass* and *force* as well as those of *utility* and *rareté* might not simply be names given to hypothetical causes. It would be essential and valid for the hypothetical causes to be incorporated in the calculations with a view to linking them to their effects, if we wish to elaborate the physico- or psycho-mathematical sciences with precision and conciseness and in a strict and clear mathematical language. Thus the *forces* would be the causes of the *traverse of space, masses* the causes of the *time elapsed* during the traverse, resulting in the *speed* of *movement* of physical causes more constant but more hidden; the *utilities* and the *raretés* would be the causes of *supply* and *demand*, from which would result the *value* of *exchange* of more visible but more variable psychic causes. Mathematics would be the special language for discussing quantitative facts and it should go without saying that economics is a mathematical science on a par with mechanics and astronomy.

Footnotes to translation

[1] H. Laurent. July, 1900. *Bulletin of the Institute of French Actuaries*. P. 84.

[2] Poincaré, in his letter of 1901. The body of this letter is translated in our commentary — P.C. & P.M.

[3] *Materialism, Vitalism, Rationalism*. 1875. Pp. 16, 17, and 18.

[4] Irving Fisher. 1892. *Mathematical Investigations in the Theory of Value and Prices*. P. 85.

[5] See Emile Picard. *Modern Science and its Actual State*. P. 106. The author is in favor of the application of mathematics to political economy; see pp. 45 and 46.

[6] See H. Poincaré. *Science and Hypothesis*. P. 124.

[7] Poinsot. *Statics*. Eighth edition. P. 178.

[8] H. Poincaré. *Science and Hypothesis*. Pp. 119–127. M. Poincaré does not prohibit our estimation of utility. He says (*The Value of Science*, p. 145) that Maxwell was accustomed to "thinking in vectors." Well! We are becoming accustomed to "thinking in raretés," which are precisely vectors.

Notes to Chapter

[1] One defense of the Walrasian program that is an exception in that it displays an awareness of some of the problems is Weintraub (1985). The myriad problems of the neo-Walrasian appeal to scientific legitimacy are surveyed in Mirowski (1987 and forthcoming). For a rhetorical analysis of the problem of scientific metaphor, see Menard (forthcoming).

[2] Such attempts to assimilate McCloskey's rhetoric to conventional "methodology" are already growing a little tedious. See, for instance, the symposium in the April 1988 issue of *Economics and Philosophy*.

[3] Unfortunately, only Pareto's side of this correspondence has survived; it has been published in Chipman (1976, pp. 45–62).

References

Bertrand, Joseph. 1883. "Compte Rendu." *Journal des Savants* (**):499–508.

Black, R.D.C.; Coats, A.R.; and Goodwin, C., eds. 1973. *The Marginal Revolution in Economics*. Durham: Duke University Press.

Boninsegni, P. 1903. "Un Nuovo Tratto D'Economia Mathematica." *Giornali degli Economisti* 30:327–336.

Bouvier, Emile. 1901a. "L'Economie Politique Mathématique." *Revue Critique de Legislation et de Jurisprudence* 30:623–629.

Bouvier, Emile. 1901b. "La Méthode Mathématique en Economie Politique." *Revue D'Economie Politique* 15:817–850.

Debreu, Gerard. 1984. "Economics in a Mathematical Mode." *American Economic Review* 74:267–278.

Etner, F. 1986. "L'Enseignement Economique dans les Grandes Ecoles." *Economies et Sociétés* 20:159–173.

Giedymin, Jerzy. 1982. *Science and Convention*. Elmsford, NY: Pergamon Press.
Jaffe, William. 1983. Donald Walker, ed. *Essays on Walras*. New York: Cambridge University Press.
Laurent, Hermann. 1870. *Traité de Mécanique Rationelle*. Paris: Gauther-Villars.
Laurent, Hermann. 1902. *Petit Traité d'Economie Politique Mathématique*. Paris: Schmid.
Markus, Gyorgy. 1987. "Why is There No Hermeneutics of Natural Science?" *Science in Context* 1:5–54.
McCloskey, Donald. 1985. *The Rhetoric of Economics*. Madison: University of Wisconsin Press.
Menard, Claude. Forthcoming 1988. "The Machine and the Heart." *Social Concept*.
Mirowski, Philip. 1984. "Physics and the Marginalist Revolution." *Cambridge Journal of Economics* 8:361–379.
Mirowski, Philip. 1987. "Shall I Compare Thee to a Minkowski-Ricardo-Leontief-Metzler Matrix of the Mosak-Hicks Type?" *Economics and Philosophy* 3:67–95.
Mirowski, Philip. 1988. *Against Mechanism*. Totawa, N.J.: Rowman & Littlefield.
Mirowski, Philip. Forthcoming. *More Heat Than Light*. New York: Cambridge University Press.
Picard, Charles. 1908. *La Science Moderne et son état actuel*. Paris: Flammarion.
Poincaré, Henri. 1952. *Science and Hypothesis*. New York: Dover.
Poinsot, Louis. 1842. *Eléments de Statique*. Eighth edition. Paris: Bachelier.
Schumpeter, Joseph. 1954. *A History of Economic Analysis*. New York: Oxford University Press.
Walker, Donald. 1987. "Walras' Theories of Tâtonnement." *Journal of Political Economy* 95:758–774.
Walras, Leon. 1909. "Economique et Mécanique." *Bulletin de la Société Vaudoise de Sciences Naturelles* 45:313–325.
Walras, Leon. 1965. William Jaffe, ed. *Correspondence and Papers*. 3 vols. Amsterdam: North Holland.
Walras, Leon. 1969. *Elements of Pure Economics*. Translated by William Jaffe. New York: Kelley.
Weintraub, E.R. 1985. *General Equilibrium Analysis*. New York: Cambridge University Press.
Zoretti, Ludovic. 1906. "La Méthode Mathématique et les Sciences Sociales." *Revue du Mois* 2:355–365.

COMMENT BY NANCY WULWICK

Philip Mirowski and Pamela Cook forcefully argue in this chapter that the Walrasian theory of demand originated as a metaphor that was drawn from nineteenth century energy physics, an origin that Mirowski and Cook see as having stymied the development of microeconomics.[1] A full understanding of their chapter requires familiarity with themes in the philosophy and history of science. My *Comment* is intended to provide some of the background material. It begins by defining the concept of scientific metaphor, surveys the context in which Walras broached the energy metaphor, and finally considers the influence of the metaphor on economics.

Scientific Metaphors

A metaphor presents an underlying analogy between one thing and another. The study of metaphor in its aesthetic aspects typically belongs to rhetoric or poetics. In contrast, the modern philosophy of science has been concerned mainly with the cognitive aspects of metaphor.[2] There are two main types of metaphor, involving a physical or a formal analogy, respectively. Physical metaphors link the attributes of an object under study with those of a known object. Most scientific metaphors set up a relational or a formal comparison between two systems. The Rutherford-Bohr model is a well-known example.[3]

Rutherford and Bohr compared a solar system with one planet that revolved around a more massive sun to a hydrogen atom with an electron that revolved around a more massive nucleus. The planet of mass m_p and the sun of mass m_s were separated by some distance d. According to Newtonian physics, the gravitational force exerted between the two bodies was

$$F_{grav} = Gm_pm_s/d^2 = m_pa_p = m_sa_s, \qquad [1]$$

where G was the gravitational constant and a the radial acceleration. The analogous relation in respect to the atom was

$$F_{elec} = -q_eq_n/d^2 = m_ea_e = m_na_n \qquad [2]$$

where F_{elec} was the electromagnetic force, -1 the electromagnetic constant, and q_e the charge on the electron. Equations 1 and 2 showed the solar and the atomic system to be isomorphic.

Scientific metaphors like the Rutherford-Bohr model are part and parcel of the process of scientific discovery. Their purpose is to suggest theoretical claims when no literal statement is available. Effective metaphors involve a shared language (everybody knew the Newtonian law of gravity). Metaphors transfer terminology from the familiar to the unfamiliar domain (the solar and the atomic system were in "dynamic equilibrium"). They require an exploration of both positive and negative analogies (the Rutherford-Bohr model missed the jumps of electrons between orbits). The viability of metaphors is subject to testing (the model could not predict energy emission). The explication of metaphors inspires problem-shifts (the solar system metaphor prompted Bohr to break with Maxwell's theory of electromagnetism).[4] Some metaphors fail, but those that are deployable are theory-constitutive.[5]

Metaphors and the Unity of Science

Nineteenth Century Views on Metaphor

Physics did not develop into a professional discipline until the nineteenth century. Even the name *physics* did not come into currency until the mid-1800s. This was a time when energy physics was encompassing a growing number of theories — optics, light, magnetism, electricity, etc.[6] In this context, philosophers of science proposed the unification of all sciences, both natural and social. Physics was to serve as the prototype and mathematics to provide the analytical tools. Metaphors, or analogies (as they were usually called), served as a method by which scientists generalized the principles of physics.[7] As Walras' predecessor, W.S. Jevons (1835–1882) insisted,

> (w)hoever wishes to acquire a deep acquaintance with Nature must observe that there are analogies which connect whole branches of science in a parallel manner, and enable us to infer of one class of phenomena what we know of another.[8]

Though the mid-nineteenth century investigators recognized the importance of metaphors as a scientific method, they differed over the appropriate role of metaphors. Three doctrines emerged, of the mechanico-molecular, the analytic, and the British schools, respectively.[9] The mechanico-molecular school was led by LaPlace (1749–1827), Poisson (1781–1840), and other famous French physicists, and was based on Newtonian methods and theories. The molecularists a priori assumed matter to be governed by a molecular attraction analogous to Newtonian gravitation, and deduced testable consequences from this analogy. Furthermore, they believed that successful tests served to confirm their a priori assumptions, a belief that the British school would challenge. The analytic school, led by the early positivist Fourier (1768–1830) and inspired by rational mechanics, derived empirical laws from primary facts, which themselves were based on common observation and confirmed by experiment. The empirical laws of the various domains were stated in terms of calculus, the progress of science being marked by the accumulation of isomorphic laws. The British school, led by Maxwell (1831–1879), the founder of electromagnetics, was based on engineering methods and theories. Uncommitted to a definite theory, Maxwell carried out physical experiments in order to develop a dynamic theory, which was stated in mathematical form. In the case of physically elusive phenomenon such as the electromagnetic field, Maxwell resorted to mechanical and mathematical analogies as heuristic devices. This use of metaphor carried over into twentieth-century modern science.

Jevons, in his work on scientific method, espoused the dictates of the British school. He remarked that scientific discoveries most often resulted from testing analogies. Himself trained and experienced in applied chemistry, he portrayed the chemistry as follows:[10]

> Having discovered what he believes to be a new element, he will have before him an infinite variety of modes of . . . investigating it. If in any of its qualities the substance displays a resemblance to an alkaline metal . . . he will naturally proceed to try whether it possesses other properties of the alkaline metals. Even the simplist phenomenon presents so many points for notice that we have a choice from among many hypotheses.[11]

The task of the scientist, he concluded, was to test which of the hypothesized analogies worked.[12]

As an economist, however, Jevons adopted the hypothetico-deductive method of the molecularists. On a priori grounds he assumed economics to work on mechanical principles and proposed to test the consequences of the analogy.

Jevon's Mechanical Analogy

For economics to qualify as a science, Jevons believed that economic statements must be stated in mathematical form. Meanwhile, mathematicians were objecting that the mathematics in his first edition of *The Theory of Political Economy* (1871) was inadequate. In particular, they

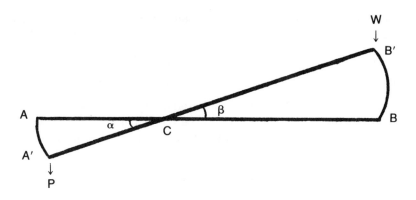

Figure 1. The Mechanical Lever

were puzzled why Jevons neglected to integrate the differential equations for utility to get total utility, which was the entity to be maximized.[13] In his second edition (1879), he responded as follows:

> The whole question is one of maxima and minima, the mathematical conditions of which are familiar to mathematicians. But, even if I were capable of presenting the subject in the concise symbolic style satisfactory to the taste of a practised mathematician, I should prefer ... to attain my results by a course of argument which is ... clear and convincing to many readers who, like myself, are not skillful and professional mathematicians.[14]

To convince readers and critics that economics was scientific, he would show that economics was like physics, in particular, rational mechanics.

Jevons drew an analogy between the workings of the mechanical lever and economic exchange.[15] As figure 7–1 shows, the lever consisted of a straight bar, BA, supported by a fulcrum, C, which divided the length of the bar into two arms, AC and BC. Two weights, P and W, appeared at each end of the bar, which displaced the lever from the horizontal, AB, along the arcs, AA′ and BB′.[16] The problem was to explain the movement of the lever caused by the forces bearing on it. The solution, known since Archimedes of Syracuse (287–212 BCE), could be derived in several ways, including by means of basic trigonometry.[17]

Mirowski shows how to derive the solution from the physics of energy. This contained two principles — of energy conservation and least action. According to the principle of energy conservation, every joule of work applied to a body could be accounted for by changes in kinetic energy (E_k, the work done by motion), potential energy (E_p, the work involving gravity) and work against friction. Assuming the frictional force in the fulcrum to be negligible, the equation of total energy E was

$$E = \underbrace{\int P \, d(AA') + \int W \, d(BB')} + \underbrace{gP(AA') + gW(BB')} \qquad [3]$$
$$\qquad\qquad\qquad E_k \qquad\qquad\qquad\qquad\qquad E_p$$

where $d(AA')$ and $d(BB')$ were infinitesimal displacements and g was the acceleration of gravity. Using Lagrange's technique — given the constraint that for small angles, the weights moved through similar triangles, so that

$$AC/BC = AA'/BB' \qquad [4]$$

— the potential was minimized when

$$W/P = AA'/BB', \qquad [5]$$

that is, the relation between the two weights was inversely proportional to the displacements from the horizontal.[18]

Jevons said that he intended to give the law of the lever (equation 5) according to "*law of energy*".[19] He extracted the picture and the description of the lever from a textbook that covered energy conservation (Magnus, 1876).[20] Yet, for his actual analysis of the workings of the lever, Jevons referred to an authority that predated the energy conservation theory, Poisson's treatise on mechanics (1833). This analysis appeared in terms of the principle of "virtual velocities," or the balance of mechanical forces, which said that the sum of the products of the respective weights and infinitesimal displacements were equal. As the notion of virtual velocities pertained to the finite movements of the lever, Jevons analyzed the position of the lever *after* movement ceased and thus avoided the integration that the mathematicians asked him to do, for "there (was) no effect to be summed up".[21]

Jevons mapped the *static* equilibrium relations of the lever onto economic exchange,

$$W/P = AA'/BB' = AC/BC$$
$$\phi(x)/\tau(y) = dy/dx = y/x. \qquad [6]$$

The marginal utilities $\phi(x)$, $\tau(y)$ corresponded to forces and the marginal rate of substitution between the goods x and y corresponded to the displacements of the lever. Assuming that consumers were rational, the marginal utilities, which were unobservable, were revealed by relative prices,

$$\phi(x)/\tau(y) = p_x/p_y. \qquad [7]$$

Then, according to Jevons, evidence that p_x/p_y was inversely proportional to dy/dx would confirm the theory of utility maximization. The whole argument, by his own admission, was circular.[22] And it did not lend any support to an analogy between energy and utility, if that was his intention.

Mirowski and Cook show that Walras, who was familiar with Jevon's work, used the lever analogy as a means to defend his general theory of exchange against the criticisms of mathematicians and physicists. Walras interpreted the workings of the lever in terms of kinetic energy ("vis viva"), which he wrongly defined.[23] As Mirowski exposes, he did not seem to understand all that much more than Jevons about the constrained extremum problem implicit in energy physics.[24]

The Legacy of the Energy Metaphor

The Formal Proofs

The production and explication of metaphors occurs simultaneously in the natural sciences. In contrast, economists took their time in demonstrating the implications of what the early marginalists understood by the energy metaphor. Economists really began to come to grips with the problem of maximization in a general equilibrium system only in the 1930s. Cassel's (1932) Walrasian textbook, the promotion of mathematical economics at the Cowles Commission, and Hicks's (1939) response to the Keynes' general model together triggered a concerted research effort. By the time of Samuelson's (1947) *Foundations*, the Lagrangian technique received an economic interpretation, appropriate to the maximization of a trader's utility subject to income. With the help of modern mathematical techniques, Samuelson along with Arrow, Debreu, Hahn, and others demonstrated the existence, uniqueness, and stability of the general equilibrium system.[25]

Not all the participants in that research effort would disagree with the gist of Mirowski and Cook's criticisms of its outcome.[26] It was unclear what was to be conserved.[27] The demonstration of the existence of a utility function given a demand curve was fraught with difficulties.[28] The treatment of time was unconvincing.[29] Once money and uncertainty were admitted, it was possible that exchange would not increase utility.[30] The assumptions of the tatonnement system without false trading were far too restrictive to have any reference to real phenomena.[31]

It was partly in response to this shortcoming that economists adopted the Phillips curve, which showed how wages changed in labor markets with false trading.[32] Here too a mechanical device (Phillips's (1950) hydraulic model) suggested an economic assumption. Phillips's attempts to empirically confirm and explain the positive analogy (that prices were flexible) and the negative analogy (that flexibility was asymmetric) of this metaphor changed the direction of economic research, but that is another story.[33]

Conclusion: The Unsolved Problem

Mirowski and Cook show that the theory of Walrasian general equilibrium originated by way of a metaphor of mid-nineteenth century energy physics, which was based on the tenet that energy was conserved through time. Yet paradoxically, the general equilibrium model contains no definite analogue to energy conservation.

It is not entirely clear why this lacuna should matter, given the optimizing framework of the static orthodox model. There are three points to be made here:

1. The Lagrange technique used to solve maximization problems in modern economics was developed in the late 1800s, well before the energy revolution.
2. While the presence in economics of the formalisms associated with nineteenth-century energy physics is indisputable, there is no logical reason why energy conservation must have an analogue in economics. In a purely mathematical sense, conservation is not necessary for optimization.
3. It is uncertain what impact the explicit importation of a conservation principle would have on the internal coherence of orthodox utility theory.[34]

Be that as it may, the authors' criticism of orthodox economics remains telling. The static general equilibrium model enabled Walras to avoid the conceptual conundrums he encountered upon his adoption of the formal energy metaphor. Although modern economists explained what economizing entailed in this static model, they neglected ex ante to argue that the conservative system as conveyed by Walras's formulations was actually analogous to the economic system. And this, in the context of scientific method, was the crucial issue.

The Mirowski-Cook chapter also tells us something about the importance of discourse analysis. The study of metaphors by economic methodologists no longer can appear to be the outlandish endeavor some members of the economics profession have made it out to be. Clearly, the role of metaphors in scientific discovery has been a standard concern of philosophers of science.

Notes

[1] Philip Mirowski is an economist with a training in the history of science. Pamela Cook's field is French literature.

[2] Beardsley (1969), p. 284.

[3] Gentner (1983), p. 163.

[4] Lakatos (1970), pp. 146–149; Cohen (1985), pp. 427–430.

[5] Hesse (1966); Boyd (1979).

[6] Mirowski (1984a), p. 365.

[7] Hesse (1974), p. 222.

[8] Jevons (1877), p. 631.

[9] Kargon (1969), pp. 424–436.

[10] Black (1972), p. 369.

[11] Jevons (1877), p. 630.

[12] Jevons (1877), p. 641.

[13] Letter from Jevons to G.H. Darwin, 29 November 1874, in Black (1977b), p. 87; Jevons (1879), p. 102.

[14] Jevons (1879), pp. xiii.

[15] Mirowski (1984), p. 363; Jevons (1879) pp. 102–106.

[16] Jevons, p. 106.

[17] Holton and Roller (1958), pp. 314–315.

[18] Mirowski and Cook (1989), pp. 25–26. Their expression for kinetic energy solves for the integral.

[19] Jevons (1879), p. 103, emphasis added.

[20] Pp. 131–132.

[21] Jevons (1879), p. 106.

[22] Jevons (1879), p. 190; Letters from Jevons to J.E. Cairnes, 14 January 1872, in Jevons (1977a), p. 246.

[23] Walras (1989/1905) defined kinetic energy as force times momentum (p. 5).

[24] Mirowski (1989), pp. 25–26. Black (1972) noted that Picard rewrote Walras's equations in light of contemporary mechanics (p. 290).

[25] Weintraub (1980), pp. 19–37.

[26] Mirowski and Cook (1989), pp. 26–27.

[27] Samuelson, quoted in Mirowski (1984b), p. 471.

[28] Samuelson (1950).

[29] Debreu in Feiwel (1987), p. 253.

[30] Hahn (1984), p. 91.

[31] Hahn (1984), p. 85; Aumann on Arrow, in Fiewel (1987), p. 308.

[32] Weintraub (1980), p. 116.

[33] Wulwick, forthcoming.

[34] For Mirowski's argument that the conservation principle renders the orthodox theory of production incoherent, see his *More Heat Than Light*.

References

Beardsley, Monroe C. 1969. "Metaphor." In Paul Edwards, ed. *The Encyclopedia of Philosophy*. New York: Collier-Macmillan, pp. 284–289.

Black, R.D. Collison. 1972. "W.S. Jevons and the Foundation of Modern Economics." *History of Political Economy* 4:364–378.

Boyd, Richard. 1979. "Metaphor and Theory Change: What is 'Metaphor' a Metaphor For?" In Andrew Ortony, ed. *Metaphor and Thought*. New York: Cambridge University Press, pp. 356–407.

Cohen, J. Bernard. 1985. *Revolution in Science*. Cambridge, Mass.: Belknap.

Feiwel, George R. 1987. *Arrow and the Ascent of Modern Economic Theory*. New York: New York University Press.

Gentner, Dedre. 1983. "Structure Mapping: A Theoretical Framework for Analogy." *Cognitive Science* 7:155–170.

Hahn, Frank. 1984. *Equilibrium and Macroeconomics*. Oxford: Basil Blackwell.

Hesse, Mary B. 1966. *Modern and Analogies in Science*. Notre Dame, Ind: University of Notre Dame.

———. 1974. *The Structure of Scientific Inference*. Berkeley: University of California Press.

Holton, Gerald and Roller, Duane. 1958. *Foundations of Modern Physical Science*. Reading, Mass.: Addison-Wesley.

Jevons, W.S. 1920/1877. *The Principles of Science*. London: Macmillan.

———. 1879/1965. *The Theory of Political Economy*. New York: Kelley.

———. 1977a. R.D. Collison Black, ed. *Papers and Correspondence of William Stanley Jevons*. Volume III. London: Macmillan.

——— 1977b. R.D. Collison Black, ed. *Papers and Correspondence of William Stanley Jevons*. Volume IV. London: Macmillan.

Kargon, Robert. 1969. "Model and Analogy in Victorian Science: Maxwell's Critique of the French Physicists." *Journal of the History of Ideas* 30:423–436.

Lakatos, Imre. 1970. "Falsification and the Methodology of Scientific Research Programmes." In Imre Lakatos and Alan Musgrave, eds. *Criticism and the Growth of Knowledge* New York: Cambridge University Press, pp. 91–196.

Magnus, Phillips. 1876 *Lessons on Elementary Mechanics*. New York: Wiley.

Mirowski, Philip. 1984a. "Physics and the 'Marginalist Revolution.'" *Cambridge Journal of Economics* 8:361–379.

———. 1984b. "The Role of Conservation Principles in Twentieth-Century Economic Theory." *Philosophy of the Social Sciences* 14:461–473.

———. Forthcoming. *More Heat Than Light*. Oxford and New York: Cambridge University Press.

Samuelson, Paul. 1950. "The Problem of Integrability in Utility Theory" *Economica* 17:355–385.

Weintraub, E. Roy. 1980. *Microfoundations*. New York: Cambridge University Press.

Wulwick, Nancy J. 1989. "Phillips' Approximate Regression." *Oxford Economic Papers*, 41:170–88.

8 DECONSTRUCTING ROBERT LUCAS

Jane Rossetti

There are at least three reasons why economists should learn about deconstruction. First, it ties together recent work about economics and language. Second, it provides a new approach to the history of economic thought. Third, it suggests a particular, and to some provocative, understanding of what economists do and why we do it.

This chapter has three sections. The first explains the theory of deconstruction. The second deconstructs two short pieces by Robert Lucas. This section is meant only to be illustrative of the principles of deconstruction and suggestive of the type of work that can be undertaken. It is not a thorough analysis of his work. The third section addresses the question, What does deconstruction mean for economists?

Deconstruction

Recent work on rhetoric and economics has focused on how economists converse and persuade, and it pays significant attention to the use of metaphor in this context.[1] Underlying this work, of course, is a denial of Popper's view that science progresses through the formulation, testing, and falsification of hypotheses. If economics progresses in a Popperian fashion, by the discovery of facts and the testing of theories relating these facts, then the vocabulary, metaphor, and style of argumentation economists use are irrelevant to economists' acceptance of the theory or model in question. We are not persuaded to believe in a model. We are shown the facts that support it and the failed attempts at falsification. On this objective basis we provisionally accept its validity. Conversely, we do not accept theories that have been falsified, no matter what rhetorical efforts their proponents make.

McCloskey (1985) argues that in actuality economists do not follow Popper's methods but instead *persuade* other economists of the appropriateness and usefulness of theory through rhetorical means. We do not go out into the world and unmercifully test theories to find one that withstands efforts at falsification; rather, we *convince* other economists that our theory or model is correct, or useful, by various rhetorical means. This may include statistical testing, because economists find such arguments persuasive. Mirowski (1987) considers economists' use of the metaphors of classical physics and their impact on neoclassical economics, including conjectures on why the metaphor has worked so successfully. Both McCloskey and Mirowski argue that there is not an objective basis to our acceptance and use of models. This position is supported and extended by deconstructive thought.

Similarly, Michel Foucault's *The Order of Things* (1970) can be interpreted using deconstructive thought. This work traces changes in the fundamental concepts organizing knowledge from the seventeenth to the twentieth centuries. Foucault argues that the categories and concepts used in the organization of knowledge are common across several disciplines, are constructed by humans in social life, and change over time. The categories he unearths (the subtitle of the book is *An Archeology of the Human Sciences*) are precisely the kinds of categories and groupings on which the deconstructionists focus. So deconstruction provides a coherent framework for understanding the work of Foucault, McCloskey, Mirowski, and the relationships between them.

What is deconstruction? It is a critical technique of the post-structuralist, or antifoundationalist, schools of literary theory. Whereas the structuralist critics of the late 1950s and 1960s believed that literature "... worked by certain objective laws, and criticism could itself become systematic by formulating them" (Eagleton, 1983, p. 91), poststructuralists deny the possibility of finding an objective theoretical foundation for literature or criticism. (Thus their label, anti-foundationalist.) Language and meaning are seen to be completely and unavoidably context-dependent. We are always trapped within some context; we can never step outside of it to attain an objective basis for our thought and our models.

The deconstruction argument revolves around language necessarily conveying meaning *only* within a context. This opposes the classical idea of language. In these theories, texts[2] contain true, discoverable, stable meaning. Words and language are capable of conveying meanings that do not require any interpretation on the part of the reader. Words have a literal meaning. Consider an example:

> A rock exists. It has a set of qualities. It is an inanimate, mineral, hard object. These are attributes the rock owns, in the sense that they are not *ascribed* to the rock, but they *are* the rock. The rock's essence, its Platonic ideal, can be describe as hard, grey, etc., but it has an essence. We experience this presence in an unadulterated, pure, almost transcendental form, unmediated by language or thought.

However, at some point language becomes necessary; we want to talk about a rock without having to point at it. So we develop a sign to stand in for the actual rock. The word "rock" captures, with no distortion, the presence of the rock. The word is the "deferred presence" of the object. The substitution of the word for the object is secondary to the original presence of the object. The sign conveys a pre-existing, original presence. This means that when "rock" appears in a text, it contains within itself a clearly understood meaning, the translation of the essence into language. "Rock" requires no interpretation, its meaning is self-evident, self-contained. The meaning is held within the word itself, the context is irrelevant. The rock's essence is immutable; therefore the meaning of the sign is fixed. The same argument is extended to concepts. They have an essence that is conveyed by language. The meaning is in the word and is context-independent. From this springs the structuralist ideas of language in which words and the structure of the language itself contain and convey meaning. These are the theories Ferdinand de Saussure and later Jacques Derrida attack.

Does a rock have an unmediated presence? No, says Saussure. It only has a set of characteristics ascribed to it. There is nothing everlasting about these descriptions. A rock need not always be conceptualized as inanimate. "Inanimate" makes sense only when we are working within a system of categories that differentiates between animate and inanimate; this system need not always exist. Imagine a culture in which any naturally occurring form has a Spirit within; or one in which there is no distinction between dead and inanimate; or one, on an isolated sandy island, where rocks are used as a store of value. What, then, is the essence of a rock? Is it an object? Is it inanimate? Is it dead? Is it valuable? Its characteristics change across space, time, and culture. It has no objective qualities, no qualities that transcend all cultural (contextual) changes. It no longer has an essence, no longer has an unmediated presence.

If an object has no presence than a word cannot convey it. The sound or shape of the word contains, in and of itself, no meaning. If you could (which you emphatically cannot) read "rock" outside any social context, it would tell you nothing. You would not be immediately informed of the rock's spiritual state or its value. Only within some context would "rock" inform you of its deadness, it inanimateness, or its worth.

The argument becomes more dizzying still. "Inanimate" like "rock" has no essence. Outside some context, it has no meaning. Within contexts, it may have as many meanings as there are contexts. Within a particular context, "inanimate" is able to convey meaning, but it does not convey presence. Since it has no essence, no particular attribute that is always and everywhere understood, the word cannot tell us what it is. Within a context, however, it can tell us what it is *not*. It is not (for us) living or dead. Within a particular context we can understand "inanimate," not because we grasp a true unalterable meaning, (which it cannot have) but because we understand what it is not.

Derrida puts this idea as follows: "The signified concept is never present in itself, in an adequate presence that would refer only to itself. Every concept is necessarily and essentially inscribed in a chain or a system, within which it refers to another and to other concepts, by the systematic play of differences" (p. 11). Words "function not by virtue of the compact force of their cores but by the network of oppositions that distinguish them and relate them to one another" (p. 10).

Words have meaning only by summing up not what they are but what they are not. This can only occur in a social context wherein we can understand the other concepts from which they differ.

Just what *do* they differ from? They do not differ from a core of meaning, from a steady stable meaning. There is no core, no presence, no benchmark, and no absolute from which they could vary. A word is the sum of a context-dependent set of negative qualities (differences), qualities it does not possess. The qualities themselves are not essences but are sums of yet other negative qualities. Meaning differs from other sets of differences. Words can have meaning only within a giant web of differences that connects and defines each word. The meaning does not lie with the word itself. It lies in the web, in the space created by removing everything it is not. It lies between the words.

Meaning is now completely context-dependent. Language conveys no essential truths, only sets of differences. Words can have no independent meaning. Meaning and understanding can only occur within the context of constructed sets of differences. It is only within the context that we know which differences are being called on and given importance. A word needs to be interpreted, placed inside its context, before its meaning can be grasped. As the context changes, the interpretation changes. New meaning is created by rearranging sets of differences. Meanings become dynamic.

Reader, do not lose heart. The difficult aspects of deconstruction are now behind us. Up to this point we have seen that objects and concepts no longer have a positive presence; words representing them sum up all they are not and declare their differences from all other sets of differences. However, some ordering has to be brought to this continuously differentiating system. The ordering is done through the construction of categories (animate, living) that will recognize specific differences. The categories have to be constructed since there are no original categories between which the differences occur. There cannot be natural or organic or correct categories since the objects or concepts unified do not share some immutable quality and so naturally belong together. Rather the categories are socially constructed, grouped around *chosen* characteristics that themselves are differences.

Once constructed, the categories appear to be organic to those living within the same context. This is not because they *are* organic categories, but because they reflect the world that they themselves have organized and created. "Living" is a constructed category. Once constructed, it imposes some order on the other groupings of differences. It arranges sets of meanings, it categorizes and organizes our knowledge, and so our world and ourselves. Once our thinking is organized around the living/ dead difference, those concepts appear to be basic to all life, everywhere. If we had built different categories, the organization of our knowledge would be quite different. The world and ourselves would differ under different systems of categorization.

In the construction of categories, Derrida argues that some set of categories (e.g., natural, male, rational) is envisioned as prior to the others. These serve as referents. Other categories (artificial, female, emotional) serve as supplements, derivatives. A hierarchy is established. The world is organized and understood around the primary, the so-called "privileged" categories, so that what is natural or rational is considered the norm. However, we know that the privileged categories have no absolute basis on which to claim privilege.

The act of deconstruction identifies these primitive organizing concepts and the hierarchy that relates them. It levels this hierarchy by showing, in the text, that the primary categories necessarily refer to and contain the secondary (supplemental) categories, and so cannot logically be considered prior to, or apart from, them. The privileges previously attached to these "primary" characteristics or concepts consequently are revoked. This must be the case as the categories are only groupings of differences that necessarily refer to each and all other sets. So, for example, the distinction natural/unnatural is shown to be an arbitrary division of objects. Since "natural" can in and of itself convey no meaning, it cannot function as a prior category. It contains meaning only when it can represent differences from other states; when it can be compared with "unnatural." "Natural" could not be a concept prior to "unnatural" but can have meaning only symbiotically. This levels the hierarchy. The categories can exist only side by side.

Deconstructing the constructed hierarchies and categories reveals the intellectual and social frameworks within which the author works (and which is part of the author — see below). It reveals the categories and hierarchies s/he "chooses"[3] to employ and so reveals the system of values underlying the work. There are four related points to make, two of which will be extended in section three, before we deconstruct Robert Lucas.

First, some words may appear to have a literal or absolute meaning. That illusion exists only because the context is so widely shared as to be unobservable. "Rock" may seem to *be* hard and inanimate. "Employed" may seem to have an entirely transparent meaning to economists because we are so thoroughly immersed in our structures of thought. We know employed means working for compensation through the labor market. It might be tempting to think that "employed" has this meaning as its essence, but such a thought misses the mark, by taking the context (market-oriented division of labor) for granted. Outside such a context, "employed" cannot convey those distinctions, and what we considered its essence would evaporate. Indeed, outside such a context, what is connoted by "employed" may not be recognized as existing, and may not exist at all. The concept itself, as well as the word that conveys that concept, are context-dependent, no matter how transparent that context may be.

Second, deconstructive thought denies the possibility of independent consciousness. There is no essential self, no self in isolation, and no self predating immersion into social life. The very word "self" immediately calls to mind the opposing ideas of groups. Self without groups can make no sense; the very concept of self in isolation makes no sense, it can only exist in opposition to other concepts. We are selves only by virtue of the fact that we differ from others, who in their differing from us, define us. Only in the structure of differences can our selves be, and in being create more differences so that other "selves" may come into being. We are created by our context, as we create it.

It is inappropriate therefore, to speak of "choosing" the categories and hierarchies for one's work. The author's thought and the author herself/ himself are created by the differences and hierarchies in which s/he works, even as s/he helps create and define new categories. An author cannot step outside the system of differences in order to choose the ones s/he prefers to employ. "Choice" is made within the significant constraints of the existing perceived sets of differences. The choices made will, perhaps, shift the web slightly, realigning or redefining some of the categories, but they cannot be made outside of the system.

Third, although there can be no essential self (no self outside some social context), the same does not hold for essential Truth. There may be Truth or God existing outside of and prior to the system of language and thought — absolute, complete in itself, and free of the need for context. However, if this Truth does exist, it is not accessible by any of us via rational inquiry. We are barred from approaching or attaining this objective, unbiased, encompassing Truth precisely because we are unable to be objective. Since ourselves exist only within a certain structure, we cannot step outside of it to evaluate or judge its content, whether or not it is true. Its content defines us, is us, we cannot leave it behind to judge objectively or comprehend Truth. If somehow we were able (which we are not) to disentangle ourselves from this web, with each broken thread we would lose part of our being, and ultimately cease to be. There is no space outside the differences from which we can objectively view the world.

Last, there can be no definitive deconstruction. The process cannot logically ever end, because there is no available definiteness, no absolute. Any deconstruction is by its very nature another construction. One text's categories are revealed only by implicitly comparing them with a different set of categories, those held by the deconstructor. The deconstructor is permanently lodged within the system albeit at a different place. Deconstructors have no choice but to bring their own interpretational angle to their work. A deconstruction is as legitimate to deconstruct as is any other text. The process has no logical end point. We will consider the implications of this further.

With all this in mind, let us turn to Lucas.

Robert Lucas

In "Unemployment Policy" (1981), Lucas begins to deconstruct the Keynesian concept of involuntary unemployment, although he does not recognize the strategy. He then reconstructs "unemployment." We know
that his deconstruction of Keynes can not be definitive. I do not intend to
deconstruct his deconstruction, but rather to use it as an example of the
strategies involved, and then deconstruct his construction.

What does Lucas do that is deconstructive? First, he recognizes
involuntary unemployment as a construct, not as an independently
existing concept. "(I)nvoluntary unemployment is not a fact or a phenomenon which it is the task of theorists to explain. It is, on the contrary,
a theoretical construct which Keynes introduced. . . ." (p. 243), and later
". . . the 'thing' to be measured does not exist" (p. 244). Keynes did not
look into the world and identify involuntary unemployment because it
unquestionably had its own existence. Rather, he constructed it for his
own theoretical purposes.

Second, Lucas denies the validity of the separation of voluntary from
involuntary unemployment, arguing that either contains elements of the
other. "There is an involuntary element in *all* unemployment, in the
sense that no one chooses bad luck over good; there is also a voluntary
element in all unemployment, in the sense that however miserable one's
current work options, one can always choose to accept them" (p. 242).
Lucas further calls this division into question by referring to it as "terminology" (p. 241) and "a carelessly drawn distinction" (p. 242) implying
lack of substantive content. Not only is involuntary unemployment a
construct, it is one that is not understandable as opposite of or supple-
mentary to voluntary unemployment. Any mutual exclusiveness between
the categories is denied. The concepts inhabit each other here in a very
concrete fashion; neither exists in a pure self-defined state. Deconstruction would take this further, arguing that these *necessarily* contain elements of each other, that not only in practice do they exist together, but
that even in thought one cannot be conceptualized without calling on the
others' existence. "Involuntary" immediately opposes itself to "voluntary." For it to exist, there must be some "voluntary" against which to
oppose it.

Lucas goes on to explain his interpretation of the purposes behind
Keynes's construction. In so doing, he identifies the use to which Keynes
puts his voluntary/involuntary distinction. Lucas claims it puts the percep-

tion of the individual worker at the center of the theory: "This terminology suggests that the key to the distinction lies in some difference in the way two different types of unemployment are *perceived by workers*" (p. 241),[4] and Keynes's analyses "begin at the individual worker level..." (p. 241). In Lucas's view, accepting the construct of involuntary unemployment led to the idea that macroeconomic policy should be focused on eliminating involuntary unemployment to ameliorate the lot of the individual workers. Lucas's Keynes views the individual as the center (the primary state) to which the macroeconomic policy is subordinate (supplementing the original state). For Lucas, such policy can only be mistaken, for it focuses on the elimination of a category he (Lucas) has shown does not exist.

Lucas has argued that since involuntary unemployment is a construct, not a fact, policy focused on eliminating it has been misguided. This is not a deconstructionist stance. It implies there are constructs that actually represent "fact" and that it is on these that policy should focus. Lucas does not argue that unemployment itself is only a construct, just that trying to divide it up into voluntary and involuntary components is an unachievable and ultimately confusing task that ought to be abandoned.

At this point Lucas moves on to constructing his own definition of unemployment and arguing it is a more coherent one than Keynes's. His reconstruction is a reversal of Keynes's hierarchy. Lucas places the macro economy at the center, the individual at the periphery. In this article Lucas does not specify exactly what "unemployment" means. This is a very short, nontechnical article that would not be the appropriate setting for a very specific definition of unemployment. His use of the word is meant only to encompass what both voluntary and involuntary unemployment meant previously. However, we know that his concept of unemployment has no better claim, in absolute terms, to superiority does the one he destroys. It cannot more fully, truly, or clearly represent "unemployment" because "unemployment" does not have an objective presence to be conveyed. Rather, Lucas's construction is an alternate construction. It redefines the meaning of unemployment, shifting the oppositions and differences the word contains. It is not inherently more or less correct than Keynes's, not a better or worse definition, but one made from a different contextual perspective. Lucas cannot prove it is a better definition, he can only argue that it is. He must persuade his readers his "unemployment" is a better, more fruitful, or useful definition than the previous one. What "better" means is not obvious here, a point we take up later.

However, Lucas knows exactly why this definition is a better one:

> First, one dispenses with that entire meaningless vocabulary associated with full employment, phrases like potential output, full capacity, slack and so on, which suggested that there was some *technical* reason why we couldn't [return to full-employment]. Second, one finds to one's relief that treating unemployment as a voluntary response to an unwelcome situation does not commit oneself to normative nonsense like blaming depressions on lazy workers.

> The effect it does have on normative discussion is twofold. First, it focuses discussion of monetary and fiscal policy on *stabilization*, on the pursuit of price stability and on minimizing the disruptive effects of erratic policy changes. Some average unemployment rate would, of course, emerge from such a policy but as a by-product, not as a preselected target. Second, by thinking of this natural rate as an equilibrium emerging from voluntary exchange in the usual sense, one can subject it to the scrutiny of modern methods of public finance. (p. 245)

With the new classical economics (NCE) definition of unemployment we no longer need to import artificial constructs (full employment) from outside the theory or turn to exogenous barriers (technical difficulties) or ad hoc behavioral assumptions (laziness) for an explanation of unemployment. New classical economics increases the (endogenous) explanatory power of neoclassical economics by defining "unemployment" in a manner consistent with microeconomic theories of behavior. The loss of the voluntary/involuntary distinction means that agents can no longer be involuntarily consigned to a state of nonwork. The individual is optimizing subject to constraints of job offers, wages, and preferences. The resultant state is an outcome of available opportunities and choice. The agent is no longer confronted by barriers beyond control but behaves in an active, decisive fashion.

Redefining unemployment in this way directly implies changes in unemployment policy for economists of the new classical and even those of the neoclassical schools, for equilibria of voluntary exchange transactions are not to be tampered with lightly. When unemployment is so characterized, interference with its level is circumscribed. For Lucas, the market-determined level of unemployment raises policy issues "only insofar as it can be shown to be 'distorted' in an undesirable way by taxes, external effects, and so on" (p. 241), which brings us back to the reference to public finance in the previous quote. Consequently, the decision of whether or not the unemployment rate is inappropriate can be determined on the basis of economic, not political, considerations and analysis. The decision no longer requires exogenous measures or judgments on the part of the policy maker as to what constitutes "full" employment. We can shift decisions on unemployment policy from the political sphere to the sphere of economic analysis.

Lucas has thus erected a hierarchy between the economic and the policy sphere. He has argued that there is no route to determining "full employment unemployment" that is contained solely within the economic sphere. An operational definition of full employment is not attainable, nor is there an explanation of "why unemployment is a problem, or as to the costs and benefits involved in economic policies which affect unemployment rates" (p. 244). Economics cannot address these issues, which arise from involuntary unemployment, because the concept itself is not an economically meaningful one. By redefining unemployment to make it meaningful in economic terms, we turn it into an economic question, for which we can find economic answers.

This shift is evident in the further work of Lucas, and others, on rational expectations, which narrows the acceptable range of policy, as well as policy goals. Nonerratic policy changes (those that are able to be anticipated) are ineffective under rational expectations. Only unforeseeable changes are effective. However, these are necessarily erratic, which imposes costs and waste on the economy. Consequently, policy needs to focus on stabilization, on minimizing the "disruptive effect of erratic policy changes" (p. 245). The implication is that if the economy is to function efficiently, it needs to be protected from these effects — insulated from the political sphere. Economics is given pride of place, with political decisions constrained not to intrude. These conclusions are all supported by neoclassical economic analysis, which stresses efficiency, equilibrium, and optimization.

Lucas has set up a hierarchy between the economic sphere and policy or social sphere. Decisions are more defensible, more efficient, and more scientific if unemployment policy is decided by economic theory rather than political expediency. With Lucas's idea of unemployment such a result is possible because it no longer requires any decision-making on just what "involuntary" unemployment is. Lucas is arguing that economic analysis itself can determine whether or not the unemployment level is an economic problem.

The economics/politics distinction is drawn again in "Rules, Discretion and the Role of the Economic Advisor" (1981). This article is initially difficult to make sense of, since Lucas is presenting several arguments simultaneously. The primary argument is that the institutional framework within which economic policy advisors work in the United States is inappropriate given the level of scientific knowledge we have about the operation of the economy. Lucas argues that the emphasis on discretionary, countercyclical, reactive, fiscal and monetary policy created by the Employment Act of 1946 and the revisions to the Federal Reserve code is foolish. What we need is a set of rules (not necessarily those Friedman suggested) to provide a stable environment for the private sector. Rules are needed not because we can never hope to know enough to apply successful discretionary policy but because "analysis of policy which utilizes economics in a scientific way *necessarily* involves choice among alternative stable, predictable policy rules...." (p. 255).

The second argument, and the one of primary interest here, concerns the role of public opinion in shaping the direction of economic policy research. Lucas asserts that the Employment Act represented a belief that government could successfully intervene in the economy and improve its performance by yearly forecasting and prescription. With the passage of the Employment Act, monetary economics recast itself as macroeconomics whose proponents were vessels for the expertise required. They accepted the roles of policy advisor, economic managers, and practical prescribers of policy; they accepted as workable the institutional and legislative guidelines within which they worked. They accepted the rules of the game as given to them by the public via the recent legislation, and turned to daily management of the economy. With the perceived failure of discretionary policy in the 1970s, the public turned both to ad hoc solutions, such as those offered by Laffer and Okun, and to legislation limiting the scope of discretionary polices (e.g., Proposition 13, the beginnings of the movement favoring a balanced budget amendment).

Lucas' view is that public opinion of the state of the discipline has had a very large impact on the role assigned to economic policy advisors, and that in the two decades directly following the Employment Act's passage, this was deleterious to the profession, since it focused research on questions of short-term discretionary policy, which were without solid theoretical foundation. More recently, however, the emphasis on limiting the scope of such policies coincides with research in rational expectations, which suggests such a predictable limited role is desirable. The public is finally asking economists to answer appropriate questions, but now we are stuck with inappropriate institutions and an inappropriate framework, which will have to be changed from the outside.

Lucas sets up an opposition between scientific research and research directed to answering policy questions. Scientific comes to mean removed from direct policy work, grounded in more fundamental analysis, research not directly influenced by policy and not subject to changes in public opinion, but rather full and thorough investigations undertaken by those not directly involved in policy decisions. Scientific work is separated from solving policy problems, from day-to-day economic management problems. In Lucas' view, management problems did not lead to scientific research or an increase in scientific knowledge.

For Lucas, scientific work is uncontaminated by policy. This scientific research is the privileged category. It is the kind of research or knowledge that is valuable and that provides a stable basis. It is pure and unmotivated by direct policy questions. This "scientific" work was, in Lucas's opinion, supplanted by research that differed from it by its focus on management questions, policy evaluation, application, and its direct reference to its context. It is to scientific work we need to return, either to work for "scientific improvements of a fundamental and basic nature" (p. 259) to allow us to "regain the intellectual control we thought we had in the sixties" (p. 259), which Lucas thinks is unlikely given institutional constraints, or perhaps to construct a framework in which we can evaluate sets of rules.

Lucas also tries to set up the opposition economist/public, again to make the point that the direction of research is guided by public opinion and perception. The public asked for fine-tuning, and we sought to provide it. This was later, correctly or not, viewed as a mistake. The public is now changing its demands for the sort of policies being prescribed. Lucas describes the direction of research as being led by public demand for certain types of policies, which economic managers then seek to provide. The public force is insurmountable. ". . . Public opinion generally . . . was far more important than were scientific considerations in influencing professional reaction to Friedman's 'Framework' and that this situation is not at all unusual" (p. 254).

Lucas detracts from his own argument about the importance of public opinion versus science in several places. He cannot separate the two, the public from the science, since each, of course, can only influence the other, and neither could ever expect to stand alone. He states parenthetically: "This observation is not intended as lament; there is little to be said for isolating economics from general contemporary social thought, and the consequences of trying to do so tend to lead to reliance on sterile aesthetic criteria in guiding theoretical work" (p. 254). Part of his own historical reconstruction reflects this unavoidable mixture. The public believed in economists since "general economic performance in the twenty years following the passage of the Employment Act was, by any historical standard, highly successful" (p. 252). During this time, some economists mistook this confidence, trust, and success as a sign of the "increasing feasibility of sophisticated, reactive countercyclical policy" (p.

257). Thus, the macroeconomists thought they were engaged in a progressing theoretical discipline, supported by everyday observations on the success of the economy. The public, living in the middle of this success, remained confident. The relationship public/economist was two-way. With public trust and good economic performance, neither economists nor the general citizenry questioned the state of the discipline.

From a deconstructionist view, Lucas's separations and rankings are manifestations of the bias of his perspective, not reflections of obvious Truths. Lucas's argument for the adoption of new classical economics theories of unemployment (i.e., the new definition) is that the new classical economics can explain and evaluate unemployment using only economic, not political, considerations. But this division and hierarchy of the economic and the political is not valid, for each informs the other and depends on the other (by how it differs from the other). Lucas admits this in "Unemployment Policy" when he says "Whether any particular level of unemployment compensation is too high or too low is a difficult issue in practice . . ." (p. 246). Both economics and political thought are created by larger forces that are fundamentally common between them, both are instances of our interpretations of our world, of how we (re)shape that world. What we call "economics" is determined by everything it is not; it includes topics that fall outside politics, psychology, and sociology. The decision of where to draw the line between these sets of ideas is a manifestation of social thought (and a facet of that thought). Disciplinary boundaries are not a reflection of the differences between the essences of the disciplines — they have none — but a creation and division of the world by economists, political scientists, sociologists, and so on.

In removing certain aspects of unemployment from the political to the economic realm, Lucas is redefining the domains of both disciplines. This is a social comment, not an advancement of objective science. Just because we could use economic techniques to solve a problem does not imply that we should solve it with economic techniques. Agreeing to depoliticizing unemployment is a political statement, a defining of what we value and how we value it. Lucas is arguing that unemployment, no matter its rate, is a natural outcome of the system. We do not need to worry about it (unless it results from distortions). Those people who are unemployed are no longer a problem. It is not a systemic flaw over which they have no control that forces them to be out of work. Rather, they accept their bad luck and choose not to accept alternative employ. Since they are optimizing, their situation is acceptable; to intercede (public works) could be construed as paternalism.

Adopting the new classical economics definition of unemployment brings its analysis out of social and political theory. It is not that economists are now forced to practice political science or sociology with respect to the unemployed — the boundaries of economics have not changed — but the problem is redefined and recast so it fits completely into economics. Considering the disciplines as intrinsically separate is incorrect. Our decisions of what we want to view as economics or politics, the change in the language, affects and reflects both fields.

Lucas not only considers economics and politics as distinct, he places them in a hierarchy, with economics on top. He couches this movement in scientific, objective terms. Not only is new classical economics preferred to Keynesian economics because it enlarges economics' domain, economics is preferred to political science because it is more objective. Lucas implies that science (here economics) can be done objectively and so is preferable to political decisions, which are intrinsically biased.

The deconstructionist point is that decisions based on economic theory are not "scientific" or are in no way *more* scientific than those arrived at via political philosophy. The "objective" economic techniques themselves are not separable from the bias, the slant, or the interpretation we live within and perpetuate. The tools that economics, but not political science, possess are permeated with language and ideas, with categories and definitions, with social opinions, from which Lucas is trying so very desperately to separate them. This attempt is doomed, for it depends on the idea of comparative objectivity. In Derrida's world, this can not be; in Lucas's writings themselves the contradictions surface.

This observation of contradictions is not a criticism of Lucas's work or method. It is, rather, an observation on what his writing reveals about his own position in the web of language and life (where "own" is not understood as perfectly independent from the rest of the world). Yes, he has created what from the deconstructive viewpoint is an ultimately presumptive distinction, and an untenable hierarchy. But in the process he reorganizes differences and casts ideas in a new light. An exposition of some of these differences from an other's perspective is not a criticism of them, but a recognition of them.

Deconstruction and Economics

What does deconstruction mean for economics? First, it means that economic research is not progressing in any fashion, linear or otherwise, towards an Objective or True Understanding or Explanation of how the economy works. Such an understanding is unattainable because objectivity as well as Truth are unattainable (at least by rational means).

We also lose the notion of practicing "objective" economics. We construct theories and models from within a certain context we all share and which shapes us. Our models are drawn from a particular, although malleable, perspective. We create our economy and our understanding of it from within our social context. From that place we interpret and explain.

With models being context-dependent and unavoidably not-objective, they cannot be accepted or rejected on grounds of their Truth, of how well they accord with some given reality, since reality is quite subjective. There is not an objective "fact"-based system for judging a theory's value — the concept simply no longer exists. Theories and models are judged and accepted on the basis of, as McCloskey puts it, how persuasive they are.

The idea that we judge theories on the grounds of their persuasiveness annoys most economists. We like to think of our work as scientific and as containing or at least promising movement towards a better, more refined, understanding of the economy. To say this movement depends on persuasiveness, on rhetoric, not scientific accomplishment, is unsettling.

But persuasiveness is not simply a question of which advocates have a stronger vocabulary, or more compelling metaphors. Persuasiveness comes from the pervasiveness of the interpretational vision of the theorists, of how well their points of view accord with the existing, stable social perceptions and intellectual organization, of how well they represent institutional assumptions, or how cleverly they redefine, redraw, or reinterpret (within strict limits) those assumptions. The cleverness or lucidity will be evaluated, as always, by the communities that share these institutions and vocabulary and assumptions, what Stanley Fish (1980) calls "the interpretive community," what Imre Lakatos referred to as "the scientific community." What we, as a group, find compelling and acceptable is viewed as progress.

This is not inviting chaos to rule over the discipline. Rather, this is recognizing that the control of method, content, and style that any discipline imposes upon itself is sociological; it is chosen, not the unavoidable result of that discipline's "true content." We all share fundamental categories and differences, structures and ways of thought, or we could never talk meaningfully to each other. Theories from outside this context will always remain outside, will have no impact, will not be even considered. If they do not incorporate the basic assumptions, they may not be communicable, and they would not be acceptable. These are models that are not "good." (See Klamer (1983) for instances of noncommunication between unlike contexts.)

Persuasiveness is not restricted to language. If the interpretive community views statistical testing as evidence, then it, too, can be used to persuade. Its persuasiveness is strictly dependent on the community's shared perception of the value of quantitative methods. If (apparent) objectivity is desired, and mathematical techniques are considered objective, their use has potentially great persuasiveness. The community develops the standards and then is developed by way of those standards, until a new view or value or measure develops. Predicting or evaluating movement in economic theory becomes synonymous with predicting or evaluating movement in how the profession defines itself and what it values. It also becomes more obviously tied to the more general social change, which both causes and is caused by changes within economics, as well as all other areas of study.

Why did Lucas feel compelled to redefine concepts of unemployment? Was it because Keynes was wrong? No. What changed was perception of economists in how we look at the economy, at what is defined as an economic question, at what ought to be considered in a purely objective, valueless, fashion (which is not a value-less judgment). Is it an historical accident that new classical economics was in its infancy as the new conservative movement was beginning to speak? I think not. Economic and political theory both shape our intellectual world, our categories, our vision, and are shaped by them. It would be more of a surprise if movements of social change were not accompanied by changes in, for example, economic theory.

So what does deconstruction do for economics? It does not offer us a new and better method that we can use to find out how the economy "really" works; rather it informs us that this is impossible to attain. It does not pass absolute judgment on the usefulness or worth of a theory, but teaches us that absolute judgments do not exist. It does not change the way we practice economics, but suggests we will continue practice as we do today. Deconstruction does not provide us with a new and better methodology as Popper, Kuhn, and Lakatos thought they had done. It shows that any method is contextual, derived from a certain perspective with the system of differences. It does not prescribe, nor demand, any changes. It removes us from objective Truth, yes, but it does not change what we do. Knowing we cannot have the ultimate explanation does not proscribe our creating and extending the "best" one we can, where best is understood as dependent on a host of cultural variables. And, economists fortunate enough to never come into contact with deconstruction or other schools of literary criticism will not find their work outdated or methodologically incorrect. Deconstruction is not a method of acquiring knowledge from out there somewhere, it accepts all methods of creation of knowledge and inquiry as legitimate if they are so understood by their practitioners.

For economists working in the history of thought, this school of literary theory suggests that one ought not view economics as a science progressing towards a fixed point. It might encourage one to undertake the sort of work of which Foucault's *The Order of Things* is an example, to look for fundamental categories and relationships. It gives us a different way to approach understanding changes in economic theories and categories, methods of inquiry and types of models, as reflecting changes in the intellectual and social world. It gives us a new framework in which to view economics, one that can only be subjective, but cannot be faulted for that. It puts economics back into the social world, and out of what we would like to consider the scientific one. Since no deconstruction is ever final, it also provides us with the opportunity for ongoing, everchanging, intriguing research and discourse.

Acknowledgments

The author is a doctoral candidate in Economics at Duke University. I am indebted to E. Roy Weintraub, Warren Samuels, Stanley Fish, Nancy Wulwick, Dan Hammond, Neil de Marchi, Craufurd D. Goodwin and other members of the Duke University seminar in the history of economic thought for their helpful comments and queries. All remaining misstatements are my own.

Notes

[1] Donald McCloskey, *The Rhetoric of Economics*; Phil Mirowski, "Shall I Compare Thee...," Arjo Klamer, *Conversations with Economists.*

[2] "Texts" should be understood to refer to both written and spoken communications, "talk" to include "write;" "word" to include both the written and spoken sign.

[3] The idea that the author chooses is not correct. I use the word here only to simplify the presentation. Its incorrectness is discussed.

[4] Emphasis in the original.

References

Derrida, Jacques. 1982. "Difference." Translated by Alan Bass. In *Margins of Philosophy*. Chicago: University of Chicago Press, pp. 1–27.

Eagleton, Terry. 1983. *Literary Theory: An Introduction*. Minneapolis: University of Minnesota Press.

Fish, Stanley. 1980. *Is There a Text in this Class?* Cambridge, Mass: Harvard University Press.

Foucault, Michel. 1970. *The Order of Things*. New York: Random House.

Klamer, Arjo. 1983. *Conversations with Economists*. Totowa, N.J.: Rowman and Allanheld.

Lucas, Robert. 1981. "Rules, Discretion and the Role of the Economic Advisor." In *Studies in Business Cycle Theory*. Cambridge, Mass.: MIT Press, pp. 248–261.

———. 1981. "Unemployment Policy." In *Studies in Business Cycle Theory*. Cambridge, Mass.: MIT Press, pp. 240–47.

McCloskey, Donald. 1985. *The Rhetoric of Economics*. Madison: University of Wisconsin Press.

Mirowski, Phillip. 1987. "Shall I Compare Thee to...." *Economics and Philosophy* 3(3):335–358.

COMMENT BY J.B. DAVIS

While Jane Rossetti nicely exhibits deconstruction as a methodology of interpretation in economics in her rendering of Robert Lucas on J.M. Keynes's concept of involuntary unemployment, she does not explore the wider philosophical implications of deconstruction as a systematic approach to the history of economic thought. Yet despite occasional disclaimers on the part of Jacques Derrida and other deconstructionists, the philosophical assumptions underlying their proposed deconstruction of texts are radical and substantial. Indeed, their adoption would require a drastic reconceptualization of the history of economic thought, as well as current practices of critique and evaluation in economics. This brief comment seeks to elicit some of these implications from a critical perspective. Its vantage point is deconstruction's tenuous *Aufhebung* — Hegel's taking up and transcending — of structuralism. The basic thesis here is that the radical poststructuralist skepticism of Derrida and others ultimately itself produces deconstruction's own critique. Suggestions for an alternative grounding of economics methodology are offered in response to these difficulties.

Structuralist thinking, beginning with the work of Ferdinand de Saussure, denies any natural or metaphysical relation between language and the world, or, in Saussure's words, between the signifier and the signified. Indeed, Saussure's founding precept is that the signified is constituted and constructed by the system of interrelated signifiers that bring it into play. Thus, structuralism denies that language possesses a referential function, rejects the notion that there is some sort of correspondence between meaning and an extra-discursive reality, and regards the idea of a reality beyond language as meaningless. Indeed, since terms never exist in a simple one-to-one relation with an underlying extra-discursive reality, whether it be things in the world or concepts, signification is essentially conventional. A Saussurian "science of signs" is accordingly entirely devoted to examining the varying play of meaning in language contexts, and since the meaning of an individual term cannot but be understood in terms of its relations to other terms, that is, its signifying contrasts, meanings across contexts are termed structures of difference.

Deconstruction embraces the structuralist critique of the referential function of language, yet extends it to the very idea that language has a structure that is somehow distinct from the play of meaning itself. For Derrida, structuralism is the last and yet the most contradictory metaphysics of meaning since its denial of language referentiality is itself posited upon the self-subsistence of a structure of language apart from the observed play of meaning. Consistency, however, demands that notion of

244

structure be taken as but metaphor, and that even the barest idea of a relation between signifier and signified which that notion might encourage be abandoned. Deconstruction, then, sets out to demonstrate "the principled, essential, and structural impossibility of closing a structural phenomenology" (Derrida, 1978, 160), when one fully suspends the referential function of language.[1]

This radical project encompasses not only the repudiation of what deconstructionists regard as the empiricist delusion, that is, that knowledge of an extra-discursive world can be achieved despite the transformative effects of language, but also its rationalist counterpart, that is, that epistemic certainty derives from recourse to the clear and distinct ideas of a self-sufficient reason.[2] For Derrida, all philosophies are metaphysical structures that presuppose formal closure and systematization based on the single great pretense and premise of Western thought — the "logocentric" bias — that meaning and truth ultimately coincide within the domain of philosophical reason. By abandoning this assumption, deconstruction seeks to open up the study of meaning to such customarily forbidden subjects as the radical undecidability of meaning, inevitable semantic slippage, the duplicitous and perverse play of metaphorical and figurative language, and the dissemination of meaning in texts of all sorts. Thus, underlying the work of deconstruction is an avowedly Nietzchean project of unmasking all claims to systematic knowledge, as reflected in Nietzsche's oft-quoted characterization of truth as but "a mobile marching army of metaphors, metonymies and anthropomorphisms . . . truths are illusions of which one has forgotten that they *are* illusions. . . ."[3]

Derrida's critique of western thought's "logocentric" bias, it should be emphasized, takes in not only any conception of a real world apart from signification but also any notion of the subject as an extra-discursive, cohesive, knowing entity that takes that world as its object.[4] Thus, just to the extent that philosophers have historically believed reason to be that faculty which guarantees a knowledge correspondent to reality itself, so this understanding has also presupposed a metaphysics of subjectivity centered upon the philosophical fiction that the thinking and knowing mind is a cohesive, coherent, intelligibilizing unity. Yet, in Derrida's view (1977), this notion of a "self-presence," the idea of a self-identical, philosophical consciousness able to render the world intelligible from its own vantage point, just derives from the accidental fact that spoken language, with its appearance of unity in the guise of the self-identify of the single speaker, has, since Plato, been believed the model for language meaning per se. A "phonocentric" bias thus undergirds the "logocentric" bias of western thought, and together they generate the illusion that in some manner at the most fundamental level of cognitive experience meaning and thought are inseparably linked and grounded in a prereflective unity that makes possible the epistemological project itself. Derrida sets out to deconstruct these illusions and, thus to uncover the radical disseminating play of meaning as it inheres in texts of all sorts. Indeed, the deconstruction of philosophical texts is but part and parcel of this exhibition of metaphorical and figurative play of meaning in language.

What, then, are the implications of this understanding for methodological practices in economics? Clearly a deconstructionist methodology of economics requires the abandonment of the traditional Schumpeterian vision of a steady progress of analytic science. Yet it also disrupts the more modern Kuhnian-Lakotosian account of science, as well as Donald McCloskey's recent strategies for explaining the practices of persuasion and rhetorical argument within the disciplinary community. While these views indeed reject the positivist notion of objective truth, they nonetheless still presuppose the vantage point of an intelligible scientific subjectivity, however fragmented and disaggregated that intentionality may be, and for deconstruction this is simply evidence of the "logocentric" bias of Western thought, albeit in somewhat more empirical-institutional garb than in more conventional philosophies of science.

Indeed, that meaning is always fully context-dependent and that language is always caught up in a conflicting and shifting play of multiple significations means that it is impossible to fix either its reference or a subjective intent behind it. The notion, then, that a contemporary text, say, that of Lucas on Keynes's concept of involuntary unemployment as in Rossetti's example, contains any element of past intended meaning that might be the object of an intended critique, however accurate or misguided, is simply illusory. In effect, the past fails to leave any residue in current texts, and those texts themselves come to exhibit a play of meaning that altogether erases their author's original intent. It simply mistaken to believe, Derrida maintains, that past authors' thought might even appear transformed in contemporary interpretation, since for the deconstructionist there are no extra-discursive point of reference for interpretation. Texts do not bear the imprint of their authors; they are simply peculiar artifacts — a pastiche of terms and symbols that are meaningful strictly in virtue of their current assembly.

Deconstruction's radical skepticism, however, as all radical skepticisms, requires an Archimedean point. Thus that there is an activity of deconstruction, it seems one must argue, indicates the presence of a deconstructor, an intentional agent engaged in deconstructing texts, however spare the conception of that agent may be. Yet this simple fact of engagement with a text certainly signals the presence of an extra-discursive subject separate from the text itself. Indeed it is fair to say that it is *only possible* to conceive of texts as pastiche, fundamentally free of authors' intentional objectives, *by postulating the synthesizing cognition of a subject engaged with that text.* Deconstruction, it might be said, elevates the dissembling disunity of the metaphorical text by surreptitiously magnifying the implicit powers of the deconstructor standing outside the text.

Moreover, the figurative and metaphorical quality of language central to deconstruction's account of the indeterminacy of meaning itself betrays the necessity for a multiplicity of extra-discursive deconstructors engaged in the reading of texts. Were it the case, that is, that a single subjectivity engaged the text, then that single deconstructor's reading of the text would be godlike and definitive. It would fix and negate the very play of meaning deconstruction regards as fundamental. Thus, to preserve the indeterminacy of meaning that texts reveal is to assume the multiplicity of perspectives that distinct readers bring to those texts. Deconstruction, then, must at the very least admit a world of minds beyond texts. In Kuhnian-Lakatosian thinking, that a disciplinary community finds itself divided over the interpretation of meanings demonstrates the extra-discursive reality of that community.

What is left of the deconstructionist project then? Certainly the sensitivity to the metaphorical and elusive character of the text deserves attention. Yet the notion that the text is a pure bricollage, an all but incoherent juxtaposition of fundamentally incommensurate elements in a structure of difference, surely goes too far in extinguishing the subjective presence of past and current authors in that text. The task for an economics methodology sensitive to these points, accordingly, is to as much as possible grasp the particular influence of past and present authors in a given text, to distinguish the sedimentation of the past from the recastings of the present.

Here the developments in the tradition from Kuhn and Lakatos to McCloskey are crucial. In the former we find elements of a macromethodology of the practical development of a discipline. In the latter we have insights and guidelines into the micromethodology of that system of disciplinary practice in the author-text-audience relationship. Together, we have a theory of economics texts embodied in a disciplinary community's theoretical practices. Rather than premising a metaphysics of unembodied texts, as does deconstruction to anchor its skeptical intent, this strategy grants a metaphysics of subjectivity loosely conceived in terms of the existence of a disciplinary community.

It is important to recognize, however, that this admission of a disciplin-

248 ECONOMICS AS DISCOURSE

ary community's subjective reality does not overturn the central idea underlying the structuralist-deconstructionist precept that the signified is constituted by the signifier. While the simple existence of a community of subjects indicates that for any given individual subject there are objects in the world — since others in the community cannot be identical with that individual subject as subject and must thus appear objectively — nonetheless, this "objective" world could still be said to be fully constituted by our system of signifiers in all respects except its simple existence. Thus, the idea that the signified is constituted by the signifier would permit speaking of a world apart from conception, but would preclude saying that anything more than this could be said about this world not strictly determined by our meaning structures. This result, it should be emphasized, tends to undermine the notion that there exists a disciplinary community of any degree of unity and cohesiveness, since, in the absence of an objectively characterizable world of things toward which that community is directed in its elaboration of meaning, it is not clear what might explain that community's unity. Put differently, without the addition of some significant realism to the disciplinary community's object world, neither can the distinctions between normal and revolutionary science be easily defended, nor the point of persuasion and rhetorical nuance be readily suggested. This demonstrates the need to consider alternative conceptual foundations for the object world.

The structuralist-deconstructionist precept that the signified is constituted by the signifier replicates Gottlob Frege's turn-of-the-century philosophical-linguistic principle that meaning determines reference. Frege (1966), together with Bertrand Russell in his well-known theory of descriptions (1956), enunciated the doctrine that language only succeeds in picking out objects in the world, the referents of terms, when one has identified the description that defines the use of that term. Yet in recent decades, a number of philosophers, most notably Saul Kripke, W.V.O. Quine, and Hilary Putnam, have argued that this view is fundamentally flawed and that alternative accounts of linguistic reference both better account for the referential function of language, and give a more plausible understanding of objects in the world.[5]

Kripke's (1980) strategy is to reverse Frege's principle that meaning determines reference, and insist — from a self-consciously post-Kantian and neo-Aristotelian perspective — that an historical practice of referring to objects by naming them underlies the determination of their meaning. On this view, neither does meaning determine reference nor does the signifier constitute the signified, since historical events within the community of speakers, not a self-contained structure of meanings, dictate how and when terms are used referentially. That is, the historical practice of "fixing a reference" and our "rigid designation" of things in the world presupposes that "we . . . as part of a community of speakers have a certain connection between ourselves and a certain kind of thing" named (Kripke, 1980, p. 118).

This view, importantly, avoids an obvious difficulty encountered in the traditional view of reference, namely, that when the description of an object changes, it seems necessary to say a different object has been referenced, though the relevant speaker's intention may simply have been to characterize a given object differently. For example, on the view that meaning determines reference and that the signified is constituted by the signifier, that the meaning of light has changed from being a certain visual impression to being a stream of photons seems to require that an altogether different phenomenon is at issue in the shift from one description to the next. Yet on the view that a naming event underlies a term's meaning, descriptions of objects may well change yet the same phenomena still be intended and picked out in virtue of a community's conventional reliance upon a past episode of naming (Kripke, 1980, pp. 129–131).

This stability of reference, it should be noted, not only suits our intuitions about the referential function of language, but, in the context of the theoretical practices of a disciplinary community, gives some basis for talking about that disciplinary community's object world apart from whatever characterization of that object world currently dominates — the difficulty noted above. Thus, that a disciplinary community tracks a history of its theoretical practice adds content to its continually evolving description of the phenomena it investigates. This is not to deny, of course, that, as Samuel Hollander (1979) has put it, each generation rightfully rewrites its own history of economics (p. 4). Rather, it is to say that the record of rewriting itself preserves some sense of the objects beyond conceptualization, specifically because it focuses upon historical contention over the sense of a name.

Proponents of the structuralist-deconstructionist precept that the signified is fully constituted by the signifier will not, it must be imagined, be persuaded by this perspective. Yet their arguments, especially in their deconstructionist formulation, cannot properly be claimed void of metaphysical assumptions, as suggested by Derrida. As argued here, the neo-Kantian, neo-idealist premise that conceptualization essentially dictates existence fails to adequately account for the subjectivity behind conceptualization. This is a matter of no little importance for economics methodology, since in recent years economics methodologists have increasingly focused upon the theoretical practices of their disciplinary community. The suggestion here, then, is that this focus lends itself more naturally to an account of meaning that emphasizes the actions of individuals that result in conception, than an account of meaning that takes the play of meaning as an irreducible datum.

Notes

[1] See Derrida's essay on Saussure (1977).

[2] Rorty takes up essentially these same themes in his own critique of the idea that philosophy is the glassy "mirror" of nature (1980). In his later work he is more explicit about his indebtedness to Derrida and the themes of deconstruction. See "Philosophy as a kind of writing" (1982, pp. 90–109).

[3] As, for example, quoted by translator Spivak in her Preface (1977) to Derrida's *Of Grammatology*, p. xxii.

[4] This is perhaps most evident in Derrida's essay on Edmund Husserl's phenomenological effort to ground knowledge in a transcendental self-consciousness (1978, pp. 154–168).

[5] For an introduction to these views and a number of the original papers adopting the new view of referentiality, see Schwartz (1977). For an argument that axiomatic general equilibrium theory is implicitly committed to the Frege-Russell account of referentiality, and that this renders that theory incapable of making statements about the world, see Davis (1989).

References

Davis, J.B. 1989. "Axiomatic General Equilibrium Theory and Referentiality." *Journal of Post Keynesian Economics*.

Derrida, Jacques. 1977. *Of Grammatology*. Translated by Gayatri Chakravorty Spivak. Baltimore and London: John Hopkins University Press.

——. 1978. *Writing and Difference*. Translated by Alan Bass. London: Routledge & Kegan Paul.

Frege, Gottlob. 1966. "On Sense and Reference." In *Translations from the Philosophical Writings of Gottlob Frege*. Revised edition. Translated by P.T. Geach and Max Black. Oxford: Blackwell.

Hollander, Samuel. 1979. *The Economics of David Ricardo*. Toronto: University of Toronto Press.

Kripke, Saul A. 1980. *Naming and Necessity*. Cambridge, Mass.: Harvard University Press.

McCloskey, Donald N. 1985. *The Rhetoric of Economics*. Madison: The University of Wisconsin Press.

Rorty, Richard. 1980. *Philosophy and the Mirror of Nature*. Oxford: Basil Blackwell.

——. 1982. *The Consequences of Pragmatism*. Brighton, Eng.: Harvester Press.

Russell, Bertrand. 1956. "On Denoting." In Robert C. Marsh, ed. *Logic and Knowledge*. New York: Allen & Unwin.

Saussure, Ferdinand de. 1974. *Course in General Linguistics*. Translated by Wade Baskin. London: Fontana/Collins.

Schwartz, Stephen P., ed. 1977. *Naming, Necessity, and Natural Kinds*. Ithaca and London: Cornell University Press.

COMMENT BY EDWARD PURO

General Comments on the Beginning of the Chapter

Rosetti points out that economics (and science generally, as many modern philosophers of science have argued) has not progressed in a Popperian fashion. Although this would clearly be interesting for those coming from a Popperian point of view, the rest of the chapter seems to suggest that this should be of interest to any "positivist." This seems to ignore the fact that most positivists were concerned with the question of justifying scientific knowledge at a point in time rather than in explaining the development of scientific knowledge over time.

Rosetti states that McCloskey and Mirowski argue that because economists use rhetoric, etc., it follows that "... there is not an objective basis to our acceptance and use of models." It is unclear whether they mean that economists do not currently have such a basis, that economists should not seek such a basis, or whether no such basis is possible. Since their position is "... supported and extended by deconstructive thought," I presume Rosetti's point is that the latter interpretation is correct, however, I am not sure that this can be established by observing economists.

There seems to be no attempt to distinguish the issue of determining the goals and methodology of science from the issue of choosing between theories within a given framework. Thus, for example, Rosetti's argument that statistics is just one more type of rhetoric used in the act of persuasion, while perhaps true on some general level, seems to ignore the fact that it can nonetheless have a special status under a given view of science.

What makes this issue particularly noticeable is Rosetti's tendency to view (positivistic) scientists as pursuing some ideal of Truth, such that they are persuaded to believe in a theory's truthfulness. In point of fact many if not most later "positivists" were instrumentalists of one sort or another, and they were certainly fallibilists. At any rate, recognition of the problems of pursuing Truth is certainly not an original contribution of the deconstructionist movement, as the author seems to imply.

Comments on the Discussion of Deconstruction

Rosetti begins by discussing the difference between the classical idea of language and the deconstructionist view of language. I question the accuracy of the author's portrayal of the classical view. The first point

251

made is the commonsensical point that a term has to be defined in order
to have any meaning. The definition is indeterminate of course, since
even if one is referring to the empirical world one thinks one sees, that
world could be divided or conceptualized in a number of ways. According
to Rosetti, the classical view is that a word is not defined by convention (and is of course subject to redefinition), but instead contains the
"... translation of the essence [of, in this example, the rock] into language." I find it hard to believe that the classical view, with which I am
admittedly unfamiliar, held the view that the collection of letters "rock"
contains some sort of essence and hence does not need to be defined.
Hence, the revelation that there is no such determinate essence contained
in "rock" does not seems especially surprising or interesting, neither does
the notion that the word can be redefined.

Trying to find a more interesting interpretation of this conflict I am
led to the idea that perhaps the classical school felt that for any given
arbitrary definition of a concept, say an empirically descriptive term such
as "rock," there are characteristics that determine whether or not something is to be considered as falling under that concept, and other characteristics that are not essential in this respect. In this case, one could refer
to the necessary characteristics as the "essence" of the definition. The
argument against the essence idea would then be the familiar line that
many (if not all) terms are underdefined, such that when they are used
no one is sure exactly what one is referring to and must therefore guess at
the definition of the term from the context in which it appears. (Of
course, theoretical terms would also be indeterminate.) This has interesting implications for the possibility of stipulative definitions as called for in
some formulations of the analytic-synthetic distinction. Anyway, I find
most of this argument convincing, especially the notion that it would be
impossible (or at least very difficult) to fully specify what is meant by any
given term. However, I am not certain that this implies that there is no
essence of the definition as described above, that is, some minimum of
characteristics a thing must have to be included as an instance of that
definition. For instance, it seems intelligible to say that some philosophers
have held that rocks are animate. It is intelligible under conventional
definitions of both rock and animate (however, one would probably want
to check the usage of animate to make sure what exactly is being said). It
is not an essential characteristic of a thing to be described by the word
"rock" that it be inanimate. Instead, it seems more likely the word refers
to some bundle of perceptual characteristics. For example, suppose one
said, "I went swimming in a rock yesterday." In this case it seems clear
that either "swimming" or "rock" is being used in an unconventional

manner (or that the individual is living in a "different world" as per the modern subjectivist theories of reality, in which case I think pragmatic and coherency considerations would govern one's reaction to this claim).

There is a very big issue made of the fact that everything must be defined in opposition to something else so that, for instance, if one's conception of the world does not contain the relevant distinction, then one could not use certain words. All of this is clearly true but, again, it seems difficult to believe that they are original ideas of deconstructionism. On the other hand, Foucault's idea of looking for sociological origins for the distinctions one does make is quite interesting. The only thing that strikes me about this idea is that it seems to deny the ability of people to consciously change their conception of the world. To many this thesis might seem empirically implausible; however, a very detailed sort of argument would have to be presented against it. This is because whenever one appears to change his/her conception of the world due to rational discussion, Foucault might answer that some sociological change had taken place that caused the change, which was then rationalized using the discussion in question. One can probably find similar ideas in pragmatism, since it seems plausible that people make the distinctions they do because they are necessary to accomplish what they would like to accomplish. Anyway, the more interesting question is the significance of this thesis. For instance, I'm not sure that one should reject the distinctions one makes because of a recognition that they are of sociological origin. It's also not clear that this makes determinate (but arbitrary) definitions of concepts impossible; however, it might make words originating in other cultures incomprehensible, at least in their original intended definitions. On the other hand, in this situation, I do not know why one would be interested in the original intended definitions.

Derrida's idea that some categories (such as "male") are "prior to" other categories, and that there is some sort of hierarchy based on this fact is not presented in a convincing fashion. It is therefore difficult to attach much interest to the levelling of this hierarchy based on the commonplace notion that "male" is defined in opposition to "female." The question of the value of rationality versus emotions in governing behavior is a normative issue that can be (and is) argued over by people within the same culture, it does not seem to be a consequence of the linguistic properties of the terms. (At any rate, I have never run across an argument for rationality that depended on "rationality" being describable in the absence of "emotion.")

Comments on the Discussion of Lucas

The main point here seems to be that there is no way of deciding between Keynes's and Lucas's definitions of involuntary unemployment and related terms since they are simply consequences of one's sociological environment. My own view is that, like any definition, these terms are indeterminate and must be given by convention; however, Lucas does have a point that Keynes's definition uses a conception of involuntary that might differ from how the word is used elsewhere in economic theory. This would suggest that for clarity the definition might be changed. However, one might want to challenge this idea based on the general (i.e., not just within economics) conventional definitions of the terms "voluntary" and "involuntary." The problem here is that Lucas's point about involuntary unemployment can be generalized to any behavior that might be called involuntary, so what he is arguing is, in effect, that this distinction should be dropped from the language. However, starting from an ordinary language perspective, there seems to be a prima facie case that the distinction is useful and should be retained, the problem is in specifying the distinction more carefully. I would start by observing the nature of the constraints involved in actions that are termed "voluntary" and "involuntary" to see if relevant distinctions can be drawn.

Regardless of whether or not one is convinced that there is a meaningful voluntary/involuntary distinction, it is clear that the problem Keynes was concerned with is not affected by definitional maneuvering. In Lucas's framework, Keynes's problem of involuntary unemployment becomes the problem of people facing such attenuated opportunities that they prefer not to work. That is, the fact that their decisions are optimal given the circumstances they find themselves in does not address the question of whether something should be done to change those circumstances. In other words, we have the familiar attempt to use economic theory to promote normative positions that are not in fact implied by that theory.

Returning to Rosetti's discussion, the attempt to use deconstructionism to shed light on this issue does not seem especially helpful. For instance, there is the repeated technique of arguing that, because concepts are defined in opposition to each other, it is impossible to observe a situation that would be classified under one or the other concept. For example, we have the argument that because voluntary and involuntary are defined in opposition, this supports Lucas's argument that the empirical situation Keynes called involuntary unemployment would also include what Keynes (presumably) would call voluntary unemployment. I find this argument unconvincing.

Another instance of this idea in Rosetti states that because science and public opinion are defined partly in opposition to each other, it is impossible to practice science without the intrusion of public opinion. (I agree with the notion that it is difficult to separate the two, but I agree on sociological, not linguistic, grounds.)

Comments on Deconstruction and Economics

I am not sure what it means to put a capital O on objective in the statement that "... economic research is not progressing ... towards an Objective...". I think that under conventional ideas of the objective of economics there has been progress. If the point is that the objective is not a priori but conventional, I think everyone already knows this.

Rosetti finally states the view that "... reality is quite subjective." This idea underlies a good deal of the chapter but is not well developed using the deconstructionist approach. This is quite different from saying that how one divides up what one perceives as reality is subjective, which I take to be the deconstructionist's point. I presume Rosetti is referring to the theory-ladeness of perception idea, however, a great deal more has to be said about this before one states that one should give up evaluating theories. For instance, it is not at all clear that this view implies that theories cannot be accepted or rejected on the grounds of how they accord "with some given reality," or whether it refers to the possibility of comparing different "realities." The latter issue is addressed most effectively from a pragmatic standpoint I believe. At any rate, I am not sure Rosetti is addressing the important issues here, particularly when she refers to the subjective reality position as doing away with the notion of Truth, which again, has already been done away with many times. Because of this it is difficult to evaluate her discussion of the implications of the relativity suggested by the deconstructionist approach.

Conclusion

I agree on independent grounds with many of the points Rosetti brings up in this chapter, both in the discussion of deconstructionism and in the discussion of Lucas. However, I feel the discussion of deconstructionism may be flawed due to the tendency of the author to attribute various ideas to the deconstructionists that seem to have been current prior to their formulations of them, and also to misrepresent the opposing theories so as to make them implausible. (I could be wrong on this point, since I may have run across discussions of points that in fact did originate with the deconstructionists but were not credited to them, and I am unfamiliar with the classical idea of language.) As far as I can tell most of the specifically deconstructionist arguments, such as Derrida's, do not seem especially convincing. An exception might be Foucault's theory, and it is unfortunate that no attempt was made to spell out the significance of this theory in greater detail. With respect to the discussion of Lucas, I am not sure whether the deconstructionist approach helps or obscures the analysis of his contributions.

Index

258